Harmony and Melody

ELIE SIEGMEISTER

HOFSTRA UNIVERSITY

Harmony

and

Melody

VOLUME I: THE DIATONIC STYLE

WADSWORTH PUBLISHING COMPANY, INC.

BELMONT, CALIFORNIA

ISBN 0-534-00245-5

Music autography by Alfredo Seville

HARMONY AND MELODY, Volume 1, by Elie Siegmeister

L. C. Cat. Card No.: 65–17537
Printed in the United States of America

16 17 18 — 84

A Prefatory Note to the 1977 Printing

Since *Harmony and Melody* was first published, I have been teaching from it, noting all student questions about the meaning of a word or phrase, the appropriateness of a musical example, and clarity and consistency in general. This special 1977 printing contains a number of refinements that, I feel, improve the effectiveness of the book as a teaching and learning tool. A few musical examples have been changed. Also, I have provided additional footnotes and more specific page references to save time in finding cross-referenced examples.

A
Prefatory
Note

The present generation has witnessed a remarkable change in the teaching of theory. Responding to the musical currents of the twentieth century and to the fresh approaches of such men as Schönberg, Schenker, Toch, Hindemith, Salzer, and Murphy, many instructors have adopted new ways of teaching harmony. Turning directly to the source—music itself— they use the works of Classical and Romantic composers both as models and as working materials in day-to-day instruction.

In the new approach to harmony, the diminished seventh chord, for instance, is presented not through abstract discussion and theoretical rules but as it appears in Bach's *St. Matthew Passion*, Gluck's *Orfeo*, and Beethoven's Sonata *Pathétique*. Thus the student first meets the chord in passages from living music; he is then asked to harmonize melodies from the literature using a variety of chords, including the diminished seventh; and finally, bearing in mind the traditional techniques, he writes something of his own.

Another new departure is the emphasis on the study and writing of melody. A hoary tradition holds that "melody is the surface of harmony"; once the student learns chords, melody comes as a by-product. But history shows that it was the other way around: melody was the original source and harmony the by-product.

Recent widespread interest in medieval and Renaissance music has revealed the high art of melody that flourished long before harmony existed. Chords first arose as the meeting of melody lines; and over the centuries harmonic structures emerged largely from the verticalization of already existing melodic patterns. For half a millenium, melody and harmony evolved together, each adding meaning to the other, in a succession of changing idioms. As we shall see, it makes sense to study them together.

The purpose of these volumes is, therefore, to reveal music from two sides at once. The first half of each chapter (except Chapter I in Volume I) deals with harmony, the second half with melody. In the beginning, the two aspects cannot always be closely related; here the groundwork is laid for correlation later on. The discussion of harmony first involves intervals, tonality, fundamental chord structures and functions, voice-leading techniques, and methods of harmonization. Later, broad harmonic motion is analyzed, as well as its role in shaping musical forms. At the same time, the early chapters explore melodic curves and motives, rhythmic patterns, and methods of developing a phrase out of smaller fragments.

Once the basic harmonic and melodic materials are mastered, the two disciplines gradually merge. The student writes his own chord progressions and learns to draw melodies from them; he writes melodies and learns to find the harmonies they imply. By analyzing the interaction of melodic and harmonic ideas in the music of the masters, and by writing original pieces in small forms, he becomes aware of the unity of the compositional act and the interdependence of melodic, rhythmic, and harmonic motion. In the second volume, the study leads from modulation and early chromaticism through late Romantic chromaticism to twentieth-century harmonic and melodic techniques—a basic interest of students in our time.

All principles in this work, all examples to be analyzed and melodies to be harmonized, are drawn directly from the musical literature, from Gregorian chant to Charles Ives; nothing has been composed to prove a point. Instead of being confronted with arbitrary rules, the student finds excerpts from actual music, as well as deductions whose source and logic he can evaluate for himself.

Thus, before he lays out a chord, designs a harmonic progression, harmonizes a melody, or plans a modulation, the student finds examples of these very processes by Orlando di Lasso, Purcell, or Brahms. Before he writes a phrase, plans a melodic curve, creates a motive, or develops an existing motive in various ways, he sees how these problems have been solved by Palestrina, Mozart, and Bartók, and also Gershwin and Cole Porter. At every stage, the student is called upon to examine and think about technical processes as they occur in a wide range of living music.

The present volumes are planned as a basic text for a two-year harmony course. Assignments in analysis, writing, singing, and keyboard exercises are contained in two workbooks, which parallel the text chapter by chapter. No hard and fast routine is intended in the plan of study; some classes may spend more time on one aspect than on another. Depending on the previous background and experience of the students, certain chapters can be mastered in a week; others may require two or three. Indeed, some sections may well form the basis for extended projects. Chapter XV of Volume I, for example, may provide the stimulus for several weeks spent in the composition of short piano pieces, and Chapter XVI for the writing of songs. A month would not exhaust the subject of altered chords (Chapter X of Volume II), nor two months the problems of twentieth-century harmony (Chapters XII and XIII of that volume). A wide variety of assignments is provided in the workbooks, to permit selection according to need. Not every class or student is necessarily expected to fulfill every assignment; the instructor will best judge which ones suit the needs of his particular group.

In the writing of this book I owe a debt to the many composers and theorists who have searched along new pathways, as well as to those whose advice has been invaluable in the preparation of the manuscript. Among the latter are my wife, Hannah; my colleagues, Professors Leo Kraft and Albert Tepper; and also Stephen Albert, Lawrence Bernstein, Philip Evans, Robert Gross, Arthur Lief, Alan Mandel, and Daniel Sabbeth.

A composer does not relinquish notes for a time and turn to words without a strong purpose. Mine has been to humanize the study of harmony, to make it more musical, and to present it in the language of our time.

Elie Siegmeister

Contents

Harmony and Melody

Prelude

A good composition forms an artistic whole. A Bach fugue, a Beethoven symphony, a Bartók quartet is more than the sum of its parts, no matter how beautiful each of them may be. In a fully achieved work, every element is conceived in relation to the others; all blend in a unity from which artistic character derives.

Harmony is one of the elements forming this unity. It cannot be isolated from melody, from rhythm, from form, above all from living music; and it is folly to attempt such isolation. Granted that harmony has certain patterns of its own, these patterns take on musical meaning only when fused with melody, rhythm, and form.

The opening of Wagner's *Das Rheingold*, for example—136 bars of E flat major triad—has little meaning from the viewpoint of harmony alone; but in association with melodic and rhythmic flow and tone color, it presents an impressive musical image of the depths of the Rhine.

The beginning of the Bach chorale *Es ist genug* (Ex. 1), with its deliberate dissonance and its radical succession of chords, is puzzling and arbitrary as a *purely harmonic* phenomenon. Considered, however, as the setting of a given melody and the delineation of an intense emotion, the harmonies have an artistic logic and beauty that supersede all purely harmonic rules.

The effect of this phrase depends, first, on the strange D sharp in the melody (a note that seems to jump out of the key of A major before that key has even been established); second, on the dramatic halting of the rhythm after only four chords have sounded; and third, on the extraordinary harmonies that have been joined to the given melody and rhythm. Only in relation to the entire musical thought does the harmonic progression take on meaning.

1

Ex. 1   Bach: *Es ist genug·*

Although generalizations can be made about the structure and relationships of chords, they have little validity as abstractions. Harmony is significant only when it functions as part of a composition.

Earlier Approaches to the Study of Harmony

In the conventional study of theory, the relation of harmony to other musical elements plays a minor role. The standard harmony exercise is an abstract problem designed to illustrate a specific technical point; it rarely reveals the artistic quality of music. Perhaps that is why the study of harmony frequently seems arid, pedantic, and lacking in reality; why it so often seems unrelated to an understanding of the musical repertory. Even in the study of composition—where theory is supposedly a vital necessity—the concentration on figured basses and given sopranos is often dry and boring; at best one accepts the assurance that "it is good for you."

Some years ago, instrumental study was conducted in a like manner. Students were confined for a year or two to scales, finger exercises, and those "original" pieces composed by the author of the method. In recent years, however, the teaching of instruments has changed. The beginning piano student no longer is restricted to technical exercises, but now is introduced to Bach, Mozart, and Bartók in the first year.

Counterpoint, once concerned mainly with the exercises called "species," now includes a study of music by Palestrina, Orlando di Lasso, and Bach. Most sight-singing courses have abandoned the dry pedagogic examples of yesteryear, using folk music and the works of the masters instead. Orchestration usually involves arranging piano pieces or other compositions of the finest composers.

But even today, some harmony courses cling stubbornly to the doctrine, "technical exercises first, real music later." Several textbooks in current use contain *not one exercise* based on actual music; the work consists entirely of solving problems—realizing given basses and sopranos contrived by the author to illustrate the theory. Dealing largely with harmony-in-isolation, the standard method fails to give the student insight into harmonic motion as it occurs in real music.

Need this necessarily be so? Must harmony students be kept isolated from the living literature? Or is the conventional method merely the last stand of an obsolete viewpoint?

New Approaches to the Study of Harmony

For some time now, musicians have been seeking a way to integrate harmony with the study of living music. As long ago as 1911 Arnold Schönberg proposed a completely new approach to the subject.* Figured basses, he maintained, were an anachronism in this day and age, when the musician is no longer called upon to sit at the clavier and realize at sight the shorthand scores containing merely bass notes and numbers, as was the practice in the Baroque period. Why put the beginning student, Schönberg asked, through a long and arduous training to develop a skill that does not bear on the central problem of harmony, the knowledge and control of chord progressions? The Viennese master astutely pointed out that the writing of figured basses was an inadequate way of learning voice-leading techniques, which may be developed far more efficiently through the study of counterpoint.† He devised a step-by-step method of studying chord formations by employing them in short phrases of the student's own composition. Only in actual use of the material, unsupported by the crutch of a given bass, he believed, can one master the art of connecting chords, of understanding the harmonic structures inherent in composition. Yet despite the fact that Schönberg was one of the great musicians of his time and a gifted teacher who influenced a whole generation of distinguished composers, so strongly entrenched have been the conventional methods that his brilliant advances in harmony teaching have had little influence in this country.

Schönberg was not alone in his search for a change in harmony study. Heinrich Schenker, in a number of theoretical works, pointed out the limited insight into harmony that even the most concentrated study along the old lines can give.‡ In his doctrine of the *Urlinie* (the basic line), he revealed the inadequacy of the conventional system of chord-by-chord analysis to account for the true harmonic structure of music. He saw harmony in the music of the masters as an over-all progression, leading from one region of a tonality to another. For him, *harmonic motion* was the prolongation of a tonal idea, its gradual transition to another tonal idea, and its equally gradual, or in some cases swift, return to the original.

* Arnold Schönberg: *Harmonielehre* (Vienna, 1911; English translation, New York, 1948).

† The study of figured bass, however, is an excellent one for the advanced student, especially the pianist who may be called upon to perform Baroque continuo parts.

‡ The only Schenker work translated into English is *Harmony* (Vienna, 1906). Important works in German include *Der Freie Satz* (Vienna, 1935) and articles in *Das Meisterwerk in der Musik* (Munich, 1925–1926, 1930). For a brief discussion of the *Urlinie*, see Willi Apel, *Harvard Dictionary of Music* (Cambridge, 1944).

Schenker's concept of harmony, as the development of broad tonal functions rather than as the step-by-step movement of single chords, did much toward restoring harmony to its integral relationship to the whole of music. His writings have influenced many composers and theorists in their understanding of musical motion. But unfortunately, since Schenker never developed his analytical theories into a practical plan of instruction, they have not replaced the conventional "harmony-exercise" method as a basis for study.

Another Viennese, Ernst Toch, made a significant contribution to theory when, in 1923, he published his *Melodielehre*.* In this book, and in his subsequent *The Shaping Forces in Music*,† the distinguished composer proposed to fill a long-felt gap in the technical training of the musician by adding a study of melody. Melody, Toch maintained, is perhaps the very heart of the musical process, the most important bearer of musical thought and emotion, yet it is the one aspect of music studied least, if at all. He made an important beginning in outlining a theory of melody which suggested a fresh approach to this most neglected of theoretical subjects. Toch's call for a study of melody was echoed in subsequent years by such diverse figures as Paul Hindemith, Howard Murphy of Columbia University, and Howard Boatwright of Syracuse University.

A group active in correlating harmony with the study of music as a whole was formed by William Schuman in the 1940s at the Juilliard School. "Theory," the Juilliard program announced, "has tended towards an unhealthy isolation. . . . It is necessary that the student, instead of mastering the 'rules' . . . understands the functional nature and organic coherence of harmony itself in its relation to rhythm and form."‡

A still further attempt to revise the old methods has been the recent trend to combine the studies of harmony and counterpoint. The merit of this procedure lies in giving the harmony student from the outset an awareness of *line*—of the onward flow of music, often neglected in the conventional block-chord approach.

Although a distinct improvement on the older method, the fusion of the two disciplines introduces new difficulties not easily surmounted. First, the mingling of harmony and counterpoint results inevitably in a type of eighteenth-century harmonic counterpoint, which, it is felt, should follow rather than precede the sixteenth-century type.§ The second difficulty is that a certain dilettantism may result. The study of counterpoint, especially in the mixed species in four voices, in double counterpoint, and in canon, is not easily combined with the complexities of harmonic structure, especially those involving

* Ernst Toch: *Melodielehre* (Berlin, 1923).

† (New York, 1948).

‡ *The Juilliard Report on Teaching the Literature and Materials of Music* (New York, 1953).

§ The Palestrina or "Golden Age" type of counterpoint enables the student to concentrate on the problems of pure linear development and free rhythmic flow, unencumbered by questions of chord progression and harmonic balance.

distant modulations, altered chords, and the like. The two fields have much in common. But the attempt to fashion a thoroughgoing mixture may lead to an unfortunate superficiality.

The Correlation of Harmony and Melody

This book is the result of a belief that a unification of theory with living music can be achieved more successfully, and without the disadvantages suggested above, by a combined study of harmony and melody.

The essence of melody is line—a continuous, flowing line. As the student investigates the nature of melody, he develops a greater awareness of purely linear qualities—such as curve, continuity, and climax—than is possible in the study of counterpoint, where the complex interweaving of voices commands his attention.

An inner affinity exists between melody and harmony. In daily musical experience, whether it be of performing or listening, the two have a natural connection. Many solo compositions for violin, cello, flute, and other instruments, a great number of piano pieces, large sections of the traditional orchestral repertory, as well as folk and art songs and operatic arias, reveal the constant interdependence of melody and harmony.

When, in the midst of a piano or violin lesson, the teacher pauses to point out an important harmonic change that needs special stress in performance, it is most often associated with a given melodic line. The teacher also frequently indicates that the melody must be played in a certain fashion because of the demands of harmony. *Interaction between these elements is a primary fact of musical listening, performance, and composition.*

If we understand melodic motion, we can more readily comprehend harmonic motion. The study of music as flowing line reveals the melodic origins of harmonic structures such as triad inversions, suspensions, and the dominant seventh chord. It adds dynamic meaning to chord progressions, the resolution of dissonances, cadential action, and modulations, as part of the movement of lines toward points of tension and rest.

The principles of melodic structure—relatively simple—clarify the more complex principles of harmonic structure. Thus the image of melody as an arc stretching from point to point in a composition makes it easier to understand harmony as a sweeping movement from point to point, rather than as a series of chords strung along like beads on a string.

The contrast between half and perfect cadences can be a somewhat dry affair when viewed purely from a harmonic standpoint. We are informed that the first cadence ends on one chord and the second on another. But when we look at an example such as the melody of Beethoven's *Ode to Joy*, with its "open" and "closed" cadences, the contrast takes on tangible reality (Ex. 2).

Ex. 2   Beethoven: *Ode to Joy*, from Symphony No. 9, Op. 125

It is no derogation of harmony to point out its relatively recent arrival on the musical scene. Melody was already an age-old art in the late medieval and early Renaissance periods, when elements of the major-minor harmonic system first emerged. By about 1500, Italian composers were using block chords in a surprisingly modern manner; the basic principles of harmonic motion were beginning to appear.* A generation later, when Clément Jannequin was writing chansons with a definite feeling for primary chord function and major tonality, the need to support strong melodic motion with strong chord progression had clearly brought harmony into being. In essence, harmonic "rules" were an extension of melodic necessities.

When, in the later Renaissance and early Baroque periods, new chord structures and functions appeared, the interaction of melody and harmony became more complex. From that point forward, and into the twentieth century, the journey of melodic ideas through more highly developed compositions has been paralleled by ever more intricate harmonic movement. Well into our own times, the two have been closely intertwined in a musical unity. They must be understood in this light.

Four additional advantages accrue from the parallel study of the two disciplines:

1. Insight into melodic structure becomes invaluable in the harmonization of melodies, where an understanding of melodic sequences, extensions, condensations, climaxes, and forms gives meaning to the selection of one or another harmonic pattern.

---

* Recent research has pushed the origins of major-minor harmony back from 1600 (a date often given) to the beginning of the sixteenth century, and earlier. See Gustave Reese: *Music in the Renaissance* (New York, 1954), especially pages 160, 185, and 642; and Edward Lowinsky: *Tonality and Atonality in Sixteenth-Century Music* (Berkeley, California, 1962). For an early frottola (1480), see Ex. 14, page 233; for a Jannequin chanson (1529), see Ex. 2, page 196.

2. Training in melody writing leads to a command of smooth bass movement, a sense of the long line of harmonic flow—essentials of good harmonic progression.

3. Awareness of the interrelationship of melody and harmony deepens one's insight into the structure of music—important to the performer as well as the composer.

4. Finally, the challenge of inventing melodic and harmonic passages encourages creative work from the start, and stimulates the powers of invention. Although very few students will ever become composers, all can benefit from the experience of writing melody and harmony in original compositions, on no matter how modest a level. No better way exists to sharpen one's perception of the inner structure and dynamics of music.

I

Musical is Motion

Whatever else it may or may not be—and the definitions are countless—there can be no doubt that music is motion. One sustained tone, no matter how beautiful, is not yet music. But the moment a change occurs from one tone to another, from one rhythm to another, from one chord to another, tonal forces are set in motion—a motion that is the beginning of music.

Musical motion appears in various ways: in melody and harmony (the basic concern of our present study); in rhythm and form (subjects we will touch on lightly); and in counterpoint, texture, and tone color. There are certain kinds of music that are pure rhythm; but they are quite exceptional. The vast majority of compositions contain two, three, or more kinds of motion blended in a single musical impulse. Even though the finished composition may seem simple to the listener, the interweaving of the various musical strands—such as melody, rhythm, and harmony—is often a subtle and complex process. To unravel the separate strands and then to examine their interweaving will be our present objective.

Rhythm is the most physical and perhaps the most basic kind of musical motion. The beating of the heart, the tapping of a foot, the repeated striking of wood or metal are elemental forms of rhythmic pulsation. Such repeated pulsations, whether simple or varied, have furnished the basic momentum for all dance music from ancient to the most recent times. In the music of African drummers (Ex. 1) and in the opening of Ravel's *Bolero* (Ex. 2), rhythm alone, without melody or harmony, creates a distinctive musical motion.

9

Ex. 1   African drum rhythm: Badouma paddlers' song

From Music of Equatorial Africa, *Harold Courlander, collector, Folkways Records. By permission.*

Ex. 2   Ravel: *Bolero*

Permission for reprint granted by Durand et Cie., Paris, copyright owner, and Elkan-Vogel Co., Inc., Philadelphia, agents.

Born of expressive cries and the chanted word, melody is another primary source of musical motion. In countless medieval plain chants, in chants of the Jewish, Hindu, and Moslem rituals, and in a vast body of folk music created over many centuries, melody is the prime mover. Lacking clear rhythmic notation and any harmonic support, the purely melodic progression of a plain chant nine centuries old still holds its interest today.

Ex. 3   Plain chant: *Kyrie Alme Pater*

Ky - - - ri - e   e - - - le-i-son.

Ky - ri - e   e - - le i   son.

Harmonic Motion

Compared to rhythm and melody, harmony is a newcomer to the musical scene. Whereas the older musical elements possess an ancient lineage, harmony has played a major role in music for a mere four or five hundred years.

Harmonic motion lends to music a special momentum—subtler and more difficult to identify than those of rhythm and melody because it is hidden, so to speak, beneath the surface of music. This momentum is sensed even by the untrained listener who is unaware of its cause. Specific knowledge of harmonic techniques—the goal of the present study—brings a conscious awareness of their generative functions.

Harmonic motion is most apparent in compositions that have a relatively inactive melody and rhythm. In the E minor Prelude by Chopin, for example, the melody shows very little movement and the rhythm scarcely changes (the dotted half and quarter notes being repeated again and again). Without harmony the composition has little forward motion.

Ex. 4   Chopin: Prelude, Op. 28, No. 4 (melody)

↑Like intro of "For No One" One note over chord progression

    With the harmony added, we see it is the chords that move the music along. Under a virtually static melody, the bass descends slowly but inexorably, the motion from chord to chord creating a continuous progression and development.

Ex. 5   Chopin: Prelude, Op. 28, No. 4

As in this prelude of Chopin, certain preludes of Bach derive their movement from harmony rather than from melody or rhythm.

Ex. 6   Bach: Prelude No. 1, from *The Well-Tempered Clavier*, Book I

Melodic and harmonic motion are closely intertwined in the music of the past several hundred years. Sometimes one and sometimes the other takes precedence. Each has unique potentialities, characteristics, and patterns, and each demands separate study. Since melodic designs precede harmonic structures in the minds of most listeners, as in many composers' sketches, we shall begin our study with the melodic aspect of musical motion.

Melodic Motion

The simplest melodic motion is the repetition of a single tone. Such repetition appears in the music of very primitive peoples, as well as in certain religious chants, presumably very ancient, that have come down to us.

Ex. 7   Plain chant: *Dominus vobiscum*

The repetition of one note is a musical device of great, almost hypnotic power. Examples of tone repetition are to be found in such widely divergent works as Purcell's *Fantasy on One Note*, Beethoven's Fifth Symphony, and Berg's *Wozzeck*.

Melodic motion in the more usual sense begins to appear when a voice moves from one tone to the next tone above (or below) and perhaps to one higher still, then returning to the original pitch.

Ex. 8   Plain chant: *Alleluia*

Stepwise motion, even when extended over a wider span than the example above, often lends to melody a flowing or gliding quality. The third movement of Brahms' First Symphony opens with a lovely example of smooth stepwise melody.

Ex. 9   Brahms: Symphony No. 1, Op. 68, third movement

Leaping motion, on the other hand, can be used to create dynamic and vigorous melodies. Examples are to be found in the symphonies of Mozart and Beethoven.

Ex. 10   Mozart: Symphony No. 40, K. 550, last movement

Ex. 11   Beethoven: Symphony No. 9, Op. 125*

Very few melodies consist solely of steps or of leaps. Composers prefer to mingle the two in a plastic and varied structure. A single leap or a series of leaps forms a good balance to a group of stepwise movements, and vice versa. Note the effective alternation of steps and leaps in two well-known melodies of Bach and Schubert.

* Unless otherwise noted, a musical example is always from the first movement of a work.

Ex. 12   Bach: Concerto for Two Violins in D minor

Ex. 13   Schubert: Symphony No. 8 (*Unfinished*)

From an examination of these and many similar examples, we can conclude that, insofar as melodic motion alone is concerned, the vigor of a passage varies directly with the proportion of leaps to steps. In general, the greater the number and size of the leaps, the greater the energy of the passage. The greater the number of stepwise movements and the smaller the leaps, the smoother the melodic line.

Thus, the Bach theme (Ex. 12), with ten wide leaps in four measures, reveals a vital, energetic quality; while the Schubert melody (Ex. 13), mainly stepwise except for four modest leaps, breathes a mood of gentleness and relaxation. One should not, however, jump to the conclusion that melodic motion alone determines musical character. Although important, it is but one of many factors influencing the quality of a passage—as we will presently see.

Range

Range is an important element in melodic structure. Melodies of a *narrow* compass, up to four or five scale steps, tend toward a close, quiet mode of expression. Whether the composer be an ancient Yemenite Jew or Beethoven, a restricted melodic range suggests sobriety of utterance.

Ex. 14   Yemenite Chant

From Jewish Music *by A. Z. Idelsohn. Reprinted by permission of Holt, Rinehart and Winston, Inc.*

Ex. 15   Beethoven: Symphony No. 7, Op. 92, second movement

Wide melodic range, on the other hand—one and a half octaves or more—suggests a more open, freer expression. The broad compass gives the melodic thought a wider area in which to expand.

Ex. 16   Mozart: Symphony K. 385 (*Haffner*)

Ex. 17   Shostakovich: Symphony No. 5, Op. 47

A great many melodies, including folk songs, religious chants, popular tunes, and theater songs, are neither especially wide nor narrow in compass, making use of the range of the average person's singing voice—an octave plus two or three tones.

Ex. 18   Emmett: Dixie

Within this *medium* range we also find many instrumental themes of Classical and Romantic composers, especially those of a lyrical character.

Ex. 19   Beethoven: Violin Concerto, Op. 61

Stepwise and leaping progression, and narrow, medium, and wide range describe the broad characteristics of melodic motion. To understand the more technical aspects of this motion, let us examine its component elements, the intervals.

Intervals

Perfect, Major, and Minor Intervals

The exact distance between one note and another is known as an *interval*. To identify intervals, we can start with a major scale. Counting up from the first tone (and always calling that first tone "one") the distance between

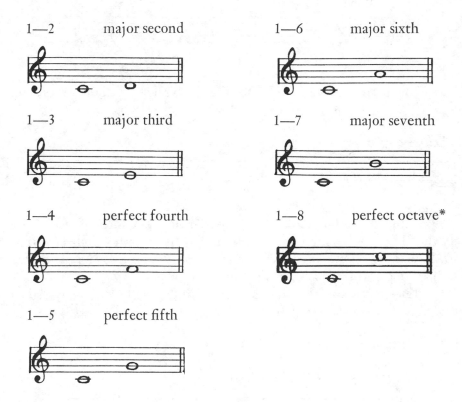

1—2	major second	1—6	major sixth
1—3	major third	1—7	major seventh
1—4	perfect fourth	1—8	perfect octave*
1—5	perfect fifth		

Why are the fourth, fifth, and octave called "perfect," while the other intervals are merely "major?" This distinction goes back at least to the middle ages, when the fourth, fifth, and octave were believed to form the only harmonious sounds, while other intervals were considered discordant.† Although ideas have changed, the name "perfect" has persisted.

* Two voices sounding the same note simultaneously form a *perfect prime*, or *unison*.

† Another possible explanation may lie in the numerical ratios of the vibrations of the sounds. See Appendix I.

Besides identifying intervals through their position in the scale, we also measure them by whole and half scale steps. Thus the *perfect fourth* consists of two steps and one half. (In Ex. 20 and hereafter, P = perfect.)

Ex. 20   Schumann: *Träumerei*, from *Kinderscenen*, Op. 15

The *perfect fifth* contains three steps plus one half.

Ex. 21   Mozart: Sonata, K. 279, second movement

The *perfect octave* duplicates the first scale step eight tones higher.

Ex. 22   Mozart: Symphony No. 41 (*Jupiter*), K. 551

Although perfect intervals appeared in only one form in medieval music, other intervals—the second, third, sixth, and seventh—each occurred in two different sizes: *major*, or large, and *minor*, or small. A minor interval is one half step smaller than a major one.

Thus a *major second* contains two half steps (or one whole step); a *minor second*, one half step. (M = major, m = minor.)

Ex. 23   Brahms: Symphony No. 1, Op. 68

Ex. 24   Bach: Fugue No. 12, from *The Well-Tempered Clavier*, Book I

A *major third* contains two whole steps; a *minor third*, a step and one half.

Ex. 25   Beethoven: *Leonore* Overture, No. 3, Op. 72a

Ex. 26   Mozart: Fantasy, K. 475

The differences between a *major sixth* (a fifth plus one whole step) and a *minor sixth* (a fifth plus one half step) are illustrated in Puccini and Beethoven.

Ex. 27   Puccini: *La Bohème*, Act IV

Ex. 28   Beethoven: Symphony No. 5, Op. 67

The *major seventh*, containing a perfect fifth plus two whole steps, is illustrated by an excerpt from Berg; the *minor seventh*, which consists of a fifth plus a step and a half, by one from Wagner.

Ex. 29   Berg: *Lyric Suite*

Ex. 30   Wagner: Prelude to *Tristan and Isolde*

So far, we have discussed only rising melodic lines. When a melody falls, intervals are measured below a given note. Illustrated are the *falling minor* and *major seconds*.

Ex. 31   Hindemith: *Mathis der Maler*

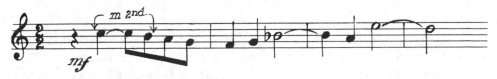

© 1935 by B. Schott's Soehne, Mainz. Used by permission.

Ex. 32   Stravinsky: *Oedipus Rex*

©1927 by Russischer Musikverlag; renewed 1955. Copyright and renewal assigned to Boosey & Hawkes Inc. English translation by E. E. Cummings © 1949 by Boosey & Hawkes Inc. Reprinted by permission.

In similar fashion, thirds, fourths, fifths, and all other intervals appear below as well as above any given note.

Two further varieties of intervals—diminished and augmented—are discussed in Chapter II.

The Expressive Character of Intervals

In Western music, from medieval to modern times, intervals have communicated a wide range of expressive intentions. Perfect, major, and minor intervals were for many centuries the basic materials of everyday music making. Whether in the music of Palestrina or in that of Bach, Haydn, or Schubert, the greatest proportion of intervals were perfect, major, and minor.

Augmented and diminished intervals were reserved mainly for moments of special intensity or dramatic power.

The expressive potentiality of intervals varies with their size. Thus, seconds, the smallest and most familiar of all, are the very essence of the smoothly flowing line; they provide melody with its connective tissue. In almost all flowing melodies, major and minor seconds are intermingled.*

Ex. 33   Beethoven: Symphony No. 9, Op. 125, last movement

When *minor seconds* are used consecutively (producing *chromatic* or half-step motion), they often generate a feeling of intensity and excitement.

Ex. 34   Bizet: Habanera, from *Carmen*

When *major seconds* alone appear in a consecutive series, the result is the special floating quality of the *whole-tone scale*, employed for a relatively short period by Impressionist composers in the early 1900s.

Ex. 35   Debussy: *Voiles*, from Preludes for Piano, Book I

Permission for reprint granted by Durand et Cie., Paris, copyright owner, and Elkan-Vogel Co., Inc., Philadelphia, agents.

*See also Ex. 9, page 13; Ex. 43, page 72; and Ex. 46, page 161.

Major and *minor thirds*, in addition to their familiar role in melody formation (Ex. 36), serve a special function in harmony. As we shall see later, thirds are the basic elements of chords.

Ex. 36   Haydn: Symphony No. 94 (*Surprise*), second movement

Perfect fourths and *fifths* often suggest a sturdy, vigorous feeling. They are the basic intervals played by the horn, trumpet, and other brass instruments, and have traditionally been used in hunting and military fanfares. In time, fourths and fifths became associated with music of a heroic or warlike character. The perfect fourth gives a special lift to anthems such as *La Marseillaise.**

Ex. 37   *La Marseillaise*

In classical music, the leaps from the first to the fifth of the scale (a perfect fifth) and from the fifth up to the octave (a perfect fourth) form one of the best means of outlining the *key*† in which a composition is written.

Ex. 38   Perfect fifth and fourth, outlining key

Beethoven often used perfect fifths and fourths to affirm a strong sense of tonality.*

Ex. 39   Beethoven: Symphony No. 3, Op. 55 (*Eroica*), last movement

* It also characterizes the march theme of Tschaikovsky's Symphony No. 6, third movement.
† Key and tonality are both defined in Chapter II.

Ex. 40   Beethoven: Symphony No. 9, Op. 125,

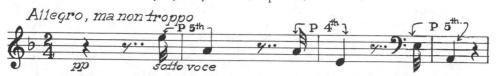

It should not be inferred, however, that fourths and fifths are always used to affirm the key or to express a virile, out-of-doors quality. Bartók used a series of fourths in a very different way in the mystery-laden introduction to his Concerto for Orchestra.

Ex. 41   Bartók: Concerto for Orchestra

© 1946 by Hawkes & Son (London) Ltd. Reprinted by permission of Boosey & Hawkes, Inc.

Perfect fifths, like fourths, may serve a variety of expressive functions: rousing (Ex. 42) or exotic and charming (Ex. 43).

Ex. 42   Haydn: Symphony No. 104 (London)

Ex. 43   Borodin: Polovtsian Dances, from Prince Igor

Beyond the range of the perfect fifth, we come to a group of intervals whose expressive potentialities are more intense than those already considered. Major and minor sixths, especially in their rising form, often project a quality of reaching or yearning. The major sixth has been used to express various kinds of amorous feeling, ranging from the innocent ardors of Prince Tamino's love song in Mozart's Magic Flute to the brooding sensuousness of Wagner's Prelude to Tristan and Isolde.

Ex. 44   Mozart: *Dies Bildnis ist bezaubernd schön,* from *The Magic Flute*

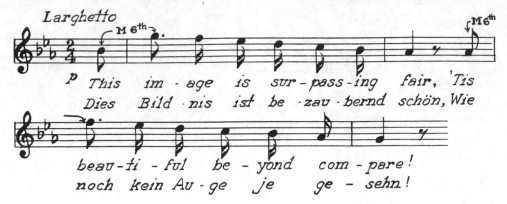

This im - age is sur - pass - ing fair, 'Tis
Dies Bild · nis ist be ·zau · bernd schön, Wie

beau – ti - ful be - yond com - pare!
noch kein Au - ge je ge – sehn!

Ex. 45   Wagner: Prelude to *Tristan and Isolde*

Major sixths may also have other expressive qualities.

Ex. 46   Negro spiritual: Nobody Knows de Trouble I Seen

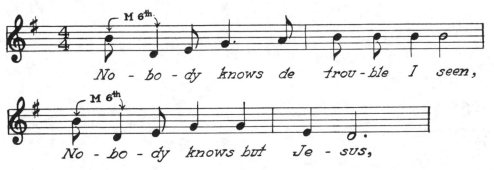

No - bo - dy knows de trou - ble I seen,

No - bo - dy knows but Je - sus,

When the major sixth is contracted by one half step to a minor sixth, its emotional possibilities become darker and more richly colored.

Ex. 47   Negro spiritual: Go Down Moses.

When Is-rael was in E-gypt land, Let my peo-ple go.

Ex. 48   Mozart: String Quintet, K. 516

For a long time, *sevenths* were considered difficult to sing. They remained, consequently, in the class of intervals labeled "forbidden." It took one rebellious period, the early Baroque, to open the door to sevenths (Ex. 49), and another, the Romantic, to establish them as a favored means of emotional utterance (Ex. 50).

Ex. 49   Monteverdi: *Orfeo*, Act II

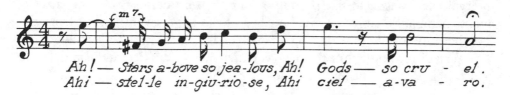

Ex. 50   Saint-Saëns: *Mon coeur s'ouvre à ta voix*, from *Samson and Delilah*

It is interesting to compare the romantic coloration of *minor sevenths* in Exs. 49 and 50 with the aggressive force of *major sevenths* in Exs. 51 and 52—all, incidentally, drawn from dramatic music of high intensity.

Ex. 51   Verdi: *O terra addio*, from *Aida*

Ex. 52   Berg: *Wozzeck*, Act I

Copyright 1926, Universal Editions, A. G., Vienna. Used by permission.

The incisive major seventh stands out in contrast to the *octave*—an interval exceeding it in size by only a half step. By comparison, the latter is almost benign. Possibly the vivid quality of the large seventh arises from the fact that it narrowly misses being an octave. The "near miss" is startling, perhaps even disturbing; while the octave, which merely duplicates the initial tone at a higher level, remains a simple interval.

Ex. 53   Major seventh and octave

The octave leap has been a familiar ingredient of melody from the days of Orlando di Lasso to the present.*

Ex. 54   Orlando di Lasso: Chanson, *Quand mon mari*

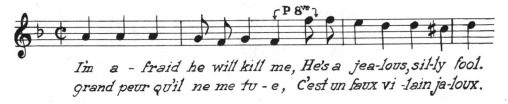

Ex. 55   Arlen: Over the Rainbow

"Over the Rainbow" by E. Y. Harburg and Harold Arlen. Copyright 1939 Leo Feist, Inc. Used by permission.

*See also Ex. 5, page 11, and Ex. 17, page 15.

This chapter by no means exhausts the subject of basic intervals, their uses and implications; the discussion will be amplified in later chapters. A few further observations, however, can be made here.

Melodic intervals are formed by two successive notes; *harmonic intervals*, by two notes sounded together.

Ex. 56   Melodic and harmonic intervals

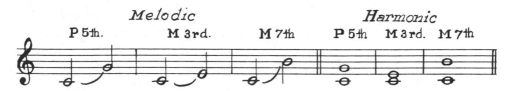

Besides its role in a given phrase, an interval may impress its character upon an entire work. The slow movement of Haydn's *Surprise* Symphony (Ex. 36) is colored by thirds; the fourth plays an important role in the opening movement of Bartók's Concerto for Orchestra (Ex. 41); and the augmented fourth, in Bernstein's *West Side Story* (Ex. 34, Chapter II).

Variation of a key interval, moreover, often produces a significant change in a composition. Beethoven, for example, created a contrast in mood in his Third Symphony by altering the first interval of the main theme from a major to a minor third (Ex. 57).

Ex. 57   Beethoven: Symphony No. 3 (*Eroica*), Op. 55

The structure of intervals is most easily learned from their positions in the scale. But once we have learned to identify them, we can regard intervals simply as units of measurement, without reference to one or another scale degree. Furthermore, although intervals have been used in various expressive ways, we must not conclude that any one is limited to a particular expressive value. Their values vary in different musical cultures. Thus a minor seventh does not have the same meaning now as it did in Palestrina's time, any more than the word "marry" bears the same connotation today as in the age of Shakespeare.

Intervals may also be employed in an abstract, non-connotative manner, simply as elements in the musical design. They are basic musical entities, each unique, all adaptable to a multitude of uses.

Summary

1. Music is motion: of melody, harmony, rhythm, form, and other elements.

2. Melodic motion utilizes both steps and leaps.

3. Melodic ranges are:
   a. Narrow (1 to 5 tones).
   b. Medium (6 to 11 tones).
   c. Wide (more than 11 tones).

4. An interval is the distance between two notes.
   a. Intervals may be formed above or below any note.
   b. The most commonly used intervals are:
      (1) Perfect primes, fourths, fifths, and octaves.
      (2) Major and minor seconds, thirds, sixths, and sevenths.
   c. Minor intervals are one half step smaller than major ones.

5. Intervals may be measured in whole and half steps:

Minor second:	½ step
Major second:	1 step
Minor third:	1½ steps
Major third:	2 steps
Perfect fourth:	2½ steps
Perfect fifth:	3½ steps
Minor sixth:	Perfect fifth plus ½ step
Major sixth:	Perfect fifth plus 1 step
Minor seventh:	Perfect fifth plus 1½ steps
Major seventh:	Perfect fifth plus 2 steps
Perfect octave:	Perfect fifth plus 2½ steps (or, simply, the same note 8 tones higher)
Perfect prime:	Two voices sounding the same note

6. Intervals are of two types:

   a. Melodic intervals, formed by two successive notes.
   b. Harmonic intervals, formed by two notes sounded together.

7. Each interval may be:
   a. Associated with certain expressive possibilities.
   b. Used in a purely abstract manner.

II

The
Tonic
Triad

Key, Tonality, and Scale

Starting with the Renaissance, a new way of creating and hearing music began to emerge in western Europe. Based on the concepts of *key* and *tonality*, it proved immensely fruitful, leading to a great expansion of expressive powers and to the evolution of important new musical forms—among them the opera, the fugue, the sonata, the concerto, and the symphony. Tonality made possible the dramatic contrasts and broad architectural values of the great masterpieces produced in the past few centuries. As we shall see, key and tonality are not identical; but between them they provided a new framework for the evolution of melody and for the emergence of harmony as a basic element of the musical language.

A *key* is a family of tones closely related to each other, but most closely related to the fundamental tone, or *tonic*. As the first and basic tone, the tonic forms a center of gravity from which the musical action springs and to which it ultimately returns. Even in the complex relationships of twentieth-century music, the tonic is often referred to as the tonal center.

Closely identified with each other, key and tonic share the same letter name. Thus, in the key of C major the tonic is C (Ex. 1) and in the key of D minor it is D (Ex. 2).

31

Ex. 1   Mozart: Sonata, K. 545

Ex. 2   Bach: *The Art of the Fugue:* Fugue No. 1

After the tonic, the tone that plays the greatest role in defining a key is the fifth, or *dominant*. Then come the remaining tones, the second, third, fourth, sixth, and seventh. They are important but not central. Thus the structure of a key comprises a hierarchy: the tonic or fundamental tone around which everything gravitates, the fifth, and the tones of lesser importance (Ex. 3).

Ex. 3   Hierarchy of tonal degrees, in C major

Another important characteristic of key structure is its internal contrast between movement and rest. Certain degrees of the key are impelled by a magnetism toward other degrees, which seem to attract them. The 2, 4, 6, and 7 tend to be active tones; they often move toward the 1, 3, 5, 7, and 8 (8 duplicates 1 an octave higher).* The tonic and 3 tend to express stability,

* Melodic tones are free to move in any direction dictated by the imagination of the composer. The tendency of, say, 7 to progress to 8 is just that—a tendency, not an eternal law. One has but to open any page of Bach or Schubert or Moussorgsky to find melodies in which 7 progresses elsewhere than to 8; the same is true of other degrees.

whereas 5 fluctuates between activity and rest. Thus the inner structure of the key is a dynamic one.

Ex. 4   Quality of degrees, in C major

The dynamic pattern of active and rest tones gravitating around a center is also referred to as *tonality*, a concept more universal than key. Tonality embraces all music possessing such a center, whether primitive or modern, Oriental or Western. Tonal music in the broadest sense makes use of many kinds of scales or *modes*.*

Key refers to music in the major and minor modes. We shall henceforth refer to compositions written in these modes as *traditional* music.

Tonality and key are inevitably linked to, but should not be confused with, the concept of *scale*. A scale is a consecutive arrangement of all the tones in a given key, moving either up or down; a key, however, can be established without necessarily sounding all the tones of its corresponding scale. Thus, in the third movement of Beethoven's *Waldstein* Sonata, only four tones of the scale—G, E, D, and C—are sufficient to establish the key of C major (Ex. 5).

Ex. 5   Beethoven: Sonata, Op. 53, third movement (*Waldstein*)

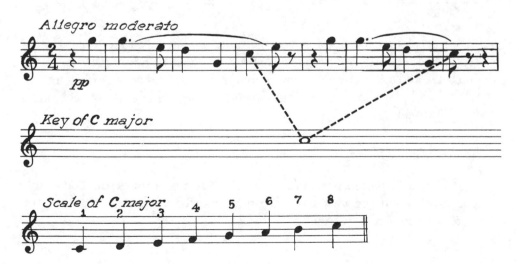

* For a discussion of modes, see Chapter V.

The steps, or *degrees,* of a key are named:

1. Tonic
2. Supertonic
3. Mediant
4. Subdominant
5. Dominant
6. Submediant
7. Leading tone

The Central Role of the Tonic

The feeling of tonality is focused on the central position of the tonic. Very often a melody starts from this tone. It passes through other tones, but almost always returns to the tonic at the end (Exs. 6, 7).

Ex. 6   French song: *Ah, vous dirai-je, maman*

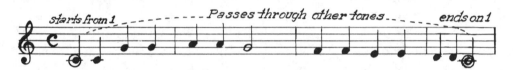

Ex. 7   Beethoven: Symphony No. 5, Op. 67, last movement

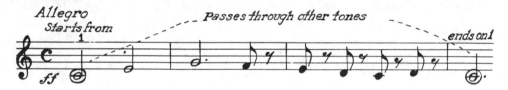

For a long time, emphasis on the tonic as a melody tone was sufficient to establish a tonality. But when the expressive needs of music grew to larger dimensions, a stronger means of projecting, masking, and then reaffirming the tonal feeling became necessary; thus developed the whole body of techniques we call harmony.

The Tonic Triad

Harmony had its roots in the *chord*—a group of tones sounded simultaneously. Around the year 850, two-tone chords consisting of a *root* (or basic tone) and a fifth were already in use.

What led man to develop the three-tone chord, the *triad,* somewhere in north-western Europe after the year 1200, we do not know. Possibly a delight in the new sonority, possibly a nascent sense of tonality. Whatever the reasons, the triad emerged after centuries of evolution as the basic chord in music.

Ex. 8   The triad

Example 8 suggests a painless definition: a triad is a three-tone chord outlined by a fifth and containing two superposed thirds; or in other words, a *root,* a *third,* and a *fifth.* A *major triad* consists of a major third topped by a minor third. Triads can be created on all degrees of the scale, but the chord based on the first tone—the *tonic triad*—is the most fundamental of all. It has played a central role in harmony for more than 500 years.

Just as the tonic note is the center of gravity of melody, so the tonic triad is the focal point of harmony—the home base from which a piece often starts and to which it almost invariably returns at the end.

Forms and Uses of the Tonic Major Triad

The tones or voices of a chord need not always be sounded together as a *block chord;* they may be played one after the other as a *broken chord* without in any way changing their harmonic structure. This is true of the tonic triad in all keys, at any pitch level.

Ex. 9   The triad as block and broken chord

In its simplest shape, a triad occurs as a chord of only three tones. It may also appear in a form in which one or more of its tones are duplicated in another octave, forming a chord of four, five, or more tones. Such duplication is called *doubling.*

Ex. 10   Tonic triad with tonic doubled an octave higher

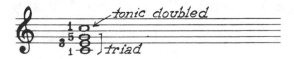

Ex. 11   Tonic triad with tonic and third doubled an octave higher

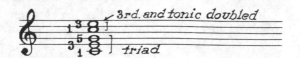

Doubling does not change the harmonic structure of a chord, although it may alter its color and resonance. No matter how often the three original tones of a triad are duplicated in one or more octaves, the chord remains identical from the harmonic point of view. Whether this doubling takes the form of a block chord or a broken chord is immaterial.

Ex. 12   C major triad, doubled

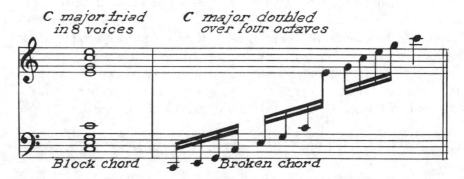

The tonic major triad—in various shapes, as block or broken chord, and in various voicings, as a three-note triad or as a triad doubled several times —has served as the opening statement of thousands of compositions from before the time of Purcell (1658–1695) to the days of Prokofiev (1891–1953).

Ex. 13   Purcell: Intrada, from Suite No. 5

Ex. 14   Chopin: Etude, Op. 10, No. 1

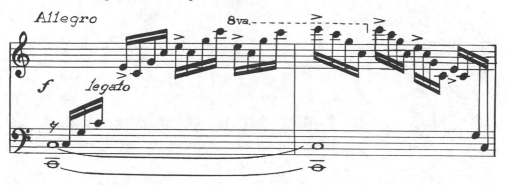

Ex. 15   Prokofiev: Prelude, Op. 12, No. 7

Examples 16 and 17 show the tonic triad in keys other than C major.

Ex. 16   Beethoven: Symphony No. 3 (*Eroica*), Op. 55

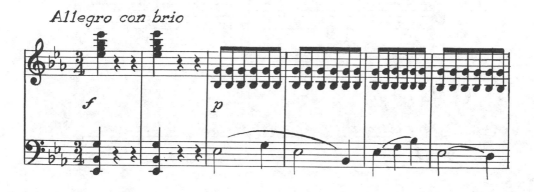

Ex. 17   Mozart: Violin Concerto, K. 219

In the seventeenth and eighteenth centuries, most compositions began with a tonic triad. Those shown above are in major; equally common were works starting with the tonic minor triad.

The Tonic Minor Triad

Major and minor triads differ in the order of their thirds. In a major triad, the lower third is major, the upper one minor. In a minor triad, the lower third is minor, the upper one major.

Ex. 18   Major triad

Ex. 19   Minor triad

As in major, the tonic triad in minor serves an important key-defining role.

Ex. 20   Vivaldi: Concerto Grosso, Op. 3, No. 11

Ex. 21 Mozart: Sonata, K. 475

Close and Open Positions

When the three tones of a triad are placed as close together as possible, the chord is said to be in *close position*. When they are spread out more widely, the chord is in *open position*. Such variations in position alter the sonority but not the harmonic meaning of a chord.

Ex. 22   Triad positions

Melody Based on the Tonic Triad

Most pieces that start with the tonic triad lead, sooner or later, to another chord. One class of composition, however—the bugle call—is based exclusively on the tonic triad, for the bugle normally plays only notes belonging to this chord. Like other tonic-triad tunes, "Taps" has an open, elemental quality.

Ex. 23   Taps

Wagner confined himself to notes of the same chord to evoke a primeval feeling.

Ex. 24   Wagner: Sword motive, from *Die Walküre*

In brief, the tonic triad, used by composers of many different persuasions for hundreds of years, has been the foundation of harmony.

Summary

1. Tonality is a pattern of tones centered around a tonic.
   a. Key is tonality in the major and minor modes.
   b. Scale is the consecutive arrangement of the tones of a key.

2. The tonic is the central tone of a key; it often begins and almost always ends a melody.

3. A key contains a contrast between active and rest tones.
   a. 2, 4, 6, and 7 tend to be active tones.
   b. 1, 3, and 8 tend to be rest tones.
   c. 5 is at times active, at times a rest tone.

4. The basic harmonic unit is the tonic triad, consisting of a root, third, and fifth.

5. A major triad = a major third + a minor third.
   A minor triad = a minor third + a major third.

6. Triads may appear:
   a. As block or broken chords.
   b. In three or more voices.
   c. In close or open position.

7. In the seventeenth and eighteenth centuries, compositions often began with the tonic triad in one form or another.

More
about Intervals

Augmented Fourth and Diminished Fifth

When medieval theorists described fourths and fifths as perfect, they encountered a slight difficulty: all such intervals fit the description except those involving the notes F and B. Sing or play a fourth or fifth between any two other notes in C major, and the interval will be perfect.

Ex. 25   Perfect fourths and fifths

Sing F—B or B—F as melodic intervals or play them as harmonic intervals, and the sound will be far from "perfect."

Ex. 26   Non-perfect fourth and fifth

To many listeners, these intervals may seem unstable or weird. The strange quality of the *augmented fourth* (F—B) and *diminished fifth* (B—F)

42

led the medieval fathers to regard them with suspicion (see Ex. 27; A = augmented, d = diminished). Known also as the *tritone* and *inverted tritone*, they were labeled *diabolus in musica*—the devil in music. Since the only trained composers then were churchmen, diminished and augmented intervals were forbidden for hundreds of years; neither the devil nor his intervals were welcome in church.

Ex. 27   Augmented fourth and diminished fifth

An augmented interval can be formed by expanding a perfect interval one half step; a diminished one, by contracting it one half step.

Ex. 28   Formation of augmented fourth and diminished fifth*

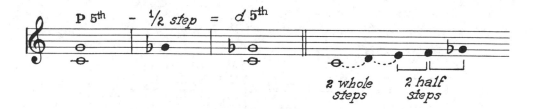

Even after the Middle Ages, the diabolical reputation of these intervals persisted. Well into the nineteenth century, they were called into action whenever a composer wished to depict ghosts, goblins, Satan, or the infernal regions.

---

*For other augmented and diminished intervals, see Chapter XIII.

Ex. 29   Berlioz: *Dream of a Witch's Sabbath*, from the *Fantastic Symphony*, Op. 14, last movement

Ex. 30   Liszt: *Inferno*, from *After a Reading of Dante*

Ex. 31   Moussorgsky: *Night on Bald Mountain*

Although it is some time now since the smell of brimstone hovered over every tritone, connotations of the strange, the wild, and the devilish still cling to this interval. Prokofiev's *Diabolical Suggestion*, composed in 1908, showed that the Evil One could still be conjured in the twentieth century by a diminished fifth.

Ex. 32   Prokofiev: *Diabolical Suggestion*, Op. 4, No. 4

In Stravinsky's *Story of a Soldier* (1917), the Devil appears "dressed as a Virtuoso Violinist," playing—no longer to our great surprise—the interval of an augmented fourth.

Ex. 33   Stravinsky: *Story of a Soldier*

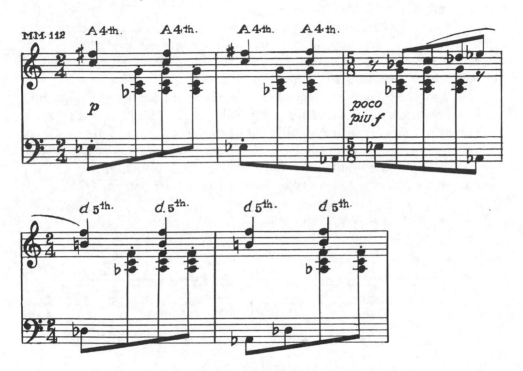

Copyright 1924 by J. & W. Chester Ltd. Used by permission.

Leonard Bernstein added contemporary meaning to the tradition when he used the augmented fourth in *West Side Story* to portray those inhabitants of today's Inferno, the hipsters and gang warriors of a slum area.

Ex. 34   Bernstein: Cool, from *West Side Story*

© MCMLVII, MCMLIX by Leonard Bernstein and Stephen Sondheim. International copyright secured. Used by permission.

We have dwelt for some time on the tritone because of its distinctive role in melodic activity. Its instability provides an important source of harmonic movement as well, in both the major and minor modes.*

* See pages 338–339.

Compound Intervals

Our discussion of intervals has been confined so far to those spanning an octave or less. Intervals surpassing an octave form a special class. Called *compound intervals,* they may be reckoned as "an octave plus a second," "an octave plus a third," and so forth.

From the harmonic viewpoint, a third and an octave plus a third serve the same function; an interval retains its identity no matter how many octaves intervene between its tones. Harmonically speaking, therefore, compound intervals are the equivalent of simple intervals.

From the standpoint of melody, however, and as sheer sound, simple and compound intervals differ markedly. The larger intervals often add special intensity and energy to a melodic phrase (see Exs. 12 and 16 in Chapter I). Their sonority, too, is distinctive. Compare the close sound of a third (Ex. 35*a*), the open sound of a third plus an octave (*b*), and the empty sound of a third plus two octaves (*c*) and plus four octaves (*d*).

Ex. 35   Simple and compound thirds

(a)	(b)	(c)	(d)
3rd.	3rd. + 8ve.	3rd.+two octaves	3rd + four octaves

In keeping with their distinctive character, certain compound intervals bear their own names. The *ninth, tenth, eleventh,* and *twelfth* are commonly referred to as such. The *thirteenth* is mentioned in connection with the chord of that number, but "fourteenth" and "fifteenth" are not used. "Sixteenth" is occasionally encountered in piano music, in the indication "16va," meaning that the passage referred to is to be played two octaves higher than written.*

Ex. 36   Minor ninth. Bach: Fugue No. 22, from *The Well-Tempered Clavier,* Book I

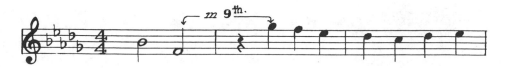

* Strictly speaking, the double octave is a *fifteenth.*

Ex. 37   Major ninth. Mozart: Sonata, K. 533

Ex. 38   Major and minor tenths. Bach: Concerto for Two Violins in D minor

Ex. 39   Perfect eleventh (harmonic interval). Ravel: *Rigaudon,* from *Le Tombeau de Couperin*

Permission for reprint granted by Durand et Cie., Paris, copyright owner, and Elkan-Vogel Co., Inc., Philadelphia, agents.

Ex. 40   Perfect twelfth. Mozart: *Per pietà, ben mio,* from *Cosi fan tutte*

Ex. 41   Major thirteenth (harmonic interval). Jazz progression

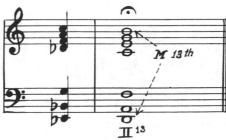

Inversions of Intervals

We have already noted that a perfect fourth plus a perfect fifth form a perfect octave. Two intervals that form a perfect octave when added together are said to be *inversions* of each other. An interval may be inverted by placing the lower note an octave higher, or the upper note an octave lower.

Ex. 42   Interval inversion: fourths and fifths

Besides fourths and fifths, other pairs of invertible intervals are (1) thirds and sixths, and (2) seconds and sevenths. It is characteristic of each of these pairs that if one interval is major, the other must be minor. Thus a major interval, when inverted, becomes a minor one.

Ex. 43   Invertible thirds and sixths; and seconds and sevenths

Diminished and augmented intervals likewise serve as inversions of each other. (Intervals larger than an octave, by definition, cannot be inverted.)

Ex. 44   Invertible tritones

As we shall see, interval inversion serves as an important melodic device, and plays a role in harmony as well.*

---

* For melodic inversion, see page 219*ff;* for the inversion of a harmonic bass, page 226 (footnote).

Relative Force of Intervals

Intervals have been described thus far one at a time. In actual music they occur consecutively, and their force is relative. In a phrase containing only small intervals (Ex. 45), the jump of a fourth (*a*) is emphatic; but in a melody containing wide leaps (Ex. 46), it seems restrained in comparison to the more active intervals.

Ex. 45   Brahms: Symphony No. 2, Op. 73

Ex. 46   Beethoven: Sonata, Op. 10, No. 1, last movement

In Ex. 46, the energetic character of the phrase grows as it passes from a perfect fourth (*a*), through a minor sixth (*b*), to an octave (*c*).

From this and previous observations, we can conclude:

1. Of the *diatonic* intervals (those formed by tones of the scale), the larger the interval, the greater its force—except in two special cases:
   a. the tritone, an extremely active interval; and
   b. the seventh (especially the major seventh), which is more forceful than the octave.
2. *Chromatic* intervals (those that contain a tone or tones not forming part of the key) are often more active than diatonic intervals of larger size.*

* Compare the effect of the chromatic seconds in Ex. 34, page 21, with that of the diatonic thirds in Ex. 36, page 22.

3. Rising intervals are more vigorous than falling ones of the same size.*

Since our immediate concern is with basic chords, we shall use only the simple diatonic major, minor, and perfect intervals for the time being in our study of harmony.

Summary

1. All fourths and fifths in the major scale are perfect, except:
   a. 4 rising to 7 (augmented fourth).
   b. 7 rising to 4 (diminished fifth).

2. Diminished intervals are one half step smaller than perfect intervals.

3. Augmented intervals are one half step larger than perfect intervals.

4. The augmented fourth (tritone) and diminished fifth (inverted tritone) are highly active, unstable intervals. For a long time they suggested the diabolical.

5. Compound intervals are those wider than an octave.

6. Invertible intervals are any two that form a perfect octave when added together.

7. Perfect intervals invert with each other; major and minor intervals form invertible pairs, as do diminished and augmented ones.

8. The force of an interval is relative to other intervals that precede and follow it.

9. Among diatonic intervals, the larger the interval, the greater the force, except for:
   a. The seventh, which is more active than the octave.
   b. The tritone, an extremely active interval.

---

* Compare the rising major sixth (Ex. 44, page 24) and the falling one (Ex. 46, page 24).

10. Chromatic intervals may be more active than diatonic intervals of larger size.

11. Rising intervals are more active than falling ones of the same size.

III

Thursday

The
Dominant
Triad

The Dominant Tone

More than a thousand years ago, musical theorists recorded a fact known intuitively to primitive and folk musicians for a long time: the fifth, after the tonic, is the most important degree in the scale. The close relationship between these two basic degrees is grounded in nature. Blow an open horn, trumpet, or bugle, and the first tone produced after the tonic will be the fifth.* Divide a string in half, and the sound it produces will be the octave above the tonic; divide it into thirds, and you get the next fifth above. The Greek philosopher Pythagoras was the first to point out the relation between this simple mathematical ratio and the musical interval of the fifth. From this and similar observations, he concluded that musical intervals embody the orderly proportions of nature.

In the musical practice of many peoples, the fifth and the tonic have the strongest of relationships, the two notes acting as twin magnetic poles. In many medieval melodies, the pattern 1—5—1 establishes the tonality. The movement tonic–dominant–tonic is both ancient and fundamental.

The movement 1—5—1 illustrates the contrast between activity and rest already discussed.† Whereas the tonic expresses stability, the dominant is all energy. It seeks to move forward and attain its goal—the tonic.

* See Appendix I for a discussion of the *overtone series*, alluded to here.

† For further examples, see Ex. 2, page 32, and Exs. 6–7, page 34.

To explore this pattern, sing Exs. 1 and 2, stopping when you come to the dominant. Can you end there? Hardly! While the preceding tones lead up to 5, the 5 itself asks to reach still further, to end on the tonic.

Ex. 1   Plain chant: *Kyrie Alme Pater*

Ex. 2   Adam de la Halle: *Robin m'aime*, from *Robin et Marion* (1284)

The Dominant Triad

Just as the dominant is the second most important tone of the key, the dominant triad is the second most important chord. A major triad, it consists of the fifth, seventh, and second degrees of the scale.

From this point on, we shall refer to triads built on various degrees by using Roman numerals written under the staff, and to single tones by using Arabic numerals written above. Thus the tonic triad = I; the dominant triad, V; the tonic tone, 1, and the dominant tone, 5.

Ex. 3   Chord symbols and tone numerals

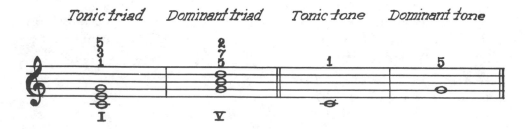

As with the tonic and dominant tones, there is a sharp contrast between the tonic and dominant chords. The I is stable, whereas the V is active and restless, and seeks to achieve rest by moving to the I. This motion from an unstable to a stable chord is called *resolution*.

Besides 5, which forms its root, the dominant triad includes as its third the seventh tone of the scale. As the leading tone, 7 is the most active of all scale steps; its dynamic quality and its urge to resolve enhance the forceful character of the V chord. When the scale moves up toward 7, there is a strong impulse not to stop there but to resolve the highly unstable tone to the eighth scale step, the tonic (Ex. 4).

Ex. 4   Resolution of 7

Conversely, when the scale descends, 2 is drawn strongly to 1. (In the course of such a downward movement, 7 moves down to 6.)

Ex. 5   Resolution of 2

The dominant triad, like the tonic, can be written in different positions and as a broken chord. It may also appear with one or more of its voices doubled. No matter what the position or the doubling, combinations of 5—7—2 always form a V chord.

Ex. 6   V in various positions and as broken chord

Ex. 7   V with voices doubled

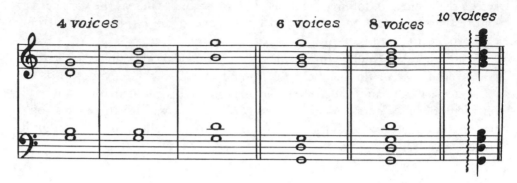

The V—I Progression

The V—I progression, fundamental in traditional music, is found in compositions of many different periods and styles.

Ex. 8   Giles Farnaby (1560–1640): *A Toye*

Ex. 9   Mozart: *Susanna, or via sortite*, from *The Marriage of Figaro*

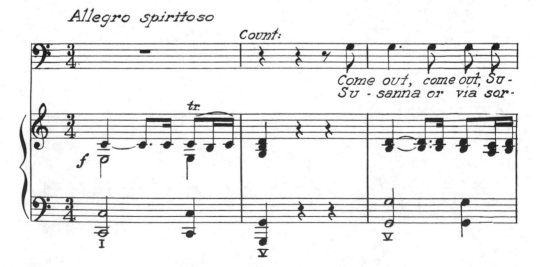

Ex. 10   Beethoven: Symphony No. 5, Op. 67

Ex. 11   Pop Goes the Weasel

Besides its other uses, the V—I progression plays a special role in traditional music, as the normal ending of a section or an entire composition. This
closing progression, which brings music to a resting point, is called a *cadence*.

Ex. 12   Haydn: Symphony No. 3 (Eulenberg edition)

Ex. 13   Mendelssohn: Symphony No. 4 (*Italian*), Op. 90, last movement

The Connection of I and V

When I and V follow one another, they are generally connected as smoothly as possible. Each tone of the I should move the smallest distance to the nearest tone of the V, then back again to the I.

Ex. 14   I—V—I

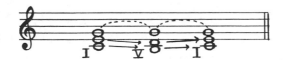

In addition to its chordal aspect, the progression in Ex. 14 may be considered as three separate lines or *voices* moving forward (→) from chord to chord. The top voice repeats the same tone (G); the middle voice moves down one step and then back again (E–D–E); and the lowest voice does the same (C–B–C). The movement of the voices and the change of chords work together to produce a smooth progression.

* Numbers in brackets are discussed later.

The I—V—I progression may be written in various positions. The tone belonging to both chords is called the *common tone*. While the other voices move, the common tone remains stationary, forming a link between the two chords.

Ex. 15   Connections of I—V—I

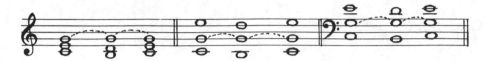

It is standard practice in traditional music to hold the common tone stationary whenever possible. In Ex. 16, note the stationary B (the lowest note in the right hand). The other voices move, but the B remains motionless throughout, connecting the I and V chords.

Ex. 16   Schubert: *Wasserfluth*

From the Schubert phrase we can make three observations concerning harmonization:

1. When a melody tone or group of tones belong to the I chord, they are harmonized by that chord; when they belong to the V they are harmonized by the V.
2. When the melody leaps, outlining a broken chord, the harmony remains stationary.
3. In the smoothest harmonization, voices move as little as possible.

Harmonization with the I and V Triads

To learn the use of the I and V chords, let us start with a short melodic phrase. The familiar folk song *Au clair de la lune* may be harmonized by adding under each melody tone the two nearest tones of the appropriate triad, I or V.

Ex. 17   Elementary harmonization

The same triads can be written as block chords.

Ex. 18   Harmonization in block chords

If a melody contains only those tones (1, 2, 3, 7) that form part of either the I or the V, but not of both, setting a chord under each tone is a straightforward matter. But what of a melody that contains the 5 repeated several times?

Ex. 19   French traditional melody: *As-tu vu la casquette?*

As the common tone between I and V, the 5 may be harmonized by either. A question then arises: Which chord should be chosen? And why, in any particular case?

We can be guided in finding the answers by Schubert's practice in Ex. 16. Following his example, we *retain the same chord whenever the melody jumps along chord lines.* Thus, the 5 could be harmonized by I throughout Ex. 20.

Ex. 20   Harmonization with I chord

This method carries out the principle well enough. Unfortunately, it leads to a boring result; constant repetition of I produces a static harmony, adding no motion to the tune.

To create harmonic movement, we introduce the V chord.

Ex. 21   Harmonization with I and V

The improvement gained by this addition leads us to modify the previous conclusions: when a melody jumps along chord lines, we retain the same harmony *except where a change of chord adds variety and motion to the phrase.*

Summary

1. The dominant (5) is the second most important tone of the key.

2. Although it may be the goal toward which other tones strive, in itself 5 is an active tone with a strong drive to the tonic.

3. Many melodies, following the pattern of rest-activity-rest, start on 1, move through 5, and return to 1.

4. The dominant triad (V) is an active chord, deriving its character from the active tones 5, 7, and 2 that make it up.

5. Like the I, V may appear in various positions and doublings.

6. I and V together provide the harmonic basis of many phrases.

7. To create the smoothest connection between I and V:
   a. The common tone should be kept stationary.
   b. The other voices should move the smallest possible distance.

8. In harmonizing melodies, when the melody leaps along chord lines the chord remains the same, except where a change of chord is needed for variety and motion.

Melodic Curves

Previously we have seen melody as the motion of a single voice or instrument, utilizing both steps and leaps, in a range that varies from narrow to wide. Another important characteristic of melody is its linear outline. Listening to a passage from Beethoven's Violin Concerto, we hear a flowing melody of medium range.

Ex. 22   Beethoven: Violin Concerto, Op. 61

Note the line gliding up and down, and then up and down again.

Such a pattern marking the outline of a melody is called a *melodic curve*.

What is the importance of studying the melodic curve? First, it enables you to grasp the pattern of melody as a whole. Second, you will understand the basic structure of melodies in the music you are studying or performing. Third, the curve serves as a framework to help you hold the total shape in mind when writing your own tunes.

Knowledge of melodic curves helps you avoid the note-by-note approach, leading instead toward the creation of long-line melodies. It is equally important in the study of harmony. A good harmonic progression has well-defined melodic curves in both soprano and bass. Awareness of melodic curve leads you to write the outer voices in well-shaped, flowing patterns.

Nine types of melodic curves emerge from a study of chants, folk songs, arias, and instrumental themes of many different periods.

1. *The Wave*

One of the most familiar types of melodies follows the pattern shown in Ex. 23.

Ex. 23   The wave

Ernst Toch, who was among the first to describe various melodic curves,* called this pattern a *wave*. Its undulations are gentle; they carry us along peacefully, avoiding the intensity of strong contrasts and big climaxes. The wave may reach its highest tone several times, without building to a climax.

In the eleventh-century plain chant of Ex. 24, the motion is placid and restrained—mostly stepwise, with an occasional small leap. Note the threefold repetition of the highest tone (*a*).

Ex. 24   Plain chant: *Kyrie Deus sempiterne*

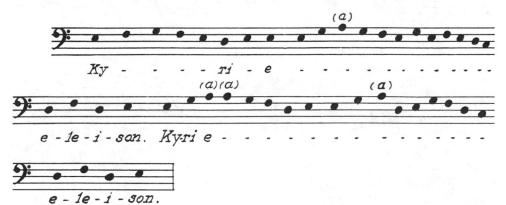

* In *The Shaping Forces in Music*, p. 78.

A wave melody may also contain wider leaps. (In Ex. 25 and hereafter, the peaks are marked with asterisks.) Characteristically, the wave weaves back and forth around a central axis, leading in no definite direction.

Ex. 25   Copland: *El Salon Mexico*

Sometimes the up-and-down movement of a wave reaches a considerable height, with swiftly rising crests and equally swift drops.

Ex. 26   Schumann: *Vogel als Prophet*, from *Waldszenen*, Op. 82

One of the most familiar patterns, the wave remains just as useful today as in the past, serving in the melodies of both serious and popular modern masters. In keeping with Stravinsky's style, the wave in Ex. 27 has a more jagged quality than do those of earlier composers.

Ex. 27   Stravinsky: *Symphony of Psalms*, second movement

Ex. 28   Carmichael: Stardust

2. *The Wave with Climax*

Often we come across a melody that hovers back and forth with no apparent goal for a few measures. Then, just before the end of the phrase, the line rises to a high point, or *climax:* the wave motion has reached a goal.* Called a *wave with climax*, this type of melody has a decisive quality different from the wave itself.

---

* The climax may be the very last note of a phrase, or it may be followed by a quick relaxing movement.

Ex. 29   Wave with climax

Ex. 30   Chopin: Waltz, Op. 34, No. 2

Ex. 31   Wagner: Siegfried's Horn Call, from *Götterdämmerung*

3. *The Rising Wave*

Most dynamic of the wave patterns, the *rising wave* was especially favored by Romantic composers. In such a curve, the melody rises up, drops back a little, rises still higher, recedes again, and reaches a grand climax shortly before the end. Its energy spent, the wave subsides rapidly. Example 32 outlines the rising wave, and Ex. 33 illustrates it.

Ex. 32   The rising wave

Ex. 33   Schubert: Waltz in A flat, Op. 9a

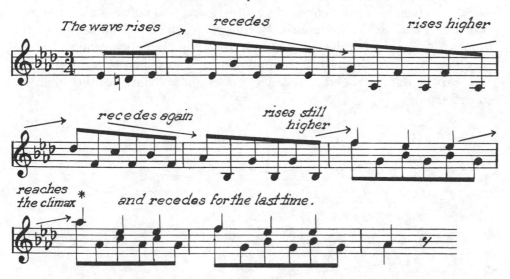

In the hands of a skillful composer, the rising wave becomes a subtle form of musical motion. Each crest rises higher than the previous one, but not by a fixed amount; nor is the distance between two crests always the same.

Ex. 34   Chopin: Nocturne, Op. 9, No. 2

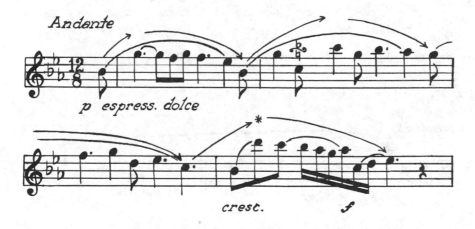

Noting the high points of this melody, observe that the first follows a leap of a sixth; the second, an octave leap; the third, the leap of a tenth. Each climactic note is not only higher than the preceding, but is also reached by a wider leap.

As for spacing, the first high point comes after one eighth note; the second, after one and a quarter measures; and then nearly two measures prepare for the final climax. The variations in height and breadth of each successive ascent add interest to this rising wave.

4. *The Falling Wave*

A fourth melodic curve, the *falling wave*, is almost exactly the opposite of the last one. Yet, interestingly enough, its emotional impact is not the
opposite. Even though the line descends instead of rising, its emotional intensity does not dwindle; instead, it often continues unabated to the end. True,
the final measures frequently reveal a gentler, more "inner" quality than the
opening ones.

Ex. 35   The falling wave

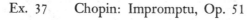

Ex. 36   Puccini: *Un bel di*, from *Madame Butterfly*

By courtesy of the publisher, G. Ricordi & Co., Milan.

Ex. 37   Chopin: Impromptu, Op. 51

Ex. 38   Tchaikovsky: *Romeo and Juliet* Overture

5. The Arch

The *arch* provides another familiar melodic curve. Like its counterpart in architecture, it has a rounded, symmetrical form.

Ex. 39   The arch

In an arch, the climax occurs at or near the middle of the phrase. The melody approaches the peak by an upward-curving movement and leaves it in a similar downward sweep.

Ex. 40   Brahms: How Lovely Is Thy Dwelling Place, from *The German Requiem*, Op. 45

Another type of arch rises and falls in a wave-like motion.

Ex. 41   Ornamented arch

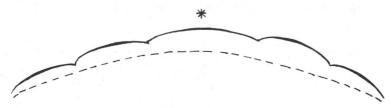

Ex. 42   Mozart: Overture, *The Marriage of Figaro*

Ex. 43   Bach: Fugue No. 6, from *The Well-Tempered Clavier*, Book II

6. *The Bowl*

The opposite of the arch is another symmetrical curve, the *bowl*. Starting at or near the highest note, it slopes to a low point in the middle of the phrase, then rises at the end to approximately its original pitch. The bowl often forms a graceful curve, paralleling the form of a valley. (In Exs. 44–46, the downward arrow indicates the low point.)

Ex. 44   The bowl

Ex. 45   Handel: Joy to the World

Joy to the world! The Lord is   come! Let earth re-ceive her King.

Ex. 46   Bach: Concerto for Two Violins in D minor

7. *The Rising Line*

As its name implies, the *rising line* forms the simplest of melodic patterns. It also poses a problem: what can one do with a scale that has not already been done a thousand times? Merely putting one note after another, always a step higher, would seem the most mechanical of procedures—yet in just such challenging situations is the master revealed. Beethoven, Brahms, and Chopin made distinguished melodies from a rising line.

Ex. 47   Beethoven: Symphony No. 1, Op. 21, third movement

Ex. 48   Brahms: Symphony No. 1, Op. 68

Ex. 49   Chopin: Mazurka in B flat, Op. 7, No. 1

8. *The Falling Line*

The *falling line*, like its converse, is difficult to present in an interesting way. Wagner used a descending scale to represent Wotan's spear in his opera *Die Walküre*. Scoring the phrase for four trombones and tuba playing staccato, he imparted theatrical effectiveness to a familiar formula.

Ex. 50   Wagner: Spear motive, from *Die Walküre*

The "Habanera" from *Carmen* (Ex. 34 in Chapter I) presents another falling line. Sinuous and seductive, it is a far cry from Wagner's spear motive! Other chromatic falling lines are provided in Exs. 51 and 52.

Ex. 51   Saint-Saëns: *Mon coeur s'ouvre à ta voix*, from *Samson and Delilah*

Ex. 52   Rodgers: Lover

9. *The Horizontal Line*

Last of the nine melodic curves, the *horizontal line* scarcely forms a **curve** at all; its hovering quality is the nearest thing to motionlessness. We have already seen examples of this pattern (Exs. 7, 14, and 15 in Chapter I). Beyond its role in ritual music, the horizontal line serves in quiet, brooding passages (Ex. 53), or—at the other extreme—in music of primitive violence (Ex. 54).

Ex. 53   Schubert: Death and the Maiden

Ex. 54   Stravinsky: Dance of the Adolescents, from *The Rite of Spring*

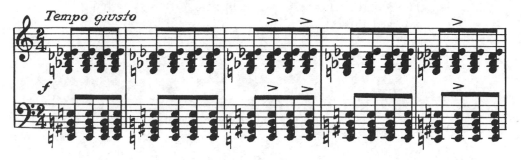

A horizontal melody is often supported by a highly directional harmony (see the Chopin Prelude, Ex. 5 in Chapter I).

Concluding this discussion of melodic curves, it would be pleasant to believe we have discovered a formula for classifying all melodies—pleasant, but scarcely accurate, for art has a way of slipping out of neat formulas. The concept of melodic curve is valuable so long as it is not rigidly applied. Some melodies are elusive; they simply resist classification. Many, however, do follow the patterns of the various melodic curves—a fact most clearly revealed when they are examined one phrase at a time.

The Compound Curve

Frequently, two or more curves are joined in a more complex pattern called a *compound curve*. In Exs. 55 and 56, for example, a wave is followed by a falling line.

Ex. 55   Stravinsky: *Petrushka*

Ex. 56   American folk song: Old Joe Clarke

The *double arch* forms another familiar type of compound curve. Note that the second arch rises a bit higher than the first, giving the entire passage an upward direction.

Ex. 57   Gershwin: I Got Rhythm

The opening section of the Beethoven Minuet in Ex. 58 forms a *double falling wave*.

Ex. 58   Beethoven: Piano Sonata, Op. 10, No. 3, third movement

As in Ex. 57, the second curve of this melody rises slightly higher than the first, imparting a sense of forward movement to the whole. Moreover, it also descends lower, reaching a *climactic low point at the end* (↓).

The Over-all Curve

We have considered thus far only the melodic curve of a single phrase, or at most a short section of a piece. It is also possible to outline the curve of an entire composition, by combining the curves of its individual sections into one *over-all curve*.

Beethoven's Minuet in G, for example, contains three parts, each with its individual curve:

> A —falling wave
> B —arch
> A'—wave

Ex. 59   Beethoven: Minuet in G

When all three are joined in an over-all curve, the result is a broad arch.*

Ex. 60   Over-all curve

For the time being, we shall be concerned with only one phrase or short section of a composition—and therefore with only simple and compound curves. Later we shall consider the over-all curve of an entire composition.

Summary

1. Melodic structure is outlined by melodic curves.

2. The nine melodic curves are:
   a. The wave.
   b. The wave with climax.
   c. The rising wave.
   d. The falling wave.
   e. The arch.
   f. The bowl.
   g. The rising line.
   h. The falling line.
   i. The horizontal line.

3. Various curves may be combined to create:
   a. A compound curve (a pattern containing two or more curves).
   b. An over-all curve (the curve of a whole composition).

*Ex. 39, page 451, also has three parts: a falling wave (bars 1-8), a rising wave (bars 10-22), and another falling wave (bars 23-31). The over-all curve is a broad arch.

IV

Four-Part
Harmony

In the early Middle Ages, the only European music in notation consisted of one-voice melodies. By the ninth century, two-part music had developed; and at the time that Notre Dame Cathedral was being built in Paris (about 1200), the great French composer Perotin had begun to experiment boldly with three- and four-part writing. Although his was a tremendous advance in musical thinking, we cannot yet call it "harmony," because it did not follow principles of chord progression later associated with the term.

Harmony began to take shape in the music of the Renaissance and in the chorales sung in Protestant churches during the Reformation. As this period progressed, the practice of writing chords in four parts gradually became standardized.

Four-part harmony has much to recommend it. Harmony in three parts is often lucid and transparent, but it can make for difficulties in creating a full sound. Five-part writing produces a rich sonority, but it presents many more problems in writing and in performance than four-part. Four-part harmony provides a balanced division of the voices into male and female, high and low.

Until now we have studied chords in three voices. How are we to create four-part settings with three-note triads? Very simply: by doubling one of the parts. Let us convert one of the chord progressions of Chapter III into four-part harmony by adding a bass part. Note that the second chord in Ex. 2 is in close position, whereas the first and third are in open.

79

Ex. 1   Three-part progression

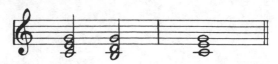

Ex. 2   Four-part progression

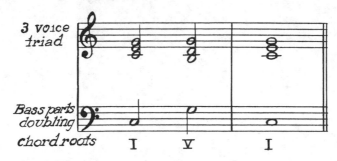

Play these two progressions on the piano. Note the fuller sound of Ex. 2; the addition of the fourth part, which doubles the root of each chord, gives solidity to the progression.

Although four-part harmony can be written for the piano or for four instruments, the best practice for the beginner is to write for chorus in four parts: soprano, alto, tenor, and bass. Written exercises should be sung aloud whenever possible, so that one can hear the parts with clarity and note the resonance of each chord.

The Range of Voices

The range of the average choral singer is shown in Ex. 3. The black notes, however, should be used only on special occasions—when a climax is desired, when there is need for some special color, or when no other note will possibly do. These notes (as you will observe when you hear them sung) often sound strained on top, thin and insubstantial on the bottom.

Ex. 3   Voice ranges

The four voices are written on two staves—soprano and alto in the treble clef, tenor and bass in the bass clef. For the upper voices on each staff, stems go up; for the lower voices, down.

Ex. 4   Notation of four voices

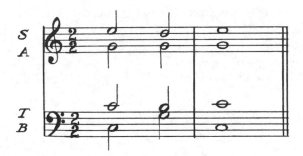

Characteristics of Four-Part Writing

Let us examine some of the basic principles of traditional four-part writing, starting with a few simple examples. First, the opening of an anthem by the early American composer William Billings.

Ex. 5   Billings: Universal Praise

O praise God, O praise God,

What characteristics of four-part harmony can be observed in this brief excerpt?

1. Four voices are present in every chord, each in its own range.
2. The voices are set in traditional order, from the top down: soprano, alto, tenor, bass. There is no *crossing*, or inverting the order, of voices.

3. Each chord is complete, containing at least one root, one third, and one fifth.
4. The chord roots are doubled.
5. The distances between soprano and alto, and between alto and tenor, respectively, are never more than an octave. The tenor and bass, however, are sometimes more than an octave apart.
6. When the melody leaps, the chord remains the same.
7. The common tone (G) between the I and V chords starts in the soprano and continues in the alto.
8. When the chords change, the inner voices (alto and tenor) move the smallest possible distance.
9. The bass, which outlines the chord changes, moves with greater freedom than the inner voices.
10. No augmented or diminished intervals are used, nor are other intervals that are difficult to sing, such as sevenths or compound intervals.

Handel's *Israel in Egypt* provides a second example.

Ex. 6   Handel: But the Waters Overwhelmed, from *Israel in Egypt*

Most of the observations made concerning the Billings anthem apply equally to the phrase from Handel. In the Handel work, however, the tenor and bass are largely in close position; indeed, they sing in unison at the beginning of measure 2. The common tone G remains in the same voice (the alto) throughout. Note that the chord changes reinforce the 4/4 meter, falling regularly on the first and third beats.

One new technique has been added in the Handel example: *the exchange of tones* between two voices. The soprano moves from 7, the leading tone, at (*a*), to 2, at (*b*). In order to avoid omitting the third of the chord at (*b*), Handel shifts the tenor from 2, at (*a*), to 7, at (*b*), effecting the exchange of tones.

A third example of four-part harmony is the *Bransle de Bourgogne*, by the French composer Claude Gervaise.

Ex. 7   Gervaise: *Bransle de Bourgogne* (ca. 1550)

From Ex. 7, further observations can be made concerning four-part harmony.

1. Chords sounded at the beginning of a bar are repeated within the bar and sometimes also in the following one or two bars.
2. Chord changes occur over the bar line.
3. The soprano is the most tuneful and active of the voices. It also has the freest rhythm.
4. There are short unaccented tones (at *a*, *c*, and *f*) that do not form part of the chords. They are embellishing tones.*
5. The fifth of the chord may sometimes be omitted and the root tripled, as at (*b*). In traditional style, the third may never be omitted. It is not usually doubled in a major triad.
6. When the bass remains stationary, the other voices sometimes all leap in the same direction (*d*).
7. The leading tone (*e*) is not doubled.

Harmonic Change and Meter

Before proceeding to harmonize melodies, let us examine the relation between chord changes and meter. In traditional music, harmonic changes normally coincide with and emphasize the metrical accent. When there has

* Discussed in Chapter VI.

been a choice between changing the harmony within the bar or over the bar line, composers have generally chosen the latter.

Example 8 presents a short melodic phrase to be harmonized with the I and V chords.

Ex. 8   Melodic phrase

There is no problem in bar 1, for it can be harmonized only by the I. The same holds for bar 2; the downbeat must be harmonized by the V, and it is logical to retain that chord when the melody leaps to the second note.

Ex. 9   Harmonization of 2 bars

There are two possible ways of harmonizing the third and fourth bars, since 5, as we know, can take either the I or the V. First, one can hold the V over the bar line, changing to I on the second beat of bar 3 (a), and holding that chord over the next bar line (b).

Ex. 10   Tentative harmonization

But this harmonization is weak: the failure to change chords between bars 2 and 3 and bars 3 and 4 contradicts the meter, weakening the rhythmic pulse.

A second way of harmonizing the phrase is to change chords over the bar line. This harmonic change reinforces the meter, strengthening the rhythm of the entire phrase.

Ex. 11   Chord changes over the bar line

Experiments of this kind reveal the extent to which harmonic change depends upon and in turn influences meter. Going a step farther, we find that harmonic change in itself may *create* meter. What, for example, is the meter of the phrase in Ex. 12?

Ex. 12   Repeated note without meter

As presented here, it is impossible to tell. The situation remains the same if we harmonize the phrase with only one chord. Without an alteration of harmony, no rhythmic effect is produced.

Ex. 13   Harmonization with one repeated chord

But the moment the chords are changed, a rhythmic impulse arises; changes at regular intervals create metrical patterns.

Ex. 14   Harmonic change at regular intervals

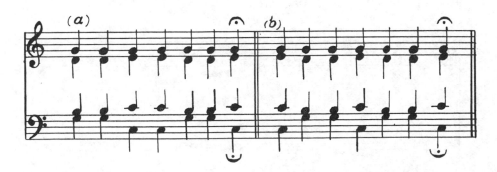

In (a), the harmony changes every two beats, producing a 2/4 meter; in (b), every three beats, forming a 3/4 meter. The pattern of regular bass movement implies the bar lines shown in Ex. 15.

Ex. 15   Harmonic change with meter indicated

It becomes apparent that harmonic change can create a metrical pulse. Most music, of course, contains other rhythm-defining elements, such as melody and accompaniment patterns. But even then, the rhythm of harmonic change, outlined primarily by the movement of the bass, is fundamental in reinforcing or negating the meter. Whether analyzing a composition, preparing a work for performance, harmonizing a melody, or writing a chord progression, the student should be aware of *harmonic rhythm* as a means of emphasizing the forward-moving impulse of music.

Contrapuntal Motion in Harmony

Two basic features of a good harmonic progression are: (1) effective choice of chords, and (2) good voice leading. Good voice leading depends on the smooth progression of the individual voices and their independence of movement. European music, as we have seen, evolved from melodic sources. When two-part music came into existence, composers sought ways of assuring the independent movement of each part. The art of creating independent melodies that combine well is called *counterpoint*.

There are four basic types of contrapuntal motion:

1. *Contrary* motion, in which voices move in opposite directions.

Ex. 16   Bach: Two-Part Invention No. 6

2. *Oblique* motion, in which one voice remains stationary while other voices move.

Ex. 17   Bach: Two-Part Invention No. 4

3. *Similar* motion, in which voices move in the same direction, by different intervals.

Ex. 18   Haydn: Symphony No. 103 (*The Drumroll*), last movement

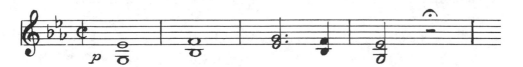

4. *Parallel* motion, in which voices move in the same direction, by the same interval.

Ex. 19   Mozart: *Papageno, Papagena,* from *The Magic Flute*

Contrapuntal motion concerns us here because harmony was a later outgrowth of counterpoint, retaining in its method the same basic voice-leading patterns found in the earlier art.

Independent movement is promoted most strongly by contrary and oblique motion; moderately by similar motion; and not at all by parallel motion. For example, look at the first phrase of Beethoven's *Ode to Joy.*

Ex. 20   Beethoven: *Ode to Joy*, from Symphony No. 9, **Op.** 125, last movement

To this part a second voice can be added, by singing the same melody an octave lower.

Ex. 21   Beethoven: *Ode to Joy*, in parallel octaves

By supplying a second voice in parallel octaves, we have neither created a new and independent melodic line nor enriched the original tune contrapuntally or harmonically. At most we have increased its sonority and perhaps its volume.

Now let us substitute, as a second part, an interval of a fifth instead of an octave.

Ex. 22   Beethoven: *Ode to Joy*, in parallel fifths

We can see that parallel fifths, besides being contrary to the style of traditional music, do not enrich a melody much more than do parallel octaves. The second voice merely duplicates the first in almost the same fashion.

During the period 1400 to 1900, consecutive parallel octaves and fifths were, for the most part, rigorously avoided. When composers wished to move voices in parallel fashion, they employed thirds and sixths—considered a smoother way of blending the voices.

Turning now to Beethoven's own method of harmonizing the *Ode to Joy*, observe, under the familiar melody, the bass shown in Ex. 23.

Ex. 23   Beethoven: *Ode to Joy*

Here, certainly, is an independent, contrapuntal melody added to the original one. In bars 1 and 2, the two lines move in contrary motion. In bar 3, we find oblique motion: the bass repeats the A while the upper voice rises. The last bar shows similar motion between (*a*) and (*b*).

Not every progression, however, can follow contrapuntal principles entirely. In many harmonic passages, the independence of parts is restricted to a contrast between the soprano and the bass. The role of the inner voices—alto and tenor—remains the more modest one of filling in the desired notes of the chord.

Another section of the Ninth Symphony illustrates this harmonic type of writing, as contrasted with the previous contrapuntal treatment.

Ex. 24   Beethoven: Symphony No. 9, Op. 125, last movement

Comparing soprano and bass, we find a predominance of oblique motion (bars 1 to 3, 5 to 8), with one bar of contrary motion (bar 4). The inner voices have less independence; the alto holds the common tone practically throughout, and the tenor, except for bars 4 to 6, moves in parallel tenths with the soprano. The second treatment of the melody (Ex. 24) is less contrapuntal than the first (Ex. 23).

In the harmonic style (Ex. 24), then, soprano and bass play a more important role than the inner voices. This style, relying mainly on block chords (later also on broken chords) will be our main concern in the present studies.

Summary

1. Harmony is customarily written for four voices: soprano, alto, tenor, and bass.

2. To form four-part chords, use complete triads (with root, third, and fifth), and double the root. The fifth of the chord may sometimes be omitted and the root tripled. The third may never be omitted; it is not usually doubled in a major triad.

3. The leading tone is never doubled.

4. Spacing:
   Soprano and alto }
   Alto and tenor   } are never more than an octave apart.
   Tenor and bass may be more than an octave apart.

5. Melodic leaps normally avoided in harmonic writing are diminished and augmented intervals, sevenths, and compound intervals.

6. Chord changes:
   a. Chords often change at the bar line.
   b. One chord may be kept for an entire bar and for part or all of the following bar or bars.
   c. When the harmony changes within a bar, it should also change over the next bar line.
   d. When chords change, the common tone is held in the same voice, whenever possible; the three other voices move the smallest possible distance.

7. Chord changes and meter:
   a. Chord changes that fall on the strong beats reinforce the meter and make for strong, well-defined progressions.
   b. Chord progressions that contradict the metrical accents involve more sophisticated rhythmic techniques. They should not be attempted at this early stage.
   c. Harmonic rhythm refers to the frequency of chord change.

8. Good harmonic progression depends on good contrapuntal motion. Desirable forms of motion include:
   a. Contrary motion (voices moving in opposite direction).
   b. Oblique motion (one voice stationary, the others moving).
   c. Similar motion (voices moving in same direction, at different intervals).
   d. Parallel motion (voices moving in same direction in thirds, sixths, and tenths, but *not* in fifths or octaves).

Melody Writing

Thoughts on Melody Writing

Surprisingly little has been written by composers (who are sometimes as prolific with words as with notes) on the subject of melody writing. Yet perhaps it is not so strange, for melody is the most personal aspect of music; through melody a composer frequently reveals the subtlest shadings of his feeling. Often a melodic idea springs to the composer's mind spontaneously, almost without conscious effort on his part. Possibly its deep-rooted quality and the spontaneous way in which it frequently appears have given rise to the ancient tradition that melody is mysterious, the "divine gift of the Muses," about which we can know nothing.

It is true that certain areas of creation are, and possibly always will be, inexplicable. Yet it would be a serious mistake to believe that melody has no technical aspects. Beethoven's sketchbooks show that many of the master's most inspired themes were only partly the product of inspiration. Between the first draft (sometimes rather trite) and the final melody there was often a long period of trial and error. Beethoven took his first sketch of a melody, bent and altered it, sometimes rewriting it 15 or 20 times before arriving at the definitive version—one that sounds so natural we can scarcely believe it did not spring full-born from the composer's mind.

Example 25 shows three of the many sketches and the final version of the beautiful slow-movement theme from the Fifth Symphony.

Ex. 25   Beethoven: Sketches for second-movement theme, Symphony No. 5,
          Op. 67

Examining the drafts in Ex. 25, we note that (*a*) is a rather banal sketch for a minuet, in which bars 3 and 4 parrot the opening bars on a higher level, in conventional fashion. (*b*) has more movement; in fact, its pitches are exactly the same as the final version. But the dotted notes of (*a*) have been lost, and the rhythm is quite stodgy and monotonous. (*c*) is an attempt in a different direction—not too successful, either. It represents an almost literal repetition of the opening, on various levels, and seems to be a retrogression from (*a*) and (*b*). (*d*) is, of course, the final version of the melody as we know it. Using the pitch contour of (*b*) and the dotted rhythms of (*a*), Beethoven arrived at a version that combines simplicity with just enough rhythmic variety to make a line of distinguished eloquence.

From this we conclude: if Beethoven and other composers used craftsmanlike methods in fashioning a melodic line, why can't the same methods be applied by everyone? Very few individuals can hope to achieve a fraction of Beethoven's melodic genius. But through study we develop an understanding of the *craft* of melody, which may help turn an indifferent inspiration into a very respectable one—or even, if we are lucky, into a beautiful one.

Unity of Style

A good melody has unity. From beginning to end, it develops one idea, one style, one feeling. Achieving unity is not easy. Often a melodic idea comes into being in rather haphazard fashion; various sections, lovely as they may be, have little relation to each other. Sometimes the proportions are all askew, or the end not worthy of the beginning.*

At this point the craftsman is distinguished from the amateur. The tyro, having fallen in love with every note he has written, looks with horror upon the idea of changing what his sacred pen has inscribed. The professional, on the other hand, looks at his first draft with a jaundiced eye, probing, questioning, testing. He cuts out a bit here, rewrites a phrase there, changes a rhythm, prepares a more gradual buildup to the climax. He may try 3 or 4—or 15—versions of the phrase. Only when convinced that all parts of a melody are closely interrelated and each note essential to the whole, does he call his work finished.

Tunes and Themes

Broadly speaking, there are two types of melodies: (1) songs or short instrumental pieces (such as "Greensleeves" or the Minuet from *Don Giovanni*) that are complete in themselves, and (2) melodies with an open end, incomplete in themselves, and therefore all the more suitable to serve as *themes* for the construction of larger works (as, for example, the first six bars of Beethoven's *Eroica*, shown in Ex. 16 of Chapter II).

Melodies of the first type, with which we are concerned in this volume, are compact and clearly articulated. They rarely last longer than the number of measures that can be remembered without difficulty by the average musical person—about 24 to 32 measures. They have a beginning, a middle, and an end; their phrases are clearly related to each other.

Points of Intensity and Rest

Melodies generally lead toward a goal. Except in horizontal, wave, and falling patterns, they move to points of intensity or climaxes, followed by moments of rest.†

Ex. 26   Beethoven: Symphony No. 1, Op. 21, third movement

*For a parody by Mozart of amateurish melody writing in which unrelated figures are crudely patched together, see Ex. 43, page 101.

† This principle applies also to harmonic motion, and, in a broader sense, to music as a whole.

Ex. 27   Schubert: *Moment Musicale*, Op. 94, No. 3

Although the climax of a phrase also involves harmonic, rhythmic, and dynamic elements, it is most clearly focused in the melodic high point. A skillful composer reserves this note for the most telling moment. One of the commonest mistakes in melody writing is to squander the climax by repeating it needlessly, thereby weakening its effect. The redundant repetitions of a high point are indicated by asterisks in Ex. 28.

Ex. 28   Repetition of high tone (student melody)

A time-honored rule of counterpoint states that the highest tone in a melody may appear but once. A single climax is certainly a most effective culmination of a phrase, as shown by innumerable examples from serious and popular music.*

Ex. 29   Beethoven: Sonata Op. 2, No. 1

* See also Exs. 30–34, pages 68–69; Exs. 48–49, page 73; and Exs. 57–59, pages 76–77.

Ex. 30   Porter: Begin the Beguine

The Repeated Climax

Like most rules, however, this one has striking exceptions. A high tone may be deliberately repeated for one of two reasons: (1) to *avoid* a climax and achieve a dreamy, relaxed quality, or (2) to render a climax still more powerful, by insistent reiteration.

In melodies having a wave-like motion, the gentle repetition of the high tone can help produce a lulling effect, as in certain religious chants and in lullabies.

Ex. 31   Plain chant: *Kyrie Deus sempiterne*

On the other hand, the insistent repetition of the melodic peak, like the orator's emphatic "I tell you again, and again, and again!" is the composer's method of driving his point home. This "hammering" of the high tone was one of Beethoven's favorite methods of achieving a climax.

Ex. 32   Beethoven: Symphony No. 5, Op. 67

Melodic Cadences

Melodic climaxes, effective as they are, would in the long run become unbearable were they not succeeded by moments of relaxation, or *cadences*. Examples 27, 29, and 30 show the peaks followed by passages of "falling away." Melodies need these breathing points to achieve a proper balance of movement and rest.

Cadences have melodic, rhythmic, and harmonic aspects, but it is the first two that concern us here. A pause, marking a breathing point at the end of a phrase, gives shape to a melody. Rhythmically, it takes place on a note of long value, or on a relatively long value followed by a rest. The momentary relaxation of movement allows the listener to absorb the content of the foregoing phrase before being confronted with the next one. Cadences, promoting articulation and clarity of thought, play the same role as punctuation marks in prose; they are essential elements of form in music.

An *incomplete cadence*, from a melodic point of view, ends on a note other than the tonic (Exs. 33, 34).

Ex. 33   Mozart: *La ci darem la mano,* from *Don Giovanni*

Give me your hand, my dar-ling, Say that you'll come with me;
La' ci da-rem la ma-no la mi di-rai di   si ;

Ex. 34   Foster: Old Folks at Home

A *perfect cadence*, on the other hand, ends with the melody on the tonic. In the lovely Gregorian *Kyrie de Angelis*, the first two pauses, on 5, form incomplete cadences; the last, on the tonic, a perfect one.

Ex. 35   Plain chant: *Kyrie de Angelis*

Melodic Direction

Melodic lines, whether written by Palestrina, Bartók, or Irving Berlin, have certain characteristics in common. The most elementary is the balance of upward and downward motion. Since these are the only directions in which a melody can move, and since melodic space is limited by the range of voices or instruments, there is always a turnabout, no matter how high a line may rise or how deep it may fall.

The turning movement was observed by Palestrina and other Renaissance masters, who followed this principle: *after a wide leap, turn back stepwise in the opposite direction.* Long after Palestrina, composers still found it a worthwhile precept.

Ex. 36   Beethoven: Symphony No. 9, Op. 125, last movement

Ex. 37   Berg: *Wozzeck*

There is good reason for this practice: a wide leap generates tension; stepwise motion in reverse relaxes the tension.

After a scale passage, similarly, the line usually turns back.

Ex. 38   Beethoven: Symphony No. 1, Op. 21, last movement

A series of leaps is often made in the same direction along the lines of a broken chord—after which we find the usual stepwise motion in the other direction.

Ex. 39   Bach: Two-Part Invention No. 8

In contemporary music, many of these procedures have been modified. But even here, a succession of leaps moving in one direction along the lines of a new type of broken chord is often followed by a stepwise returning movement. (See, for instance, the third bar of Ex. 41, page 23.)

Dynamics, Phrasing, Timbre, Tempo

In addition to its melodic curve and general style, there are other factors that influence the character of a melody: dynamics, phrasing, timbre, and tempo.

Dynamics—the level of sound at which a melody is to be played—can radically affect the character of a melody. The same composition will sound different when played *pp* and *ff*.

Phrasing has several meanings in music. In the present connection it refers to the slurring together or separation of the individual notes or segments of a melody.* The quality of a melody can be altered quite radically by changing from legato to staccato phrasing, or even by changing the number of notes included within a *slur* or phrase mark. Note how the broad sweep of the second theme of Beethoven's Violin Concerto (Ex. 22, page 64) is broken up by a phrasing (*a*) in which each note is played separately. A staccato phrasing (*b*) completely alters the nature of the melody.

Ex. 40   Beethoven: Violin Concerto, Op. 61, theoretical phrasing

(a)

*In another meaning, a *phrase* is defined (page 259) as a musical thought ending in a cadence.

(b)

The *timbre* of a melody is produced by the color of the voice or instrument by which it is performed. Obviously, a melodic line sounds different when sung by a soprano and a bass, when played on a cello and a trombone, or when played in a high or low register of any instrument.

Tempo, of course, refers to the rate of speed at which a composition is to be played. Exact tempo indications are essential to the notation of a melody. In writing original melodies, be careful to indicate their dynamics, phrasing, timbre, and tempo.

Pitfalls

Some common weaknesses in writing melodies are:

1. Too frequent repetition of one tone (indicated by asterisks in Ex. 41), resulting in static or "dead" melody.*

Ex. 41   Franck: Symphony in D minor

2. Leaps in the direction of a preceding scale passage, especially over the bar line.

Ex. 42   Student example

---

* To some listeners, the static melodic quality is counterbalanced by the harmonic motion underneath. Others find the harmonies themselves too obvious and cliché-ridden, no justification for a trite melodic pattern.

3. The appearance, in the middle of a phrase, of notes, intervals, or rhythms alien to the style of a melody. The entry of a foreign element acts as an intrusion, breaking the unity of a melodic line. In the hands of a master, such an intrusion, done deliberately, can provide humor of a very high order. Note particularly the incongruous entry of the triplets in bar 6 of Ex. 43.

Ex. 43   Mozart: *A Musical Joke*, K. 522, third movement

4. The monotonous repetition of a short, choppy rhythm. Such repetitions create a stiff, box-like feeling and impede the unfolding of the melodic line.*

* For *effective* ways of using rhythmic repetition, see pages 152–159.

Ex. 44   Student example

When composing your first melodies, it is best to start from personal experience and enthusiasm. If you are a choral singer who loves *The Messiah*, start with something sacred; if you are a jazz player, write a popular tune; or if an admirer of Stravinsky, try a piece in shifting rhythms. Whatever technical problems are posed, the *form* in which you write should meet the given requirements; the *style* should wherever possible derive from personal taste and imagination.

Summary

1. Good melody writing involves:
   a. Choice of a melodic curve.
   b. Alternation of movement and rest.
   c. Careful handling of the climax or climaxes.
   d. Willingness to rewrite.
   e. Unity of style.

2. The high tone of a phrase normally appears only once, to form a climax. Deliberate repetition of the high tone is used:
   a. To produce a dreamy, relaxed quality, as in lullabies or certain religious chants.
   b. To create a particularly forceful climax, as in dramatic moments of a symphony or opera.

3. Melodic cadences are:
   a. Incomplete (any tone but the tonic).
   b. Perfect (the tonic).

4. After a wide leap or series of smaller leaps, the line turns back, usually stepwise.

5. After a scale, the line turns back; it does not leap in the same direction.

6. Dynamics, phrasing, timbre, and tempo indications are important in defining the character of a melody.

7. Some pitfalls to be avoided in melody writing are:
   a. Too frequent repetition of one tone.
   b. Leaps in the direction of a preceding scale line.
   c. Intrusion of an element alien to the general style.
   d. Monotonous repetition of a short, choppy rhythm.

8. Melodic style should reflect personal background and imagination.

V

The Subdominant Triad

Although it is possible, by a diligent search through the history of music, to find short compositions based entirely on the tonic and dominant triads, such examples are few and far between. Tonic and dominant chords can define a tonality, but obviously they provide only a restricted area for tonal motion, since between them they include only five of the seven tones of the scale.

When we add the subdominant triad, containing the fourth, sixth, and eighth degrees, all the tones of the scale are included.

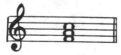

We now have the trio of *primary chords*, I, IV, and V, which have played a fundamental role in traditional music.

The IV chord has been one of the pillars of harmony since the very beginning of the chordal style. Although its root lies four tones above the tonic, it is also found five tones below.

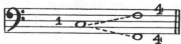

105

The progression from tonic to subdominant (down a fifth) has, therefore, the same elemental quality as the progression from dominant to tonic (Ex. 1).

Ex. 1   Progressions: I—IV compared to V—I.

We can now see why the tonic has such strength as the center of tonality. Flanked on one side by the dominant and on the other by the subdominant, both of which move to it in the strong progression of a fifth, it is the keystone of the tonal arch.

Ex. 2   Tonal arch: IV—I—V

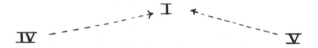

From the days of Renaissance madrigalists to those of Ozark folk singers, the IV triad has played a basic role, together with the I and V, in defining tonality at the beginning of a composition.

Ex. 3   Orlando di Lasso: *Bon jour, mon coeur*

The I, IV, and V form the harmonic basis of a delightful English virginal piece from the Elizabethan period.

Ex. 4   Anonymous: *A Toye* (from *The Fitzwilliam Virginal Book*)

In a Chopin Nocturne, we find the same chords beautifully scored to reveal the poetic resonance of the piano.

Ex. 5   Chopin: Nocturne Op. 37, No. 1

The basic chords appear again in the rich sonorities of the "Valhalla" motive from Wagner's *Das Rheingold*.

Ex. 6   Wagner: "Valhalla" motive, from *Das Rheingold*

Thus, Exs. 3–6, which span three centuries, show the I, IV, and V affirming tonality in the strongest manner.

Connection of IV with I and V

IV and I are connected most smoothly when the common tone, the tonic, remains stationary while the other voices move the smallest possible distance. In this progression, Lasso, Chopin, and Wagner use the same voice-leading techniques. In the Wagner excerpt (*c*), note that the middle voice holds the common tone; the upper voice makes a short skip.

Ex. 7   Connection of IV and I

The connection of IV and V is not quite so simple. The problem stems from the location of the two chords one tone apart, with no common tone. In moving from IV to V, one can easily fall into the trap of parallel fifths.

A sure way to avoid this pitfall and to effect a smooth connection between IV and V is to use contrary motion, with the three upper parts moving in opposite direction to the bass.

Ex. 8   Contrary motion between IV and V

We find this voice-leading employed by Lasso (Ex. 3); by the unknown composer of the "Coventry Carol" (Ex. 9); by Brahms in his Fourth Symphony (Ex. 10); and by hundreds of composers in between and since.

Ex. 9   The Coventry Carol (1520)

Ex. 10   Brahms: Symphony No. 4, Op. 98

B:

Cadences with IV, V, and I

As we have noted, the V—I progression frequently forms a final cadence. Such a cadence is rounded out by the addition of the IV, in the order IV—V—I. Grouping the three primary triads in this manner brings the primary key-defining tones into action to form a decisive conclusion.

The Perfect Cadence

When the soprano comes to rest on the tonic in such a progression, the result is a *perfect cadence**—the most definitive of all phrase endings (Exs. 11, 12). Such a cadence serves like a period in language—to mark a complete stop at the end of a sentence.

Ex. 11   Perfect cadence with IV—V—I

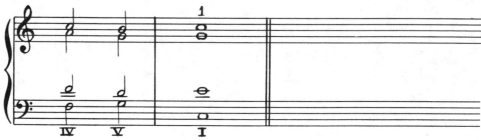

Ex. 12   Greensleeves

* This cadence is also known as the "perfect authentic cadence."

Because it creates a feeling of finality, the perfect cadence is generally avoided *during the course of a phrase*, where it tends to halt the musical flow.

The Imperfect Cadence

To produce an ending less final than the perfect cadence, the progression IV—V—I may close with the third or fifth in the soprano, forming an *imperfect cadence*. Such a cadence acts as a breathing point, suggesting by its unfinished quality that there is more to come.

Ex. 13   Imperfect cadences

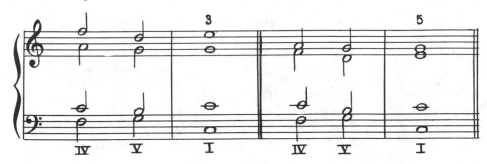

Ex. 14   Bach: *Lobt Gott, ihr Christen alle*

Ex. 15   Corelli: Concerto Grosso, Op. 6, No. 8

The Plagal Cadence

Still less emphatic than the imperfect cadence is the ending based on the IV and I, the *plagal cadence*. Lacking the directional drive brought to other cadences by the V, the plagal close is a mild one. From its frequent appearance at the end of church anthems, it became known also as the "amen cadence."

Ex. 16   Handel: Hallelujah Chorus, from *The Messiah*

Often a plagal cadence will occur *after* a perfect cadence. The hymn "O God, Our Help in Ages Past" comes to a perfect cadence, followed by the traditional plagal ending on the word "Amen."

Ex. 17   Hymn tune: O God Our Help in Ages Past

The Half Cadence

Another type of close, the *half cadence*, resting on V, is often employed in pieces having two equally balanced phrases. The first phrase ends at the midway point with a half cadence, creating a feeling of suspense ("we have not finished yet"); the second closes with a perfect cadence ("now we have done"). Two phrases with contrasted cadences form a *period** (Exs. 18–20).

Ex. 18   Period, with half and perfect cadences

* The period is fully discussed in Chapters I–III of Volume II.

Ex. 19   Brahms: Symphony No. 1, Op. 68, last movement

Ex. 20   American folk song: Gambler's Blues

Although the V remains the most common choice for the half cadence, occasionally a IV chord may be used. Ex. 21 shows a half cadence resting on the subdominant.

Ex. 21   Auld Lang Syne

Harmonizing Melodies with I, IV, and V

Many folk singers and other "natural" musicians use the primary triads with the greatest of ease in accompanying songs on the guitar, banjo, and other instruments. Yet the naturalness conceals a long period of training—a training informal, to be sure, but nonetheless extensive. The folk singer does not pick his knowledge of music out of the air; he has listened closely to a relative or neighbor who has a strong feeling for tunes and chords. His ear is trained over many years—not in an ear-training class but at a songfest, a fiddler's contest, a square dance.

Those who have not had the good fortune to imbibe a knowledge of harmony in so painless a fashion can find the equivalent in another way. Recordings and paperback collections of folk music are legion. Those who don't play the guitar can, in little time, learn several tunes accompanied by the I, IV, and V chords on the piano—a fine way to develop a basic feeling for the relation of melody and harmony.

The use of the IV chord along with the I and V in harmonizing melodies introduces several new voice-leading problems and procedures. They are illustrated, together with some already familiar techniques, in Ex. 22.

Ex. 22   Little David, Play on Yo' Harp

Example 22 shows the following voice-leading procedures:

1. Since the tonic can be harmonized by both I and IV, which chord is chosen? At (*b*) the I was selected because it is best to keep the chord unchanged when the melody leaps.

2. But when the leap is to a tone of another chord (*c*), a change to IV becomes mandatory.

3. The common tone is held in the alto from (*d*) to (*e*) while changing between I and V; and likewise between (*f*) and (*g*) in changing between I and IV.

4. When both melody and harmony repeat (as at *h*), variety may be created by different voicing. At (*h*) the bass shifts to an octave above its original position (*a*). The octave leap down to (*i*) adds a little further variation.
5. At (*j*), in the interests of good voice-leading, the fifth of the chord is omitted and the root tripled.

Summary

1. The IV triad completes the trio of primary chords (I—IV—V), with which every degree of the scale can be harmonized.

2. The progression IV—V—I is one of the strongest means of affirming the tonality.

3. Many melodies can be harmonized with the I—IV—V.

4. The movement I—IV, like V—I, is basic and vigorous.

5. The connection IV—I is most smoothly achieved when the common tone (1) remains stationary and the other voices move the smallest possible distance.

6. The progression IV—V is best achieved when the three upper voices move the smallest possible distance in contrary motion to the bass.

7. The following cadences are possible, using the IV, V, and I:
   a. The perfect cadence V—I (or IV—V—I) occurs when the soprano rests on 1. It creates a feeling of finality.
   b. The imperfect cadence V—I (or IV—V—I) occurs when the soprano rests on 3 or 5. Its effect is less final than (a).
   c. The plagal cadence IV—I is less forceful than the perfect and imperfect cadences. Often it follows a perfect cadence.
   d. The half cadence rests on V (rarely, on IV). It creates a feeling that there is more to come.

8. In harmonizing melodies with the I, IV, and V:
   a. Familiar principles are applied (see page 63 items 7 and 8; and page 90, items 3 through 7).
   b. New procedures are introduced (see pages 116–117, items 2, 4, and 5).

The
Modes

Like the hero of Moliere's *The Bourgeois Gentleman*, who had been speaking prose all his life without realizing it, most of us have been hearing modal music for a long time in total innocence of the fact. "When Johnny Comes Marching Home," "What Shall We Do with a Drunken Sailor," "Old Joe Clarke," and other modal melodies are part of our folk heritage. Modal music is also found in the standard repertory: in the Bach chorales, Chopin's Mazurkas, Brahms' Fourth Symphony, Dvorak's Cello Concerto, Stravinsky's *Rite of Spring*, and Gershwin's *Porgy and Bess*—not to mention countless works of the medieval and Renaissance periods, the great ages of modality. Long ignored by academic theorists, the modes are once more part of living musical practice. Their revival has greatly refreshed the art of melody.

There is no difference in principle between the scales commonly referred to as "modes" and the major and minor scales. Major and minor are modes, too—simply two among many. We shall examine all alike, and use each for the special possibilities it may suggest in the creation of melodic ideas.*

Major and Minor Modes

As we have seen, a scale is a series of steps rising from a tonic to its repetition an octave higher. Scale steps ordinarily consist of three sizes: half steps, whole steps, and steps-and-a-half.

A *mode* is a particular ordering of scale steps; modes differ according to the order of steps of various sizes. Thus, in the *major* mode, half steps occur

---

* For the present, modes will be used only in melody writing.

118

between 3—4 and 7—8 (Ex. 23), while in *harmonic minor* they lie between 2—3, 5—6, and 7—8 (Ex. 24).

Ex. 23   Half steps in major

Ex. 24   Half steps in harmonic minor

The different positions of the half steps create the difference in character of the two modes and of music utilizing them. Note also in Ex. 24 the step-and-a-half between 6—7, a special characteristic of the harmonic minor mode.

In the *melodic minor*, whose structure varies with its direction, there is yet another order of steps. Half steps occur when rising, between 2—3 and 7—8; when falling, between 3—2 and 6—5.

Ex. 25   Melodic minor, rising and falling.

The varied order of steps in the major and minor modes represents but a few of the many possible arrangements. The music of the world's peoples includes a vast number of different modes, each characterized by a different sequence of steps of various kinds. The diversity of scale structures is especially great in the Orient, where the Hindus alone are said to use 70 different modes in their daily music making.

In the West, for whatever reason, the number of modes in practical use has been much smaller ever since the days of the Greeks. Besides major and minor, folk musicians and composers of western Europe since the Renaissance have relied mainly on five modes: *Dorian, Phrygian, Lydian,*

Mixolydian, and *Aeolian.** In addition to these, we shall consider a distinctly American invention, the *blues* mode, as well as the *Ahavoh Rabboh,* an example of the innumerable Oriental modes. We shall also touch on a pattern—not strictly a mode, but nonetheless widely used—the *pentatonic scale.*†

Tetrachords

Analysis of modal structure is simplified by dividing each mode into two groups of four notes each, called *tetrachords.* The octave comprises two tetrachords, placed one above the other, with a whole step in between. We shall speak of the *first* (lower) and *second* (upper) tetrachords in each mode.

Ex. 26 First and second tetrachords

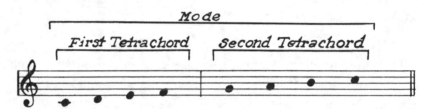

Most tetrachords include one half step and two whole steps. The half step may occur in one of three positions: at the bottom, in the middle, or at the top of the tetrachord.

Ex. 27 Position of the half steps

Dorian Mode

One of the noblest and most familiar of the old modes is the *Dorian.* This mode is easy to remember: its half steps lie in the middle of both tetrachords.

Ex. 28 The Dorian Mode

* Dorian, Phrygian, Lydian, and Mixolydian were the chief modes of medieval music. Together with certain variants, they were known for many centuries as the *church* modes. These, in turn, traced their ancestry to the Greek modes, used well over two thousand years ago.

† Not every mode can be covered here. For a more detailed discussion, see John Vincent: *The Diatonic Modes in Modern Music* (New York, 1951).

Dorian-mode melodies often give the feeling of spaciousness and grandeur. Many impressive plain chants* and some of the most beautiful English, French, and American folk ballads are in the Dorian mode.

Ex. 29   Sequence: *Victimae Paschali Laudes*

Vic -ti - mae pa-scha-li lau-des   im-mo-lent Chri-sti-a - ni.

A - gnus red-e-mit o - ves: Chri-stus in-no-cens Pa-tri

re - con - ci - li - a - vit   pec - ca - to - res.

Ex. 30   English folk song: Henry Martin

There were— three bro-thers in mer-ry Scot-land, In

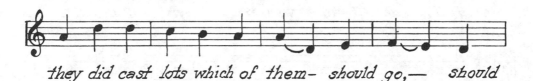

mer-ry Scot-land there were three,———   And

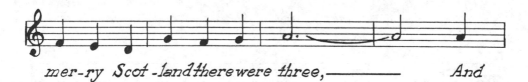

they did cast lots which of them— should go,—   should

* Ex. 33, page 442, for instance.

go,— should go, And— turn rob-ber all

on the salt sea._____

Aeolian Mode

Closely allied to the Dorian—differing from it in fact by just one tone—is the *Aeolian* mode, also called *natural minor*. Aeolian, which has provided the framework for many traditional songs and instrumental melodies, contains a half step in the middle of the first tetrachord and one at the bottom of the second.*

Ex. 31 Aeolian mode

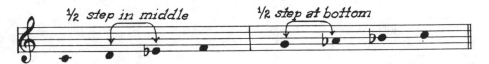

½ step in middle   ½ step at bottom

Ex. 32 German traditional song: *Der Tod als Schnitter*

There   is   a   reap - er   cal — led
Es   ist   ein   Schnit - ter,   der heisst

Death, His pow-er is giv-en by God._____
Tod, Hat G'walt— vom gros - sen Gott._____

—   He sharp-ens his blade__ and cuts with-out
—   Heut wetzt er das Mes - ser, es schneidt schon viel

*See also Ex. 38, page 264 and Exs. 3-4, pages 288-289.

pi - ty, Now soon he'll be here, – we trem-ble in
bes-ser, Bald wird er drein schnei-den,wir müs – sen's nur

fear. —   Take   care, oh, lit -tle flower!
lei - den.   Hüt   dich,schön's Blü-me - lein !

Phrygian Mode

The *Phrygian*, one of the most striking of the modes, has a strong downward tendency due to the position of the half steps at the bottom of both tetrachords.

Ex. 33   Phrygian mode

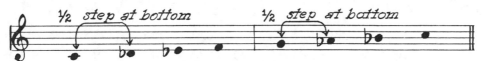

This mode has given rise to melodies of great intensity, sometimes of a brooding quality. Examples 34 and 35 present two Phrygian melodies: an old German chorale tune, favored by Bach; and, by contrast, a florid, pseudo-Oriental passage from Rimsky-Korsakov's *Scheherazade*.

Ex. 34   Chorale tune: *Aus tiefer Noth*

From deep-est need I   cry to Thee,Oh, God in Hea - ven,
Aus tie -fer Noth schrei ich zu dir, Herr Gott er-höhr mein

hear my prayer! For now Thou soon will look and see, How
Ru - fen!   Denn so du   willst das se - hen an, was

men do sin most ev-il- ly. We all bow down be-fore Thee.
Sünd und Un-recht ist ge-than, wer kann,Herr, vor dir blei - ben.

Ex. 35   Rimsky-Korsakov: *Scheherazade*

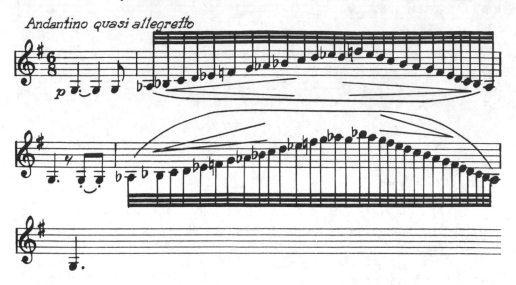

Lydian Mode

The *Lydian*, a highly colorful mode, has an unusual character. Its first tetrachord contains three successive whole steps—the only mode with this peculiarity; the missing half step appears *between* the two tetrachords. In the second tetrachord, the half step is on top.

Ex. 36   Lydian mode

Especially favored in Polish folk music, the Lydian mode also appears in Chopin's Mazurkas and in the Polacca from Moussorgsky's *Boris Godunov*.

Ex. 37   Chopin: Mazurka, Op. 24, No. 2

Ex. 38   Moussorgsky: Polacca from *Boris Godunov*

Mixolydian Mode

The Mixolydian mode has a brighter quality than Dorian, Phrygian, or Aeolian. Its half steps are found at the top of the first tetrachord and in the middle of the second.

Ex. 39   Mixolydian mode

Two American folk songs illustrate this mode. The first is well known to all square dance callers; the mood of the second borders on the blues.

Ex. 40   American folk song: Old Joe Clarke

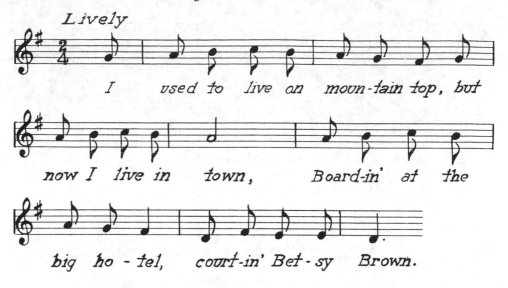

I used to live on moun-tain top, but now I live in town, Board-in' at the big ho-tel, court-in' Bet-sy Brown.

Ex. 41   American folk song: Every Night When the Sun Goes In

Eve-ry night when the sun goes in, Eve-ry night when the sun goes in, Eve-ry night when the sun goes in, I hang down my head and mourn-ful cry.

Blues Mode

The *blues* mode—one of the distinctive products of this country's music—is characterized by a variable third, a tone sometimes flat and sometimes natural. This variable third is often performed as a "hot" or "blue" note, with the voice or instrument sliding from the flat to the natural or vice versa. In the lower tetrachord, the half step occurs either at the top or in the middle; in the upper tetrachord, the half step occurs in the middle.*

* In some blues, the seventh tone likewise varies between flat and natural, with the characteristic slide.

Ex. 42   Blues mode

In the folk blues shown in Ex. 43, note, at (a) and (b), the E flat followed by an E natural. This is the variable third, which provides so much flavor in the blues.*

Ex. 43   American folk song: Darling Corie

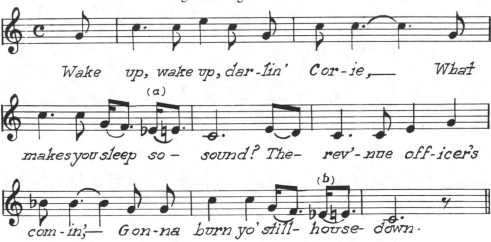

Wake up, wake up, dar-lin' Cor-ie,— What
(a)
makes you sleep so— sound? The— rev'-nue off-icer's
com-in;— Gon-na burn yo' still- house- down.
(b)

Ahavoh Rabboh Mode

Any attempt to describe the wealth of modes in Oriental music would go beyond the scope of this book. Oriental music, as is well known, relies very largely on the intricacy and variety of its scale patterns, many of which cannot be captured in our notation. However, one characteristic mode, from the Near East, should be mentioned. The *Ahavoh Rabboh* mode derives its quality from the step-and-a-half, or augmented second, in the middle of its lower tetrachord, flanked on either side by half steps. The upper tetrachord is a familiar one, with a half step at the bottom (Ex. 44).

Ex. 44   Ahavoh Rabboh mode

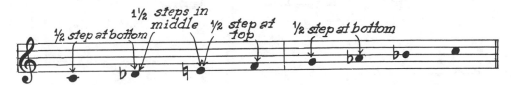

* For another use of the blues mode, see Ex. 40, page 452.

Used extensively in the music of the Near East, the Ahavoh Rabboh penetrated into the folk melodies of southeastern Europe and the Synagogue chants of east European Jews. (The step-and-a-half is indicated by an asterisk in Exs. 45–47.)

Ex. 45   Arabic prayer

From Jewish Music by A. Z. Idelsohn, published by Holt, Rinehart and Winston, Inc. Reprinted by permission.

Ex. 46   Bartók: Roumanian Folk Dance, No 4

Ex. 47   Synagogue chant (Ashkenazic)

Tik-kan-to shab-bos ro-tsi-so kor-be-no - se - ho,

Tsiv-vi . . . . . so   pe - ru-she-ho im sid - du -

ri ne-so-ch - ho,   Me-an-ge-ho le-o-lom

Ko - vod yin-cho-lu,   to - a-me-ho cha-yim zo-chu,

ve - gam ho-o-ha-vim de-vo—re-ho ge-du-lo bo-cho-ru.

From Jewish Music *by A. Z. Idelsohn, published by Holt, Rinehart and Winston, Inc. Reprinted by permission.*

Pentatonic Scale

Before leaving the subject of modes, we should take note of the *pentatonic* scale. Although not a mode, it is a very old scale pattern; some theorists believe that it antedates the modes. Containing only five tones (sometimes identified with the black keys of the piano), the pentatonic is also referred to as the "gapped" scale because, in relation to the familiar seven-tone pattern, it lacks two tones.

Ex. 48   Pentatonic scale

Ex. 49   Mongolian song: *Kara Sada*

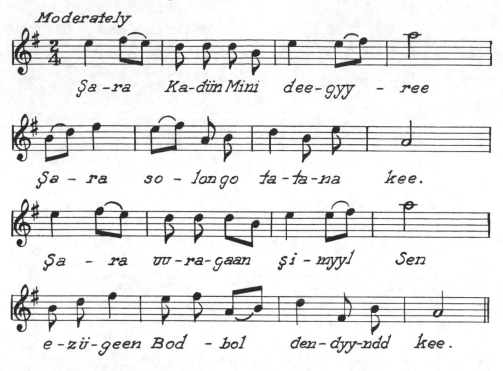

Moderately

Şa—ra   Ka-dün Mini   dee-gyy — ree

Şa — ra   so - longo   ta-ta-na   kee.

Şa - ra   uu-ra-gaan   şi - myyl   Sen

e - zü-geen Bod - bol   den-dyy-ndd   kee.

Ex. 50   American white spiritual: Poor Wayfaring Stranger

Slowly

I   am a poor way-far-ing stran-ger,— while trav'-ling

through this world of   woe,   Yet there's no sick -ness,toil or

dan-ger— in that bright world to which I   go— I'm go·ing

home to see my   fa -ther,— I'm go-ing there no more to

A study of modal melodies reveals several important characteristics. They frequently begin with the tonic or with the fifth soon followed by the tonic. This tone often recurs during the opening phrase or is firmly stressed at the end of the phrase. The tonic triad, too, is commonly outlined at or near the beginning.* In this way tonality—generally vaguer in modal music than in major and minor—is firmly established at the outset.

The modes other than the familiar major and minor offer the student, as they have offered many famous composers, a world of fresh musical possibilities. Knowledge of modal music may stimulate the young musician to explore new melodic patterns and unfamiliar pathways.

The best way of learning the unfamiliar scales is to sing plain chants and old English, Appalachian Mountain, and Russian folk songs; and to play the *Mikrokosmos* of Bartók, as well as pieces by other composers, such as Moussorgsky, Borodin, Dvorak, Debussy, Ravel, Falla, Villa-Lobos, or Kodaly, who have written extensively in the modes.

Summary

1. The modes offer a wide range of melodic possibilities for the writing of melodies.

2. The structure of the modes is determined by the position of the various steps within the first and second tetrachords, as shown in Ex. 51.

Ex. 51   Summary of modes

Position of half steps in tetrachord	
1	2
top	top

*See Exs. 30, 37, 43, and 50 on pages 121-130.

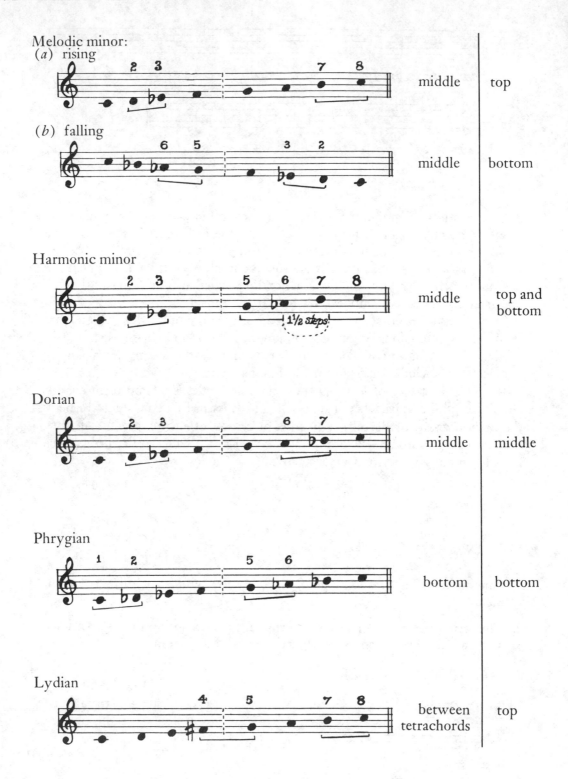

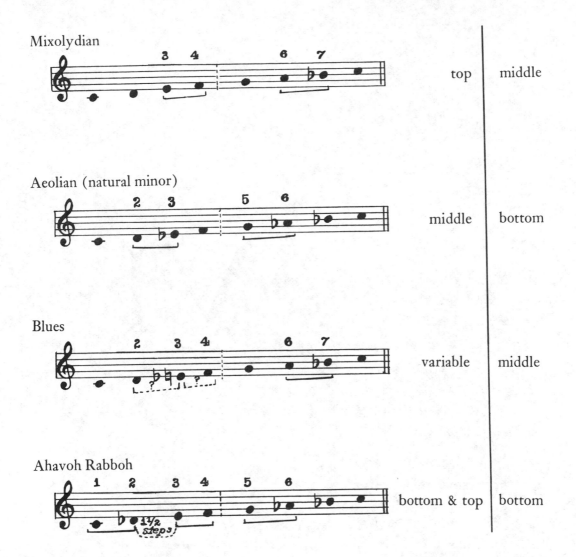

VI

Embellishing Tones

Up to this point we have been rather spare in our harmonization of melodies—a result of being bound to only three chords. But melody cannot be limited solely by chord patterns. Even in the case of simple folk songs accompanied by the I, IV, and V, the tunes often flow around the chords with much freedom. For example, the first measure of "Red River Valley" (Ex. 1) has tonic harmony. The melody, however, goes its own sweet way, unrestrained by the notes of the chord. On the words "they" and "you," the voice sings two A's—notes not included in the G major triad underneath.

Ex. 1   American folk song: Red River Valley*

* For the entire tune, see *Workbook*, Volume I, Exercise 3(d) on page 83.

Further on (Ex. 1a), we find a D on the first beat, a note foreign to the accompanying IV triad. And in Ex. 1b a B appears on the fourth beat, although that note does not form part of the V triad below.

Ex. 1a

Ex. 1b

How do we account for melodic tones that move independently of chord structures?

The melodic impulse and melodic motion are primary musical forces. They preceded harmony by thousands of years, and can never be entirely bound by harmonic rules. In music, the two currents of melodic and harmonic motion flow along together. Now one, now the other asserts its rights; neither ever quite relinquishes its inner necessities. In the works of the masters, both forces are free, yet intertwined.

The fluid character of melody caused some difficulties for eighteenth-century theorists, who considered harmony the foundation of music. To account for embarrassing melodic movements that do not derive from chord structures but function independently of them, they invented the concept of "non-harmonic tones." In this category they placed melodic tones that, although sounded together with a chord, do not form part of the chord structure (the non-conforming notes of "Red River Valley," for example).

The theorists were thus able to retain an ideal vision of music as a progression of lawful harmonies going their orderly, well-mannered ways, while melody oscillated between "harmonic" and "non-harmonic" tones. The implication existed that there was something inherently less important about non-harmonic tones—an implication spelled out by those theorists who labeled them "unessential" tones.

Returning once more to "Red River Valley," are the circled tones in the examples "unessential?" The melody could scarcely do without them! Are they, for that matter, "non-harmonic?" Even though not congruent with tones of the accompanying chords, they lend spice to the harmonies by providing a delightful friction with them. The color produced by the clash of tone with chord is assuredly a *harmonic* effect. From a modern vantage point, it does not make sense to call tones that create a harmonic effect "non-harmonic" simply because they clash with the chord instead of blending with it.

Let us call the flowing or leaping notes that move independently of the chord structure *embellishing tones*. Melodic movement can then be considered on its own terms, and the misnomer "non-harmonic" avoided.

Traditionally, tones forming part of a triad are called *consonant*, and embellishing tones not part of a triad, *dissonant*. Yet the two concepts are not sharply divided; there are degrees of dissonance, ranging from gentle to strong. Embellishing tones falling on weak beats or between the beats form extremely mild dissonances; accented embellishing tones, moderate or harsh ones. It should be clear from this discussion that dissonant tones, far from being objectionable, provide a sense of movement and a necessary tension in music; they form an indispensable part of almost any composition.*

Passing Tone

In *Frère Jacques* (Ex. 2), whose melody outlines the C major triad, the notes marked (*a*) are embellishing tones. D bridges the passage between C and E; F smooths the way between E and G. In these positions, the embellishing tones are called *passing tones*, since they help the melody pass in steps between the various tones of a chord.

Ex. 2   French folk song: *Frère Jacques*

* For further discussion of consonance and dissonance, see page 406.

Passing tones are part of the flowing motion of melody, occurring normally on weak beats or between the beats.* The opening phrase of Bach's Chromatic Fantasy sweeps up and down the D minor scale, then up once more to a peak on E.

Ex. 3   Bach: Chromatic Fantasy

In the first arch of the line that outlines a D minor triad, D, F, and A are chord tones, and the other notes passing tones. Between the root and third of the triad, there is one passing tone; between the third and fifth, another; and between the fifth and the upper octave tonic, two more (PT = passing tone).

Ex. 4   Passing tones between the tones of the D minor triad

Passing tones also occur between the notes of two different chords. In Ex. 5, the three notes at (*a*) are passing tones between the V chord and the I of the next bar. C sharp, the last of the three, is a chromatic passing tone, but it behaves no differently than a diatonic one, except that it forms a half step not belonging to the key.

Ex. 5   Haydn: Symphony No. 101 (*The Clock*), second movement

* For accented passing tones, see page 140.

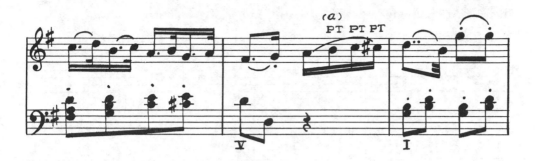

Sometimes passing tones occur in two or more voices simultaneously. In the second, third, and fourth bars of Ex. 6, *double passing tones* in thirds give an exotic flavor to the music.

Ex. 6   Bizet: Gypsy Song, from *Carmen*

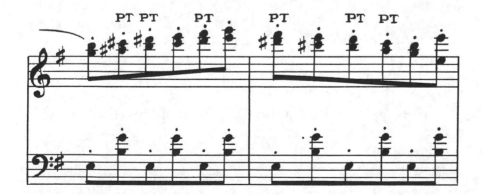

The third bar of Ex. 7 contains a passage with *triple passing tones* (in soprano, alto, and bass).

Ex. 7   Jannequin: *Assouvi suis, mais, sans cesser, désire*

The *accented passing tone* differs from those already discussed in that it occurs *on* the beat, often forming a dissonance with other notes of the chord. Like the unaccented variety, it is approached and left by steps.

Ex. 8   Beethoven: Sonata, Op. 22, last movement

The E flat at (*a*), an accented passing tone, adds emphasis to the downbeat—but a mild emphasis, since it is part of a flowing line. The same applies to the chromatic accented passing tone at (*b*).

In Ex. 9, the passing tones (*a* and *b*) are slightly more dissonant because of the aggressive minor ninths they form with the upper notes of the chords in the left hand.

Ex. 9   Beethoven: Sonata, Op. 10, No. 3, third movement

Neighboring Tone

A *neighboring tone* occurs when a voice, leaving a chord tone, moves one step up or down, returning then to its original position. Neighboring tones (NT) generally fall on weak beats or between the beats—like the D in the first measure of Ex. 10.

Ex. 10   German folk song: *Ach, du lieber Augustin*

Often, both upper and lower neighbors are called into play—especially in music of a decorative character. In Ex. 11, the upper neighbor skips directly to the lower one before returning to the original tone.

Ex. 11   Mozart: Sonata, K. 284, third movement

A five-note group, starting and ending on a chord tone and including both upper and lower neighbors, was a favorite ornamental figure in eighteenth-century Rococo music. Called a *gruppetto*, or *turn*, it is represented by the symbol ∿ . In Ex. 12, the actual sound of the *gruppetto* is written out above the passage as notated by Beethoven.

Ex. 12   Beethoven: Sonata, Op. 10, No. 1, second movement

Like passing tones, upper and lower neighbors may be diatonic or chromatic. Half-step embellishments add delicacy and color to a phrase.

Ex. 13   Chopin: Etude, Op. 25, No. 2

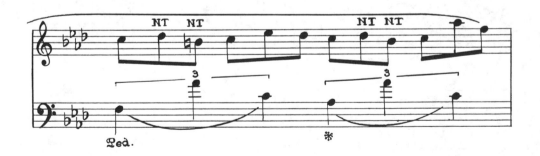

Neighboring tones may also occur on strong beats, sometimes in two voices simultaneously. They are then called *accented* neighboring tones.

Ex. 14   Beethoven: Sonata, Op. 2, No. 3

Three other types of embellishing tones are the appoggiatura, the anticipation, and the escaped tone.

Appoggiatura

An *appoggiatura* is a tone one step above or below the tone whose place it takes in the chord. While passing and neighboring tones usually occur on the weak beat, concealing the dissonant element, the appoggiatura falls on the strong beat, throwing the dissonance into sharp relief. Unlike the accented passing tone, it is approached by leap (App. = appoggiatura; Res. = resolution).

Ex. 15   Appoggiaturas

The term appoggiatura comes from the Italian verb meaning "to lean": it "leans against" a chord tone, producing a moment of tension, which is relaxed by stepwise resolution to the chord tone we have been awaiting. Thus the appoggiatura is more than an ornament; it is often an expressive accent adding emphasis to a given point in the melodic line.

Ex. 16   Chopin: Mazurka, Op. 17, No. 2

When writing appoggiaturas in four-part harmony, one traditionally avoids sounding the note of resolution in another voice at the same time as the appoggiatura itself. A dissonance has greater effect when the note of resolution is held in abeyance until the tension is released by the next chord.

In Ex. 17 (a), E is omitted from the chord; when it arrives on the second beat, it produces all the greater feeling of satisfaction. Compare the awkwardness of (b), where E is sounded in the tenor on the downbeat. When the soprano resolves on the second beat, it is anti-climactic; the effect of the appoggiatura has been lost.

Ex. 17   Resolution tone not doubled, and doubled

An exception occurs in the case of an appoggiatura in an upper voice proceeding to the root of a chord while the bass sounds the root one or two octaves below. Because wide spacing softens the clash between the voices, good practice permits the sounding of such an appoggiatura simultaneously with the root in the bass.

Ex. 18   Beethoven: Sonata, Op. 79, third movement

Further exceptions may be found, especially in Beethoven, who often wished to create strong, even harsh harmonic clashes through dissonance (*a*).

Ex. 19   Beethoven: Sonata, Op. 26

Bach, whom an unaccountable tradition pictures as a model of musical coolness and restraint, produced a work that must have burst explosively upon eighteenth-century ears. The last four bars of his Chromatic Fantasy contain a series of dissonant appoggiaturas that sounded bold even to nineteenth-century musicians.*

Ex. 20   Bach: Chromatic Fantasy

Although an appoggiatura most commonly approaches the chord tone from above, appoggiaturas from below are not infrequent. Leonard Bernstein

* As late as 150 years after Bach's death, bowdlerized editions still appeared in which the dissonances were softened to consonances.

makes excellent use of a lower appoggiatura in his song "Maria." The repeated A natural resolving up to B flat starts the song on a note of urgency and tension.

Ex. 21　　Bernstein: Maria, from *West Side Story*

The intensity of the appoggiatura can be heightened by using the device in two or three voices simultaneously (sometimes called *appoggiatura chords*). At the end of his *St. Matthew Passion*, Bach expressed a profound lamentation for the death of Christ in a passage containing such appoggiatura chords.

Ex. 22　　Bach: Closing chorus, from *The St. Matthew Passion*

Anticipation

An *anticipation* is produced by a voice sounding a tone of the next chord before the other voices move to that chord. The anticipatory action on a weak beat forms a dissonance with the other voices of the chord that are still sounding—a dissonance eased when the other voices "catch up."

Eighteenth-century composers often anticipated the final tone of a cadence chord.

Ex. 23   Gluck: Ballet music from *Orfeo*

Beethoven used the anticipation to lend rhythmic bite to a very charming minuet.

Ex. 24   Beethoven: Sonata, Op. 49, No. 2, Menuetto

Escaped Tone

There are two types of *escaped tone* (ET), both of which occur on the weak beat: (1) a neighboring tone that leaps instead of returning to the original chord tone (Ex. 25); and (2) a neighboring tone that is *approached* by a leap but resolves by a step to a chord tone (Ex. 26).

Ex. 25   Schubert: Impromptu, Op. 142, No. 1

Ex. 26   Beethoven: Sonata, Op. 14, No. 2

Passing and neighboring tones, appoggiaturas, anticipations, and escaped tones are various means of ornamenting a melody and creating expressive harmonic accents. They enable the composer to devise a more graceful turn or add a tart sprinkle of dissonance to a given passage.

Embellishments can be mere decoration, as they often were in eighteenth-century music. On the other hand, they may reveal the workings of a highly original mind, as in Bach's Chromatic Fantasy (Ex. 20). Seen in the large, they are a seminal part of the musical language. Many procedures that started as mere ornaments slowly took on more substance, emerging in time as new chord formations. What were once embellishing tones later took shape as the $^6_4$, the dominant seventh, the dominant ninth, and other basic chords. Thus the search for melodic variety led to the development of harmonic structures.

Summary

1. Embellishing tones do not form part of a chord, but are sounded together with the chord, forming dissonances. They may create a more flowing melody, enrich the texture of the music, or produce points of expressive intensity.

2. Passing tones are created by stepwise motion from one chord tone to the next above or below.

3. Neighboring tones are created by stepwise movement away from and back to a chord tone.

4. Passing and neighboring tones normally appear on weak beats or between the beats. When occurring on the strong beat, they are called accented passing and neighboring tones. They may be diatonic or chromatic, and may occur in one voice or in two or three voices simultaneously.

5. Appoggiaturas are dissonant tones on the beat, approached by leap; they replace chord tones, to which they resolve by stepwise motion.
   a. Appoggiaturas approach a chord tone commonly from above; more rarely from below.
   b. When an appoggiatura is sounded in one voice, the note of resolution is not, as a rule, sounded simultaneously in another voice.
   c. Appoggiaturas may be diatonic or chromatic; single, double, or triple.

6. Anticipations are chord tones that arrive in one voice before the rest of the chord; they frequently appear as short notes before the bar line.

7. Escaped tones are neighboring tones occurring on the weak beat; they are either approached or left by leap.

Melodic Rhythm

One cannot study melody for long without recognizing the importance of its rhythmic element. Besides playing an independent role in music, rhythm serves as an integral part of melody. Just as the melodic curve shapes the pitch contour of a line, rhythm outlines its pattern in time.

Rhythm may contribute to melody formation in a variety of ways. As a start, let us define a few basic concepts: beat, meter, and rhythm.

The fundamental unit of all rhythm is the *beat*, a constantly repeated pulse from which all rhythmic patterns are developed. The musical beat derives ultimately from the heartbeat, whose steady pulsation is a basic phenomenon of life.

Meter is a regularly repeated pattern of strong and weak beats (> = accented or strong beat).

Ex. 27   Metric patterns

And what of *rhythm?* The word has two meanings in music: (1) a broad one, embracing every aspect of time, and (2) a specific one, referring to particular patterns of time values.

To clarify the latter, a rhythm may be a grouping of half notes, quarters, and perhaps a few rests, arranged in a certain order. Or it may simply be three eighth notes and a half (the beginning of Beethoven's Fifth Symphony):

It may be the pattern of "Glory, glory, hallelujah":

"Jingle bells" is a rhythm:

and so is the opening of Ravel's Bolero (Ex. 2, Chapter I).

Many songs and many symphonic themes derive their identity mainly from rhythm. A D major scale, for example, is scarcely a melody.

Ex. 28   D major scale

Yet when rhythm is added,

melody appears.

Ex. 29   Handel: Joy to the World

A rhythmic pattern, then, may be the most distinctive feature of a melody. Out of the endless possibilities of rhythmic design found in music throughout the world, we shall study seven broad types.* Three of these are symmetrical or evenly balanced types, and four are asymmetrical or free-form.

Symmetrical types of rhythm:	Asymmetrical types:
Repeated rhythm	Changing meter
Rhythm with varied repetition	Polyrhythm
Double repeated rhythm	Free-flowing rhythm
	Non-metrical rhythm

Repeated Rhythm

The most basic of all rhythmic structures is simple repetition. This common rhythmic process has fallen into disrepute in certain circles today, but it characterizes the opening phrases of a great number of masterpieces. Some of their rhythms are shown in Ex. 30.

Ex. 30   Rhythms of symphonic themes

(a)

The examples quoted are the beginnings of (a) Schubert's *Unfinished* Symphony,† (b) Mozart's *Eine Kleine Nachtmusik*,‡ (c) Beethoven's Ninth

* A serious study of further possibilities is offered in Curt Sachs: *Rhythm and Tempo*, New York, 1953.

† See *Workbook*, Volume I, Exercise 4 on page 85.

‡ See *Workbook*, Volume I, Exercise 1(ii) on page 1.

Symphony,* and (d) the fourth movement of Bartók's Concerto for Orchestra.†

Insistent Repetition

Sometimes a phrase or section of a composition will consist almost entirely of one rhythmic pattern repeated over and over. Such insistent repetitions occur in four different kinds of music.

1. In dance music, repeated rhythms produce a kind of physical intoxication.‡

Ex. 31   Chopin: *Grande Valse Brillante*, Op. 18

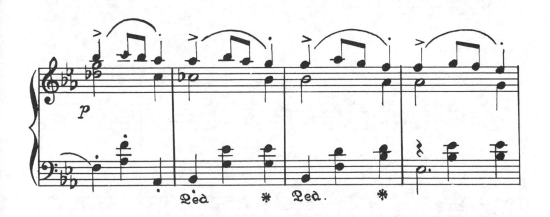

---

* See Ex. 40, page 23.

† See *Workbook*, Volume I, Exercise 4(g) on page 87.

‡ See also Ex. 54, page 164; Ex. 2, page 196; and Ex. 27, page 298.

2. In phrases having a sharply outlined melodic curve, rhythmic repetition adds force to the sweep of the line.

Ex. 32   Mozart: Menuetto, from Symphony No. 40, K. 550

3. In compositions marked by strongly directed harmonic movement, rhythmic repetition adds further momentum.*

Ex. 33   Beethoven: Sonata, Op. 106, second movement

* In Chopin's Prelude in E minor (Ex. 5, page 11), the constant downward motion of the harmony contrasts vividly with the fixed rhythm and static melody.

4. In music having a driving, obsessive quality, reiterated rhythms are often the key factor. Stravinsky's "Dance of the Adolescents" from *The Rite of Spring* (Ex. 54 of Chapter III) provides a familiar example. We find another in Beethoven's Fifth Symphony, in which the entire opening section (56 bars) grows from a repetition of the opening rhythmic figure.

Ex. 34   Beethoven: Symphony No. 5, Op. 67

Example 34 illustrates both (3) and (4). Note the dramatic opposition of the fixed, constantly repeated rhythm and melody in the right hand and the active motion of the harmony in the left. Note also how the repeated rhythm of the bass adds strength to the rising line.

Rhythmic repetition thus gives articulation and force to many different kinds of melodies. Most suitable for repetitive treatment are clear, sharply defined rhythms. Such rhythms generally vary from one half a bar to four bars in length.

Rhythm with Varied Repetition

Music would remain in a lockstep if every pattern were repeated literally. Rhythmic variation often brings a welcome freshness to a repeated figure. Such variation may be slight or considerable (Exs. 35–37).

Ex. 35   Byrd: The Carman's Whistle

Ex. 36   Debussy: String Quartet

Permission for reprint granted by Durand et Cie., Paris, copyright owner, and Elkan-Vogel Co., Inc., Philadelphia, agents.

Ex. 37   Bartók: Music for Strings, Percussion, and Celeste

Frequently a rhythmic pattern is repeated literally once, then varied.*

Ex. 38   Brahms: Rhapsody , Op. 7, No. 1

Ex. 39   Siegmeister: Flute Concerto, third movement

Double Repeated Rhythm

Greater variety is offered by the combination of two rhythmic patterns in one phrase (*a* and *b* in Ex. 40). Such a design permits a longer melodic sweep, because the first rhythm needs time to become established before the second takes over. Generally each pattern is repeated immediately at least once: a, a′, b, b′. The repetition may be exact or varied.

Ex. 40   Bach: *Brandenburg* Concerto, No. 2

* For other examples of rhythmic variation, see Exs. 54–57, pages 220–221.

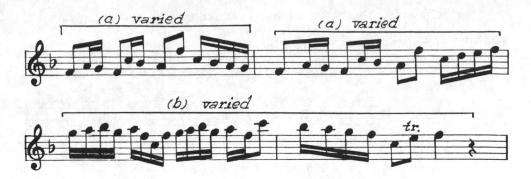

Tchaikovsky was fond of the two-rhythm structure, which he employed frequently. In the excerpt shown in Ex. 41, he added to the interest by using rhythms of unequal length: a two-bar pattern followed by a one-bar pattern, each repeated.

Ex. 41   Tchaikovsky: March, from the *Nutcracker* Suite, Op. 71²

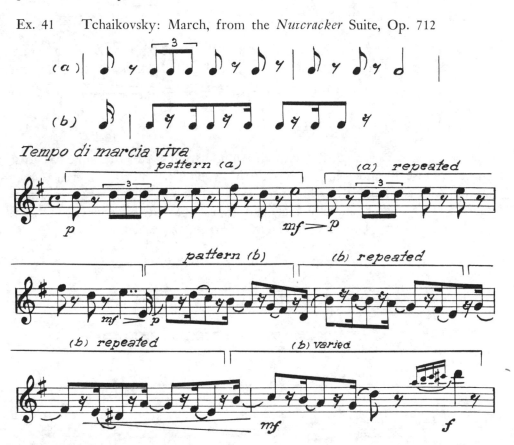

Mozart is not commonly thought of as a composer of extremely rhythmic music. Yet his rhythmic construction is often subtle and intriguing. At the opening of the *Jupiter* Symphony, an incisive two-bar rhythm alternates with a second, broader one. These are followed in turn by a hammering one-bar pattern, repeated five times, then varied. The three rhythms are sharply contrasted, launching the symphony on a vivid, dramatic note.

Ex. 42   Mozart: Symphony No. 41 (*Jupiter*), K. 551

In the three rhythmic types just discussed, repetition leads to symmetry and balance. In the four remaining types, rhythmic variety leads to an asymmetrical structure.

Changing Meter

Changing meter is the twentieth century's answer to what has been described as "the tyranny of the bar line." Having invented the bar line to facilitate the writing of scores, seventeenth-century musicians proceeded to treat it as a law of nature. Delight in the newly found harmonic style with its four-square patterns led Baroque composers to discard the supple rhythms of the Renaissance. Once having started with a given meter, it was now obligatory for a composer to maintain it unchanged to the end of a movement or until another meter was formally installed in its place. Fixed, regular meter was destined to rule supreme in Western music for nearly 300 years.

The twentieth century opened new rhythmic pathways. But the predecessor of many modern innovators was a nineteenth-century composer, Modeste Moussorgsky.* Taking the rhythms of Russian folk music as his point of departure, he used changing meters with great boldness. *Pictures at an Exhibition*, written in 1870, starts with an alternation of 5/4 and 6/4.

Ex. 43   Moussorgsky: Promenade, from *Pictures at an Exhibition*

One of Moussorgsky's musical descendants, the young Stravinsky, followed the older master in many respects—and not least in the field of changing meters, which he developed into a complex rhythmic art.

Ex. 44   Stravinsky: Ritual Dance, from *The Rite of Spring*

* Isolated examples of changing meter can also be found in earlier nineteenth-century compositions—among them Beethoven's Symphony No. 3 and Brahms' Variations, Op. 21, No. 2.

Further examples of changing meter can be found in such works as Bartók's *Mikrokosmos*, Copland's *Appalachian Spring,* and Piston's Fourth Symphony.*

Free-Flowing Rhythm

In much medieval, Renaissance, and Oriental music, the rhythms are *free-flowing.* Whether metrical or not, such compositions contain no rhythmic duplications; their time values are in constant flux. Many compositions by Josquin des Prés, Okheghem, Palestrina, and their contemporaries seem to float in air, free of earthbound repetitions.

Ex. 45   Palestrina: Mass, *Ascendo ad Patrem*

With the growth of meter and harmony, free-flowing rhythms gave way to repetitive ones. Bar lines, block chords, and harmonic changes made it much more difficult to write a free rhythmic line. But the tradition was not entirely lost, and here and there a composer remembered the possibilities inherent in free-flowing rhythms.

Ex. 46   Beethoven: Symphony No. 4, Op. 60, second movement

In the twentieth century, free-flowing rhythms began to be widely used once more.

Ex. 47   Ives: Walt Whitman †

* See also Ex. 37, page 156; Ex. 57, page 221; and Ex. 40, page 452.

† Words by Walt Whitman.

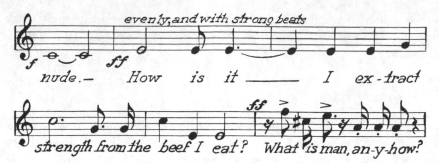

Ex. 48   Shostakovich: Symphony No. 5, Op. 47

Polyrhythm

Polyrhythm is, strictly speaking, a misnomer. It should be called *polymeter*, for that is precisely what polyrhythmic music is: one meter superposed on another. Since the accents do not coincide, a rhythmic conflict results.*

A meter of four beats over one of three provides an example of a polyrhythm—let us say a march over a waltz rhythm.

Ex. 49   Polyrhythm: 4/4 over 3/4

Obviously, the one-two-three-four of the march does not coincide with the one-two-three waltz pattern, thus provoking a clash of accents.

* A famous early example of polyrhythms occurs in Mozart's *Don Giovanni*. Three different orchestras performing at a ball play simultaneously: (1) a minuet in ¾, (2) a country dance in ¾, and (3) a waltz in ⅜ time.

Two over three was a polyrhythm frequently used in Romantic music; Chopin's *Minute* Waltz provides an example. The left hand contains the standard three-beat meter of the waltz.

Ex. 50   Chopin: Waltz, Op. 64, No. 1, left hand

The right hand, however, presents a 2/4 meter.

Ex. 51   Chopin: Waltz, right hand

Since it was not customary in the nineteenth century to notate such music by two different, simultaneous time signatures, Chopin wrote the right hand as though it, too, were in waltz meter.

Ex. 52   Chopin: Waltz, Op. 64, No. 1

Sensitive performances of the waltz should, however, reveal its polyrhythmic character, as though it were written in separate meters.

Ex. 53   Chopin: Waltz, written in two meters

Polyrhythms are, of course, part and parcel of much twentieth-century music, especially jazz. Gershwin's song "Fascinating Rhythm," written when jazz rhythms were still a novelty, shows a distinct polyrhythm: the melody in 7/8 meter over a bass in 4/4. The sheet music does not indicate the 7/8 meter (which would frighten off most amateur pianists). Example 54 shows (*a*) the printed version of the song, and (*b*) a version in which the contrasted meters are notated as they actually sound.

Ex. 54   Gershwin: Fascinating Rhythm

American composers—notably Ives, Gershwin, Copland, Gould, and Bernstein—developed jazz polyrhythms into a characteristic element of American symphonic and theater music; but they were not alone in using this technique. Such European and Latin American moderns as Stravinsky, Milhaud, Bartók, Revueltas, and Villa-Lobos have also enriched music with the vitality of their polyrhythmic writing.

Besides polyrhythms that contain an obvious clash of patterns, there is a subtler type in which a phrase departs temporarily from the basic meter of a movement. In Prokofiev's Second Violin Concerto, the chief melody starts with a five-beat pattern, although the meter of the composition is 4/4.

Ex. 55   Prokofiev: Violin Concerto No. 2

Richard Strauss, in *Till Eulenspiegel*, depicts the capricious character of his hero by a 7/8 pattern within a meter of 6/8.

Ex. 56   Strauss: *Till Eulenspiegel*

Non-Metric Rhythm

The last of the seven rhythmic types dispenses not only with the bar line but with any regular rhythmic accent whatsoever. Such non-metric music is conducive to an escape from the physical. It leaves the mind floating in a realm far removed from that of dancing feet, moving bodies, or physical action of any kind.

Oriental, Hebrew, and Gregorian chants provide examples of non-metric music. The melodies are free-flowing,* with a subtle irregularity that often enhances their solemnity and grandeur.

Non-metric rhythms may result from setting to music prose texts, whether from the Bible (as in the Hebrew and Gregorian chants and Renaissance masses) or from modern literature. *Recitative* passages in opera often achieve dramatic vividness through the free rhythmic inflections of prose. Mimi's recitative from *La Bohème* is an excellent example. †

Ex. 57   Puccini: Recitative, from *La Bohème*, Act I

Composers sometimes use non-metric rhythm in cadenzas for instrumental concertos. Such use may produce a striking contrast after passages of great rhythmic drive. A non-metric phrase in Bartók's Concerto for Orchestra almost gives the feeling of improvisation.

* See Ex. 14, page 14; Ex. 24, page 65; Ex. 49, page 219; Ex. 24, page 240; and Ex. 17, page 277.

† For another example of recitative, see Ex. 18, page 278.

Ex. 58   Bartók: Concerto for Orchestra, fourth movement

© 1946 by Hawkes & Son (London) Ltd. Reprinted by permission of Boosey & Hawkes Inc.

Rhythm and Melodic Motion

Rhythmic motion, as we have seen, provides music with one of its elemental forces. Many of the rhythmic techniques already discussed—especially insistent repetition, changing meter and polyrhythm—contribute to the energy of a phrase. Melodic motion is strongly promoted by clearly defined, sharply accented rhythms.

Three further aspects of rhythm serve to enhance the movement of a melody: (1) fast tempo, (2) fast rhythmic values, and (3) syncopation.

Fast tempo and rhythmic values add force to many compositions—the finale of Beethoven's Ninth Symphony, for example. The *Ode to Joy* melody exudes vigor when its sturdy quarter notes are first sung in 4/4 time by the solo baritone.* Later in the movement, when a feeling of high exhilaration develops, the same melody appears in eighth notes, and in double tempo (sounding, therefore, *four* times as fast). The quickening of tempo and rhythm creates a sense of dazzling animation.

Ex. 59   Beethoven: Ninth Symphony, Op. 125, fourth movement

Syncopation—accenting the weak beat or between the beats—is sometimes considered an invention of jazz musicians. While frequently found in American melodies, it is hardly an American invention, having been used for centuries in the music of many different nations. In metrical music, the dis-

* See Ex. 20, page 88.

placement of the accent to an unexpected position in the measure serves to increase the sense of rhythmic movement and energy, as shown by the asterisks in Exs. 60–62. *

Ex. 60   Bach: Cantata No. 4, *Christ lag in Todesbanden*

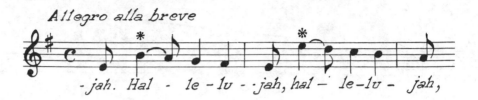

Ex. 61   Mozart: Overture to *The Magic Flute*

Ex. 62   Negro spiritual: Didn't My Lord Deliver Daniel?

* For other examples of syncopation, see Ex. 20, page 113; Ex. 22, page 115; Ex. 37, page 156; Ex. 39, page 157; and Exs. 41–42, page 413.

Summary

1. Rhythm is an integral part of melody.
   a. The beat is the basic unit of rhythm.
   b. Meter is a repeated pattern of strong and weak beats.
   c. Rhythm, in the specific sense, is a particular pattern of time values.

2. A rhythmic pattern may be the most characteristic feature of a melody.

3. Symmetrical types of rhythm form evenly balanced patterns.
   a. Repeated rhythm is the literal reiteration of a pattern.
   b. Rhythm with varied repetition is a freer version of (a).
   c. Double repeated rhythm occurs when a phrase has two clearly contrasted rhythms, each repeated: a, a', b, b'.

4. Asymmetrical types of rhythm produce irregular, free-form patterns.
   a. Changing meters occur when the number of beats per measure varies during the phrase.
   b. Free-flowing rhythms occur when a phrase contains no repeated rhythmic pattern.
   c. Polyrhythms occur when a phrase contains two different meters produced simultaneously.
   d. Non-metric rhythms occur when a phrase contains neither bar lines nor regular rhythmic accents.

5. Rhythm is one of the basic sources of melodic motion.
   a. Various rhythmic techniques, especially insistent repetition, changing meter, and polyrhythm, enhance the activity of a phrase.
   b. Fast tempo, fast rhythmic values, and syncopation serve further to increase rhythmic momentum.

VII

Harmonization
and Voice Leading

Harmonization of Melodies with Embellishing Tones

The harmonization of melodies with embellishing tones presents new opportunities and problems. As long as we are limited to chord tones alone, the choice of harmonies for a given note is restricted to one or two at most, and can almost be decided by rule of thumb. Melodies of a more ornamental character offer more choices.

There is no one correct way of harmonizing a melody. Even the simplest folk songs have been arranged in different but equally effective settings by various composers. Beethoven, Rimsky-Korsakov, and Moussorgsky harmonized the same Russian folk tune, each in his own manner.* Bach made as many as ten different settings of the same chorale.

The first step in harmonizing a melody is to study its character. Sing or play the tune over two or three times, searching for clues to its style and meaning. If it has words in a foreign language, obtain a translation. Note the dynamics, if any, and especially the tempo. Is the tune fast or slow, strongly accented or evenly flowing, playful or serious?

Once the character of a melody has been grasped, look for its harmonic rhythm. A folk dance, a children's song, a courtly air need lighter harmonic underpinning and fewer chord changes than a hymn tune or a lament for a lost love.

* Beethoven: String Quartet, Op. 59, No. 2, third movement; Rimsky-Korsakov: *Collection of 100 Folk Songs;* Moussorgsky: see Ex. 32, page 405.

Without violating any rules, one could harmonize *Ach, du lieber Augustin* as in Ex. 1.

Ex. 1   *Ach, du lieber Augustin*, block-chord harmonization

This harmony, theoretically "correct," would be suitable for a slow-paced anthem. But could poor Augustin survive under the weight of these block chords? Comparison with another setting (Ex. 10 on page 141 shows the disadvantage of over-harmonizing; such a tune needs only the simplest of chord patterns.

Beethoven used a light treatment in sections of his *Pastoral* Symphony.* The passage in Ex. 2 has an airy accompaniment—mostly tonic chord, with a few changing notes and the V sounded briefly near the end.

Ex. 2   Beethoven: Symphony No. 6 (*Pastoral*), Op. 68, third movement

* Bela Bartók once said he believed the first theme of the *Pastoral* was a folk song. He had listened to it played on a bagpipe by a Croatian peasant who surely had never known the Beethoven symphony. "Beethoven must have heard it when he was in the country with one of those counts," Bartók said.

In contrast to such a folk-like tune, other melodies not only need but cry out for a change of harmony under each note. The Bach chorales are examples of this continuous harmonic change.*

The great majority of melodies falls somewhere between the two extremes. The question remains, just how far to go, how many chords to use in a particular case? Although no pat answer exists, we can find valuable suggestions in a tune like "Susie, Little Susie," from Humperdinck's *Hansel and Gretel*.

Ex. 3   Humperdinck: *Suse, liebe Suse*, from *Hansel and Gretel*

A practical procedure in writing a harmonization might be as follows:

1. Find the harmonic rhythm. Does the tune need one or more chords per bar, or shall the rate of chord change vary from bar to bar?
2. Try to determine which notes are chord tones and which embellishing tones.
3. Mark the cadences. Are they half, imperfect, plagal, or perfect?

* See, among others, Ex. 14, page 111.

Having profited by the experience with *Ach, du lieber Augustin,* we quickly discard the idea of using cumbersome block chords; a different chord on each note would swamp a lively, naïve tune such as this. The harmonization in Ex. 4 would be tasteless.

Ex. 4   *Suse, liebe Suse,* block-chord harmonization

Some experimentation will show that the D and B flat in the first bar are best treated as neighboring and passing tones, respectively:

Ex. 5   *Suse, liebe Suse,* sketch no. 1

We quickly sketch in the cadences: (a) imperfect, (b) perfect, (c) plagal, and (d) perfect. The sketch will now look like Ex. 6.

Ex. 6   *Suse, liebe Suse,* sketch no. 2

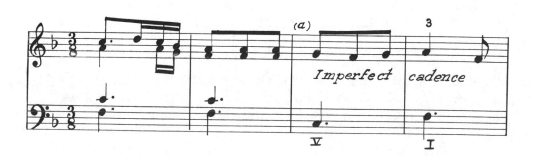

With the general style of the harmonization established and the cadences sketched in, we now write the bass part—a fairly simple task, since the
piece takes the I and V chords throughout, except for bar 11, in which the IV
makes a brief but telling entrance.

Only the inner parts remain to be filled in. Since embellishing tones
add flow and elegance, let us distribute them between alto and tenor (Ex. 7).
At (a), the F makes a good neighboring tone, accompanied in thirds by the
alto. The thirds continue from (b) to (c), where the tenor has a chance for a
passing tone. The sixths at (d) provide a welcome change from several bars
of thirds. At (e), matters are varied a bit by the motion of the tenor in parallel tenths with the soprano; this motion changes at (g) to parallel sixths. An
escaped tone, G, fits well in the tenor line at (f). Example 7 illustrates one
version of the completed harmonization.

Ex. 7   *Suse, liebe Suse,* harmonized to show possibilities of embellishing tones

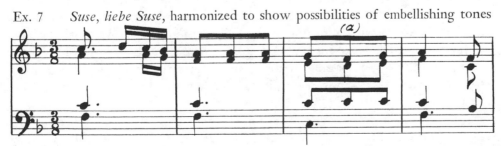

 ·The harmonization finished, it is important now to check for parallel fifths and octaves; then to test the voice leading by singing each of the parts from beginning to end. Beyond a doubt, if the writer himself has difficulty singing any of the voices, others will find the same difficulty. The voice leading had best be simplified!

Parallel Octaves and Fifths

Among the musical values most prized in the traditional period were elegance and clarity of part writing. Baroque, Classical, and Romantic composers constantly sought for a natural melodic flow of individual voices and for the smoothest possible blend among them. Traditional harmony, with its full, euphonious sound, was—in the beginning at least—partly a reaction against the medieval style of parallel fifths, fourths, and octaves, which probably struck men of the early Renaissance as somewhat hollow, rough, and old-fashioned.

This background helps us to understand the centuries-long distaste for parallel octaves and fifths. To the ear of the classically trained musician, these intervals represented a primitive manner of writing; and, to be sure, when inserted into a passage of traditional harmony, they do sound like an anachronism.

Making comic use of such an anachronism, Mozart wrote a clumsy pair of parallel fifths in *A Musical Joke*, his delightful satire on the crudity of village musicians.

Ex. 8   Mozart: *A Musical Joke*, K. 522, second movement

Another source of the prejudice against parallel fifths and octaves can be found in the prevalence of empty fifths and octaves in folk music, especially in the drone of the bagpipe and the group singing of peasants. Here, no doubt, is the explanation for the deliberate use of the forbidden parallelisms by such composers as Beethoven, Chopin, and Moussorgsky in compositions suggesting the wildness of a peasant dance or village festival.

Ex. 9   Beethoven: Symphony No. 6 (*Pastoral*), Op. 68, third movement

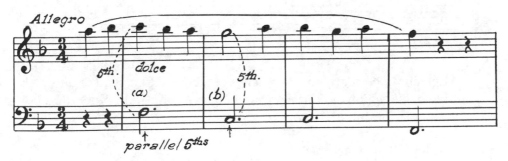

The hollow sound of parallel fifths (rather delightful to modern ears) was emphasized by Beethoven when he placed fifths on downbeats in two successive measures.

Such emphasis—as well as the sound produced by consecutive fifths or fifths on successive accented beats—was avoided in the vast majority of traditional compositions. And, unless one wishes to suggest a peasant festival or a grotesque scene, they had best be eliminated in harmonic writing for the present.*

* There will be ample opportunity for writing parallel fifths in contemporary-style composition (see Chapters XII and XIII, Volume II).

Covered Octaves and Fifths

Closely allied to the traditional aversion to parallel fifths and octaves was a similar feeling against certain so-called *covered* (or *hidden*) fifths or octaves—a curious name, for these intervals are not always covered, often being quite apparent to the ear. A covered interval is one formed by two voices moving in similar motion.

Ex. 10   Covered octave and fifth

Covered octaves and fifths have been freely used when the approach to the upper voice has been by stepwise motion. Haydn provided a fine example of *horn fifths*—so-called because of their frequent occurrence in fanfares played by hunting horns. The passage from his *Drumroll* Symphony is scored for horns. The stepwise approach to the upper voice of the open fifths at (*a*) and (*b*) introduces them smoothly into the phrase.

Ex. 11   Haydn: Symphony No. 103 (*Drumroll*), fourth movement

Equally smooth are the approaches to a covered octave (*a*) and fifth (*b*) in the *Gagliarda* of the Elizabethan composer John Bull. Note the stepwise motion of the upper voice.

Ex. 12   John Bull: *Gagliarda*

A slightly different problem is encountered when a covered fifth does not involve the upper voice. More latitude has generally been allowed in such cases: covered fifths or octaves were permitted if *either* the bottom or the inner voice was approached by stepwise motion. Note the approach to the fifth in the last chord of a Bach chorale, in which the bass part moves down by step.

Ex. 13   Bach: *Herr Jesu Christ, dich zu uns wend*

> Lord Je - sus Christ, Oh turn to us.
> Herr Je - su Christ, dich zu uns wend.

A third type of covered fifth has been widely used in traditional music; this type occurs in a shift from one to another position *of the same chord*. Since no harmonic change is involved and therefore no harmonic accent, composers have felt free to approach such covered fifths by a leap of both voices.

Ex. 14   Bach: *Herr, ich denk an jener Zeit*

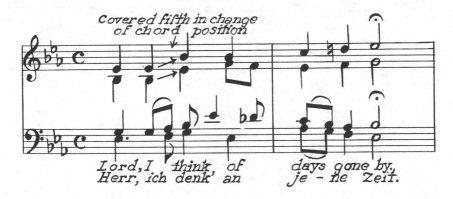

> Lord, I think of days gone by,
> Herr, ich denk' an je - ne Zeit.

When the chord *changes*, however, it has been considered crude to approach a covered octave or fifth by a leap to the upper voice, or to both voices.

Ex. 15   Covered octave by leap (student example)

Use of the Leading Tone

Because of its strong need to resolve, 7, as we have seen, is practically never doubled; such doubling almost always produces a clumsy, unbalanced chord. The obligation to resolve 7 to 8 is relaxed in two situations:

1. When 7 forms part of a falling scale line, 8—7—6, as in Ex. 29, Chapter VI, or 14, Chapter VIII.
2. When there is a need for a complete tonic chord at the cadence. Together with a falling movement of the soprano from 2 to 1, the 7 in an inner voice may resolve by *a leap down* to 5, filling out the final chord, which would otherwise lack a fifth (Ex. 16, *a*). In such case, a covered fifth approached by leaps in both voices is considered acceptable.

Ex. 16   Bach: *Herr Gott, dich loben alle wir*

Use of the Unison

Another voice-leading problem concerns the unison. Traditionally, one avoids entering or leaving a unison by similar motion of two voices, because of the resultant heaviness.

Ex. 17   Unison by similar motion (student example)

Exception is made, however, for the resolution of tenor and bass to a unison on the *tonic*.

Ex. 18   Palestrina: *O bone Jesu*

Overlapping of Voices

A moot question among traditional composers concerns *overlapping*. This procedure occurs when, in a progression of two chords, a lower voice moves above the pitch of an upper voice in the preceding chord, or vice versa (Ex. 19). Some musicians have felt that such a process causes confusion between the two parts. Others, however, indulged in it freely. The better part of wisdom is to avoid overlapping until one has achieved sufficient skill to handle the procedure with taste and meaning.

Ex. 19   Overlapping

Overlapping in changes of position of the *same chord*, however, is considered excellent style, because no undue heaviness results.

Ex. 20   Beethoven: String Quartet, Op. 59, No. 1, second movement

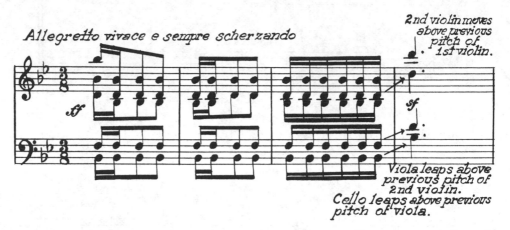

Doubled Thirds

It is often effective to double the third of a minor triad (see Ex. 22, page 348). The third is not usually doubled in major triads, however, except when the doubling is produced by two voices moving in stepwise, contrary motion. (See the second bar of Ex. 14, page 179, where soprano and tenor voices double the third—C—while passing in opposite directions.)

Difficult Melodic Leaps

In their desire for the smoothest possible voice leading, composers of the traditional period normally avoided leaps that were difficult to sing, such as most augmented and diminished intervals and leaps of a seventh or ninth. They also generally avoided *two successive leaps* adding up to a seventh, a ninth, or a larger interval. When such leaps were introduced, it was usually for a specific expressive or dramatic purpose. The student should reserve all such difficult intervals for moments of special emphasis or intense expression.

Summary

In harmonizing melodies that contain embellishing tones, the following order should be followed:

1. Sing or play the melody several times, studying its character.

2. Decide how frequently the harmonies shall change:
   a. A chord for every tone, or
   b. A chord for every few tones.

3. Try to determine which notes are chord tones and which embellishing tones.

4. Harmonize the cadences.

5. Write the entire bass part.

6. Fill in the inner voices.

7. Check for and correct:
    a. Parallel octaves and fifths.
    b. Poorly introduced covered fifths and octaves.
    c. Poor approach to or exit from the unison.
    d. Overlapping.
    e. Difficult melodic leaps.

The Motive

A melody makes its impression on the listener as a complete musical thought; but often it does not come to a composer this way. Sometimes it arrives as a series of bits and fragments that must be com-posed (literally: put together) to form a smoothly flowing line. The fragments that go to make up most melodies are called *motives*.

A motive is a group of tones *used as a unit* in forming a phrase, a melody, or an entire composition. Whether short or long, simple or complex, a motive forms the core from which a melody evolves. Take any phrase that comes to mind, and the chances are it springs from a motive. Beethoven's Fifth Symphony (Ex. 21) grows from a dramatic motive, and "Skip to My Lou" (Ex. 22) from a playful one; "I Got Rhythm" (Ex. 23) is based on a motive, and so is the *Crucifixus* from Bach's B minor Mass (Ex. 24). There are motives in the "Star Spangled Banner" as well as Berg's *Wozzeck*.

Ex. 21   Beethoven: Symphony No. 5, Op. 67

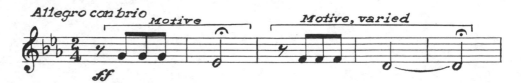

Ex. 22   American folk song: Skip to My Lou

Ex. 23   Gershwin: I Got Rhythm

Copyright 1930 by New World Music Corporation. Used by permission.

Ex. 24   Bach: *Crucifixus*, from the B minor Mass

Identifying the Motive

In studying the structure of a melody, a question often arises: Just what is the motive? The identity of a motive is established by its continued use in a phrase or composition. Its ending is marked in three different ways: (1) by its immediate repetition, (2) by a rest, or (3) by the entry of contrasting material.

Each of the excerpts above starts with a well-defined motive. In Examples 21, 23, and 24, the motive ends with a rest. In Ex. 22, the motive is repeated (a tone lower) in the third bar. In Bach's *Crucifixus*, which is contrapuntal in style, each successive statement of the motive appears in a different voice; each, however, ends with a rest. (Note that the entries are dovetailed: the second voice starts the motive before the first has completed it.)

A motive achieves its identity through repetition, whether literal or varied. (If a group of tones is *not* repeated at all, it cannot act as a motive.) Almost always the repetition of a motive follows immediately upon its first statement (see Ex. 21). On occasion, however—especially in longer works— the restatement may be delayed by the intervention of contrasting material.

Ex. 25   Beethoven: Symphony No. 3 (*Eroica*), Op. 55

Melodic and Rhythmic Motives

Many motives are distinguished by melodic and rhythmic features, but some by one, some by the other.

A *melodic motive* is usually characterized by its intervals or melodic curve, while its rhythm remains neutral. Bach's Fugue in C sharp minor, for instance, draws its distinction from the diminished fourth (*a*).

Ex. 26   Bach: Fugue No. 4, *The Well-Tempered Clavier*, Book I

Chopin's Nocturne in E flat commands attention by the swiftly rising major sixth with which the motive starts.

Ex. 27   Chopin: Nocturne in E flat, Op. 9, No. 2

Sliding chromatic intervals characterize a melodic motive in Gershwin's *Rhapsody in Blue*.

Ex. 28   Gershwin: *Rhapsody in Blue*

Copyright 1924 by New World Music Corporation. Used by permission.

A *rhythmic motive*, on the other hand, is distinguished by an interesting rhythmic pattern—particularly if its melodic shape is of little moment. Few listeners would sit patiently through the opening of the slow movement of Beethoven's Seventh Symphony were it not for the hypnotic effect of the insistently repeated rhythmic motive.

Ex. 29   Beethoven: Symphony No. 7, Op. 92, second movement

Several rhythmic motives have already been discussed in Chapter VI, where they were called "rhythmic patterns."* We see now that a rhythmic pattern, when repeated, takes on the character of a motive. Some other rhythmic motives are the familiar theme of Rossini's *William Tell* Overture, the first movement of Beethoven's Violin Concerto, and Mime's *leitmotif* from Wagner's *Siegfried*.

Ex. 30   Rossini: Overture to *William Tell*

Ex. 31   Beethoven: Violin Concerto, Op. 61

* See Exs. 30–33, pages 152–154.

Ex. 32   Wagner: *Siegfried*

Mässig bewegt

Rhythmic-melodic motives, by far the most common variety, are marked by a combination of interesting rhythmic and intervallic features. The opening motive of Mozart's Symphony No. 40 grows from a rhythmic germ* that is stated three times and then capped by a striking melodic leap of a sixth. Rhythmic and melodic elements merge in one motive.

Ex. 33   Mozart: Symphony No. 40, K. 550

Bach's Two-Part Invention No. 8 starts with a motive that combines rhythmic and melodic features: a series of eighth notes succeeded by a group of running sixteenths; a leaping broken chord followed by a rapid scale passage.

Ex. 34   Bach: Two-Part Invention, No 8

Roy Harris' Third Symphony contains a three-bar motive whose interesting rhythm (3/2 alternating with 6/4) is matched by a distinctly American melodic line.

Ex. 35   Harris: Third Symphony

* Some writers believe this germ to be the motive. For a discussion of the relation of germ to motive, see Appendix II, page 458.

Motive Complexity and Length

Motives may be simple or complex, short or long. Typical of the pithy motive often used as a "motto" theme in nineteenth-century music is the opening of the César Franck Symphony.

Ex. 36   Franck: Symphony in D minor

Such three-note motives are about the utmost in simplicity; but Sibelius went one step further in creating a two-note motive.*

Ex. 37   Sibelius: *Finlandia*, Op. 26

Copyright 1899, 1900 by Breitkopf and Haertel. Used by permission of Associated Music Publishers, Inc.

More complex motives are often found in music of a theatrical or exotic character—the colorful themes of Rimsky-Korsakov's *Scheherazade*, for example, and Gershwin's *Rhapsody in Blue*.

Ex. 38   Rimsky-Korsakov: *Scheherazade*

Ex. 39   Gershwin: *Rhapsody in Blue*

Copyright 1924 by New World Music Corporation. Used by permission.

*For another two-note motive, see Ex. 53, page 220.

To carry the inquiry one step further, where do motives begin, and how long can they be?

Many start at the beginning of a bar; some on an upbeat; and others on another beat of the bar.* There are motives as short as one half bar, but the majority extend to one, two, or four bars in length. Motives of various lengths are shown in Exs. 40–43.

Ex. 40   One half bar. Bach: Fugue II, from *The Well-Tempered Clavier,* Book I

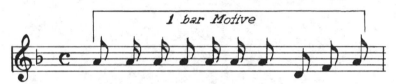

Ex. 41   One bar.† What Shall We Do with the Drunken Sailor?

Ex. 42   Two bars.‡ Tchaikovsky: Symphony No. 5, Op. 64

* For motives starting on an upbeat, see Exs. 27, 30, and 33. For those starting elsewhere in the bar, see Exs. 21, 34, and 40.

† Other illustrations of the one-bar motive are Ex. 13, page 36; Ex. 51, page 74; and Ex. 56, page 75.

‡ For further examples of the two-bar construction, see Ex. 12, page 14; Ex. 50, page 25; Ex. 22, page 64; and Ex. 15, page 111.

Ex. 43   Four bars.* Porter: Begin the Beguine

Perhaps the omission of the three-bar motive seems strange. Such motives were rare in the symphonic literature of the eighteenth and nineteenth centuries, and virtually non-existent in popular song and dance music of the recent past. They are often found, however, in folk songs, in music of the Renaissance, and in modern compositions.

Ex. 44   Three bars. Russian folk song: The Birch Tree

Ex. 45   Milhaud: *Protée* Suite, third movement

* Other four-bar motives are found in Ex. 16, page 37; Ex. 6, page 174; and Ex. 48, page 218.

Rarely do we find motives longer than four bars or motives that do not fit into a regular metric pattern. Five-bar motives, however, sometimes appear in folk songs, in music influenced by folk style, and in contemporary works (Ex. 46).

Ex. 46   Bartók: *Mikrokosmos*, Book II

Tell me, Tell me, have you got a rake to show?
Va - ne, va - ne, va - ne ne´ - ked ge - veb - lyéd?

© 1940 by Hawkes & Son (London) Ltd. Reprinted by permission of Boosey & Hawkes Inc.

Certain motives are of irregular length, and do not fit within a measure. The opening of "Fascinating Rhythm" (Ex. 54 of Chapter VI) covers seven eighth notes of a 4/4 measure. Prokofiev's Second Violin Concerto (Ex. 55 of Chapter VI) starts with a five-beat motive occupying one and one-quarter measures. Another example of motivic asymmetry is the bassoon solo that opens Stravinsky's *Rite of Spring*. The motive is exactly two and one-third beats long, in a 4/4 meter.

Ex. 47   Stravinsky: *The Rite of Spring*

© 1921 by Edition Russe De Musique. Copyright assigned 1947 Boosey & Hawkes Inc. Reprinted by permission.

We have seen how motives may vary in size, shape, length, and structure. In Chapter VIII we shall examine their growth into phrases.

Summary

1. The motive is a unit of musical thought used to form a phrase or a melody.

2. Motive endings are determined by:
   a. A rest.
   b. Repetition of the motive.
   c. The distinct appearance of new material.

3. Motive types are:
   a. Melodic.
   b. Rhythmic.
   c. Rhythmic-melodic.

4. Motives may be simple or complex.

5. Motives usually vary in length from one half to four bars.
   a. Occasionally longer motives can be found.
   b. Occasionally motives are of irregular length—for example, ⅞ or ⅝ of a bar.

VIII

Secondary Triads

Although discussion has centered thus far on the primary chords, I, IV, and V, triads are found on every step of the scale. The *secondary triads* include the II, III, VI, and VII.*

Primary triads differ from secondary triads in structure and function. In the major mode,† I, IV, and V are major triads; II, III, and VI, minor.

Ex. 1   Primary and secondary triads in major

The primary chords serve to express the tonality and to harmonize melodies of a forthright, elemental character. The II, III, and VI play a variety of roles:

1. They provide a more varied, subtler, and richer harmony than do the primary chords.

---

* The VII chord is discussed on pages 312–314.

† For triads in the minor mode, see Chapters XII and XIII.

2. They make for a more flowing bass line.
3. They serve as substitutes for the primary chords.
4. They are used to suggest modality, providing a contrast with the key-affirming primary chords.

Secondary Triads Providing Richer Harmony and More Flowing Bass

The potentialities of the secondary triads were already well known to composers in the sixteenth century, when the chordal style was still in its early stages of growth. Clément Jannequin employed the II, III, and VI with taste and elegance in his delightful chanson *Ce mois de mai*. Example 2 shows (a) the melody alone; (b) a harmonization with primary triads only; and (c) the composer's harmonization, using both primary and secondary triads.

Ex. 2 (a)   Jannequin: *Ce mois de mai*

(b) Theoretical harmonization with primary chords

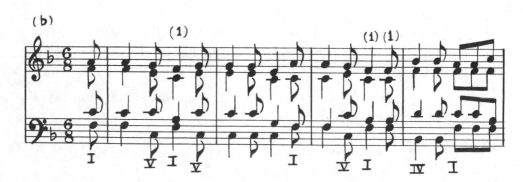

(c) Composer's harmonization

In comparing (b) and (c), the superior effectiveness of the composer's version becomes apparent.

Example 2(b) demonstrates that, although it is theoretically possible to harmonize the melody with primary chords alone, such a setting is repetitious to a fault. The constantly repeated chords produce a static feeling and a dull bass line, showing that a ponderous harmonization can weigh down even the most elegant of melodies.

The harmonization in (c), with its imaginative use of secondary triads, imparts forward motion to the melody by adding to it a well-shaped bass line. Note the contrast between (b) and (c), especially in the six places where Jannequin allows the soprano to sound the tonic (1). In (b) the note is accompanied five times out of six by the tonic triad. In (c) it is given three different harmonies: VI the first four times; then IV; and I only the last time.

Obviously, Jannequin valued harmonic variety. He knew, furthermore, how to employ suspense to create harmonic motion. By associating the all-important tonic five times with chords not central to the key, he gave it an unresolved quality; by harmonizing it with the tonic triad the last time only, he reserved the feeling of finality for its proper place—the end of the phrase.

The final cadence merits special notice. The progression V—VI—IV—V—I forms a very effective way of closing a phrase.

Chord-by-chord comparison of versions (*b*) and (*c*) reveals the value of secondary triads in producing harmonic variety and a more interesting bass line.

Secondary Triads as Substitute Chords

Each of the secondary triads discussed has a special relation to the primary triad a third above it. Two common tones link VI to I, II to IV, and III to V.

Ex. 3   Relation of primary and secondary triads

This partial identity of structure permits the minor triad to serve as a *substitute chord* for the major one when it would be awkward or impossible for the latter to appear. For example, the opening phrase of the anthem "America" contains in its melody several repetitions of the tonic and the third.

Ex. 4   America, melody

If "America" were harmonized with primary chords alone, the tonic triad would be used six times—a monotonous effect.

Ex. 5   America, with primary triads

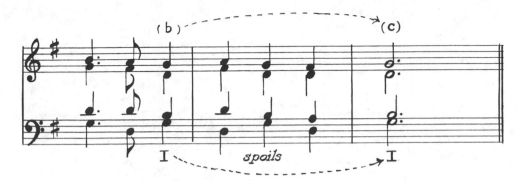

An appearance of the tonic triad at (b), just two bars before the end, is especially awkward because of the final quality of the tonic in both outer voices. By anticipating the last chord so near the close, it halts the movement prematurely, spoiling the impact of the cadence.

Ex. 6   America, traditional harmonization

In the traditional harmonization of "America," VI serves twice as a substitute for I (at a and b), creating a more varied harmonic line. It is particularly valuable at (b), where it gives the first degree a different harmony than it will have at (c). The final chord is not anticipated, as in Ex. 5. The substitute chord provides smoother harmonic motion and a more flowing bass line.

A virginal piece by William Byrd illustrates the use of II as a substitute for IV.

Ex. 7   Byrd: *La Volta*

At (*a*) the melody moves from 4 to 5 (*b*). The choice of the IV and V chords, respectively, to harmonize these tones would result in parallel octaves.

Ex. 8   Harmonization of bar 6 of *La Volta* with primary triads

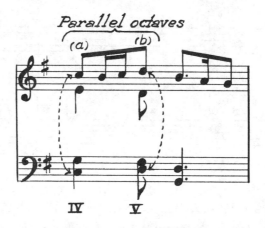

The substitution of II in Ex. 7 avoids this pitfall and makes for a more varied harmony. The use of VI in bars 2 and 3 should also be noted.

Substitute chords serve not only where primary chords cannot appear, but also where such chords, although possible, would be awkward. In setting harmony to the English folk-dance melody "The Crested Hen" (Ex. 9) it would be *possible* to harmonize bars 9 to 12 with I—IV—IV—V (Ex. 10).

Ex. 9   English folk melody: The Crested Hen

Ex. 10   The Crested Hen, harmonization with I, IV, V

But how much better is Ex. 11. The substitution of the II for IV at (a) promotes harmonic motion and avoids the lame repetition of IV.

Ex. 11   The Crested Hen, harmonization with I—IV—II—V

Often the need for a secondary triad becomes apparent from the melodic line itself. In Schubert's Waltz in A flat, there is no question of which chord to use at (a); the melody outlines the II as a broken chord, making its use in the bass mandatory.

Ex. 12   Schubert: Waltz in A flat, Op. 9, No. 3

Note that the same chord pattern used in "The Crested Hen" occurs here: I—IV—II—V; it is a common progression in traditional music. We meet it once again in harmonizing the American folk song "The Foggy Dew."

Ex. 13   American folk song: The Foggy Dew

The use of II in the second bar is once more obligatory; no other triad contains both the 2 and the 6. Thus the II and other secondary chords are embedded in the structure of many melodies.

Similarly, III is often used as a substitute for V in harmonizing a descending scale passage. The falling pattern 8—7—6 frequently takes the progression I—III—IV.

Ex. 14   Brahms: Symphony No. 4, Op. 98, third movement

The III is related to VI in the same way that the V is to I. A fifth above the VI, it acts as a kind of dominant to the latter, analogous to the relation of V to I. When a melodic pattern harmonized by I—V repeats a third lower, what is more natural than to use the chords a third lower—VI and III? A falling melodic line is paralleled by a falling harmonic line: 3—2—1—7 harmonized by I—V—VI—III.

Ex. 15   Descending melodic and harmonic patterns

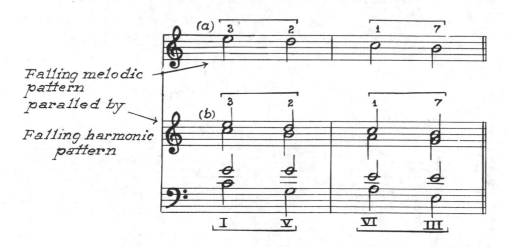

This progression occurs in an early American folk song, "Old Colony Times" (Ex. 16, a–b).

Ex. 16   American folk song: Old Colony Times

The Deceptive Cadence

When a phrase approaches a perfect cadence, but its final melody tone arrives with an unexpected harmony, the result is called a *deceptive cadence*. The VI often acts as the "surprise" chord, substituting for the expected I in such a cadence (Ex. 17, *a*). By delaying the appearance of the tonic chord, the "deceptive" VI requires an extension of the phrase, heightening the listener's satisfaction in the perfect cadence when it finally arrives (*b*).

Ex. 17   Mozart: *Bei Männern welche Liebe fühlen*, from *The Magic Flute*

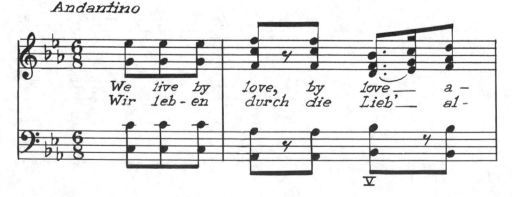

A deceptive cadence near the end of a composition is usually followed by a perfect cadence. This pattern is sometimes referred to as a *double cadence*.

Secondary Triads as Modal Chords

One final function of secondary triads in the major mode is to create an intermediate area between tonal and modal harmony.*

In the works of some sixteenth- and late nineteenth-century composers, tonal and modal harmonies are intermingled in the same composition, producing a distinctive harmonic style. At certain points in such works, the key is emphasized by primary chords; at other points, modality is suggested by secondary harmonies. This contrast between the tonal quality of the primary triads and the modal quality of the secondary ones receives vivid illustration in the opening movement, Promenade, of Moussorgsky's *Pictures at an Exhibition*, whose melody first appears without harmony.

Ex. 18   Moussorgsky: *Pictures at an Exhibition*, bar 1

In the course of the movement, Moussorgsky harmonizes the melody of the first bar in two different ways. In bar 3 (Ex. 19), secondary triads (VI and III) provide the harmony for three of the tones. Later in the movement, these same tones are harmonized by primary triads (IV and I—Ex. 20).

---

* Modal harmony is found in music of the medieval and Renaissance periods and also in some contemporary music, where it serves to accompany modal melodies and to create a freer, more colorful kind of tonality. See Chapter XII, Volume II.

Ex. 19   Moussorgsky: *Pictures*, bar 3

Ex. 20   Moussorgsky: *Pictures*, bars 4 and 3 from the end

Equally beautiful, the two settings present a sharp contrast. The harmonies of Ex. 19 have a modal character; in themselves they do not emphasize the key. The second harmonization, on the other hand (Ex. 20), clearly affirms the key, B flat major.

Nineteenth-century Slavic composers—Moussorgsky, Tchaikovsky, Borodin, and Dvorak—made imaginative use of the secondary triads within a framework of tonality. Their emphasis on the II, III, and VI lends a special modal color to their work. Had Dvorak harmonized the second theme of his *New World* Symphony with primary chords alone (as in Ex. 21), it would not have half its flavor.

Ex. 21   Dvorak: Symphony No. 5 (*From the New World*), Op. 95, harmonization with primary triads

The composer's harmonization (Ex. 22), employing the VI and III, gives the music its "Dvorak" quality.

Ex. 22   Dvorak: Symphony No. 5 (*From the New World*), Op. 95

Tchaikovsky's use of the same chords, in his Fourth Symphony, emphasizes the music's Russian style.

Ex. 23   Tchaikovsky: Symphony No. 4, Op. 36, third movement

I VI I VI I VI I (I⁶) V (VI⁶) III (IV⁶) I (II⁶) VI V

Twentieth-century composers—among them Ravel, Vaughan-Williams, Bartók, Revueltas, Villa-Lobos, Gershwin, and Ives—expanded the concept of tonality to embrace both modal and tonal elements, thus adding greatly to the expressive possibilities of harmony.

Summary

1. The primary triads of a key are I, IV, and V. They express the tonality most strongly, serving for the simplest harmonizations.

2. The secondary triads are II, III, VI, and VII. The II, III, and VI are minor triads in major.

3. The secondary triads serve:
   a. To create a rich, varied harmony.
   b. To provide a flowing bass line.
   c. As substitutes for the primary chords (each primary triad has a substitute triad a third below it).
   d. To suggest a modal area within the major mode.

4. Special uses of secondary triads:
   a. III serves to harmonize 7 in the pattern 8—7—6.
   b. VI serves in the deceptive cadence (V—VI).

5. The deceptive cadence is part of the double cadence: V—VI followed by V—I.

Techniques
of Motive
Variation

When a composer has found a motive he likes, how does he develop it into a melody?

Trained in the techniques of his craft, he may turn the motive over in his mind: shall it go this way or that? Shall it develop a swift intensity or rise in a slowly mounting curve, be repeated literally or find a variety of shapes? These questions do not present themselves consciously to the professional composer; but every student musician must start very deliberately by asking them and seeking their answers.

Some two and a half centuries ago, the composer of the Minuet in G, from *Anna Magdalena Bach's Notebook*,* started out with a two-bar motive.

Ex. 24   Minuet, from *Anna Magdalena Bach's Notebook*

* Once attributed to J. S. Bach.

How did the composer develop the motive into a phrase? We find:

(a) Repetition of the motive on a higher level.
(b) The first bar turned upside down and slightly varied.
(c) The same material a tone lower.
(d) The motive with changed intervals.
(e) A breathing point in the right hand, while a hint of the motive appears in the left hand.

The entire phrase arises out of the two-bar motive; the composer of the Minuet in G was evidently trained in the techniques of motive variation.

Two hundred years later composers were still using the same basic techniques. In the ballet *La création du monde* by Darius Milhaud, the second section consists of a jazz fugue based on a five-note motive.

Ex. 25   Milhaud: *La création du monde*

Four appearances of the motive constitute the phrase. At (*a*) it has one added note; (*b*) starts a fifth higher, and is extended to two bars; (*c*) starts a fourth lower, and contains seven notes.

Despite obvious differences in style, the techniques of motive variation are basically the same in Exs. 24 and 25: literal repetition; varied repetition; repetition on a higher pitch level; inversion; and shortening or lengthening of the motive. The vast majority of melodies from plain chant to contemporary music have been written with these and similar methods of variation.

Eight different techniques have long been the mainstays of melody writing:*

Literal repetition	Extension
Sequence	Inversion
Interval change	Rhythm change
Fragmentation	Ornamentation

The basic method for developing a motive into a phrase usually involves some form of repetition.

Literal Repetition

By its very nature, music is an evanescent art; no sooner has a musical idea been heard than it is gone. Repetition serves to impress it on the listener's mind. *Literal* repetition, obviously, cannot figure as a type of variation. Yet it occurs so frequently as a method of working with a motive that it cannot be overlooked.

Examples of literal repetition are legion; Exs. 26–28 show one each from Beethoven, Brahms, and popular music—which, of course, thrives on repetition.

Ex. 26   Beethoven: Piano Concerto No. 5 (*Emperor*), Op. 73

Ex. 27   Brahms: Concerto for Violin and Orchestra, Op. 77

* For seven other techniques, see Chapter IX.

Ex. 28   Arlen: Blues in the Night

Copyright 1941 by Harms, Inc: Used by permission.

Sequence

A less literal form of repetition occurs when a motive is repeated on a higher or lower level. Called *sequence*, this technique is found in all periods and styles of music.

A rising sequence can add intensity to a motive—as in Exs. 29 and 30.*

Ex. 29   Beethoven: Sonata, Op. 13 (*Pathétique*)

Ex. 30   Rimsky-Korsakov: *Scheherazade*, Op. 35

The falling sequence, an equally familiar technique, appears in a Mozart symphony.

Ex. 31   Mozart: Symphony No. 41 (*Jupiter*), K. 551, fourth movement

*See also Exs. 42, 43, and 45 on pages 216-217.

In Rodgers' song "Lover," the two-bar motive recurs in chromatic sequence, a half step lower each time.

Ex. 32   Rodgers: Lover

By Lorenz Hart and Richard Rodgers. Copyright © 1932 and 1933 by Famous Music Corporation. Copyright renewed 1959 and 1960 by Famous Music Corporation.

Melodic sequences are often paralleled by harmonic ones, which intensify their impact. Melodic-harmonic sequences* are a valued means of musical development.

Ex. 33   Handel: Sarabande, from Suite No. 11

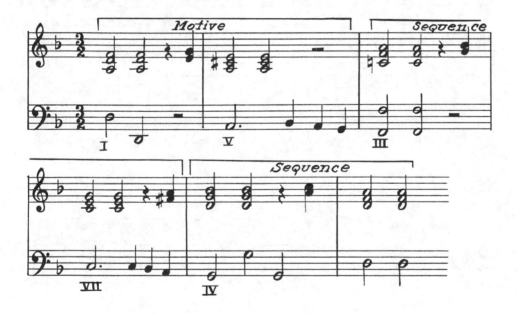

The technique of sequence may be used literally or in varied form.

Ex. 34   Mozart: Minuet in F

* For a discussion of harmonic sequence, see Chapter V, Volume II.

The motive (*a*) is repeated sequentially at (*b*), with one interval—the falling sixth—changed to a fifth; at (*c*) the varied sequence is repeated on a lower level and extended to two bars. By varying the sequences, Mozart holds the listener's interest while maintaining the unity of the phrase.

Interval Change

Interval change constitutes another type of motive variation. When a primitive or folk musician sings a motive two or three times, he often has an unconscious impulse to change one or another of its notes. This spontaneous quest for variety appears in countless folk songs. In Ex. 35, the interval variation is a slight one: the third note, G, changes to A upon repetition.

Ex. 35   English folk song, Appalachian Mountain version: Edward.

The interval change may be slight in composed music as well; thus, although the interval change in Satie's *Gnossienne* No. 1 is small, it is musically significant.

Ex. 36   Satie: *Gnossienne* No. 1

Sometimes a composer will expand an interval one or more steps each time it appears, producing the effect of a rising line.*

Ex. 37   Mozart: *O Isis and Osiris*, from *The Magic Flute*, K. 620

*See also Ex. 31, page 153.

Ex. 38   Scarlatti: Sonata in C

The opposite technique—contracting an interval one step in each repetition—is less common.

Ex. 39   Schubert: Waltz, Op. 18a, No. 5

Ex. 40   Haydn: Allegro in F

A final form of interval variation involves a complete alteration of *all* pitch relationships of the original motive. In such cases the rhythmic pattern gives identity to the motive and holds the phrase together.

Ex. 41   McHugh: I'm in the Mood for Love

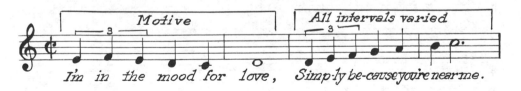

"I'm in the Mood for Love" by Jimmy McHugh and Dorothy Fields. Copyright 1935/Copyright renewal 1963 Robbins Music Corporation. Used by permission.

Fragmentation

If motive repetitions of the same length occur too frequently, rhythmic monotony may set in. Several nineteenth-century composers erred by writing a series of sequences in square patterns that seem mechanical to twentieth-century ears.

Ex. 42   Rimsky-Korsakov: *Scheherazade*, third movement

At an early period, composers learned to avoid monotony in a repetition by altering the length of a motive. One technique, *fragmentation*, involves breaking the motive apart and repeating one of the fragments. Recurring more quickly than in the original motive, the repeated fragment produces a rhythmic intensification.

Ex. 43   Beethoven: Piano Sonata, Op. 2, No. 1

At (*a*) the two-bar motive is presented.
   (*b*) it is repeated in sequence.
   (*c*) the second half alone appears as a fragment.
   (*d*) it is restated a tone higher.
   (*e*) the phrase reaches a climax, with the motive fragment extended to two bars.

Other instances of fragmentation appear in "Joshua Fit de Battle of Jericho" and in *Wozzeck*.

Ex. 44   Negro spiritual: Joshua Fit de Battle of Jericho

Ex. 45   Berg: *Wozzeck*, Act I

Copyright 1926, Universal Editions, A. G., Vienna. Used by permission.

Extension

In Ex. 37, a one-bar pattern, after being repeated, has been lengthened to two bars. This lengthening process, when it occurs at the end of a phrase, is called *extension.** Acting in the opposite manner from fragmentation, it is yet another means of producing rhythmic variety.

Extension may be accomplished in two ways: (1) by addition of new material to the motive (Ex. 46); and (2) by reiteration of a fragment. Extension through the persistent repetition or sequence of a fragment often builds intensity in a rising wave.

Ex. 46   Brahms: Rhapsody, Op. 79, No. 1

* When such lengthening occurs during the course of a phrase it is called *expansion*. See page 243.

Ex. 47   Mozart: Rondo *alla turca*, from Piano Sonata, K. 331

In the *Leonore* Overture No. 3, Beethoven spins a great crescendo out of a motive repeated over and over in a long rising wave. As the wave mounts, the four-bar motive is shortened to a two-bar fragment (*a*), then to a one-bar fragment (*b*).

Ex. 48   Beethoven: *Leonore* Overture No. 3, Op. 72a

Inversion

Inversion, or turning the motive upside down, is a basic melodic device.* When a motive moves up in steps, the inversion will move down in steps by the same interval; when the motive leaps up, the inversion will counter with a downward leap of the same size.

Compare the opening motive of a Gregorian *Sanctus* with the inverted statement.

Ex. 49   Plain chant: *Sanctus* (from the Mass *cum jubilo*)

One of the most useful tools of the composer, inversion enables him to repeat the motive in a form manifestly new, yet recognizably linked to the original. From medieval to modern times, composers have made frequent use of this device.†

Ex. 50   Bartók: Concerto for Orchestra

© 1946 by Hawkes & Son (London) Ltd. Reprinted by permission of Boosey & Hawkes Inc.

Ex. 51   Riegger: Variations for Piano and Orchestra, Op. 54 ‡

© 1955 by Associated Music Publishers, Inc., New York. Used by permission.

* Melodic inversion must not be confused with interval inversion, described on page 48.
† See also Ex. 57, page 76.
‡ Example 51 illustrates the use of inversion in twelve-tone music—one common twentieth-century style.

In Wallingford Riegger's Variations for Piano and Orchestra, the four bars at (*a*) are a literal inversion of the notes in the preceding three bars (with rhythmic variation).

Inversions may be exact or approximate. Approximate inversions are found in some of the most familiar works of the repertory.

Ex. 52   Brahms: Violin Concerto, Op. 77

Ex. 53   Haydn: Symphony No. 94 (*Surprise*), second movement

Rhythm Change

Although *rhythm change* would seem to be a basic technique of motive variation, it does not occur nearly so often as one might imagine. The simplest method of rhythmic variation is to keep the length of the motive constant, while changing the time value of certain notes or adding repetitions of the same notes in shorter time values. In Moussorgsky's *Baba Yaga*, the quarter notes of bar 1 are changed to eighths and a quarter in bars 3 and 5; and to eighths in bar 7.

Ex. 54   Moussorgsky: *Baba Yaga*, from *Pictures at an Exhibition*

In the Russian Dance from Stravinsky's *Petrushka*, the first and third bars contain the same notes with different time values.

Ex. 55   Stravinsky: Russian Dance, from *Petrushka*

Another type of rhythmic change is called *rhythmic shift:* the beginning of the motive shifts to a different beat in successive measures, due to the changed value of one or another note.

Ex. 56   Brahms: Intermezzo, Op. 119, No. 3

Ex. 57   Ives: The Se'er

In the Ives song, the motive starts on an afterbeat at (*a*), is followed by a bar of changed meter (5/8), and reappears on the downbeat at (*b*). Beginning at (*c*), the bar line itself seems to have shifted, for the strong beats now fall on the second half of the measure. The song, written in 1920, is a striking anticipation of the jazzy rhythmic shifts favored by a later generation of American composers.*

* The entire song is worth examining; notice the piano accompaniment, full of intricate polyrhythms—remarkable for its, or any, period.

Ornamentation

Ornamentation involves decorating certain tones of the motive with grace notes, neighboring tones, appoggiaturas, and the like. It also includes filling in leaps with passing tones and replacing long notes by faster-moving rhythmic values. The basic structure of the melody, however, remains the same.

Ex. 58   Beethoven: Piano Sonata, Op. 53 (*Waldstein*), last movement

Romantic composers were fond of ornamentation; we find some of the most florid embellishments in the nocturnes of Chopin.

Ex. 59   Chopin: Nocturne, Op. 9, No. 1

Summary

The composer may develop a motive into a phrase by the following techniques:

1. Repetition: literal restatement of the motive.

2. Sequence: repetition of the motive on a higher or lower pitch level. It may be:
   a. Literal.
   b. Varied.

3. Interval change: repetition with one or more intervals expanded or contracted.

4. Fragmentation: repetition of only a part of the motive.

5. Extension: repetition of the entire motive plus an added segment consisting of:
   a. New material.
   b. Repetition or sequence of a fragment.

6. Inversion: repetition of the motive turned upside down. The inversion may be:
   a. Literal.
   b. Approximate.

7. Rhythm change: repetition with altered rhythmic values.

8. Ornamentation: repetition in embellished form.

Root
Movements

Strong, Medium, and Weak Progressions

Just as the foundation of a building is usually not visible to the eye, so movements from chord root to chord root—the foundations of harmonic structure—are not heard by the average listener. Yet these movements beneath the surface of music create much of the forward drive of a composition. Strong, medium, or weak root progressions produce dynamic, moderate, or weak movement. Such gradations do not necessarily imply value judgments; powerful harmonic motion may occur in music of no great value, and little motion in a very beautiful composition.

Before the sixteenth century, strong root progressions were rarely used; medieval and Renaissance composers relied more on flowing lines. Centuries later, in the time of Debussy and Ravel, vague, floating harmony was once more important in the musical language.

In traditional music, however, strong harmonic progression was the rule. As Stravinsky has suggested in his foreword to the excellent book of Edward Lowinsky,* the post-Renaissance period gave rise to the modern spirit of dynamic activity, which found its counterpart in forceful root movements.

The dynamic harmonic techniques of the post-Renaissance period are central to our study. In addition to their role in Western culture of the time,

* Edward Lowinsky: *Tonality and Atonality in Sixteenth-Century Music* (Berkeley, California, 1962).

225

they still serve in large musical areas today; nor has the last word been said on their future. Let us examine them closely.

There are six diatonic root movements possible from any one bass tone, listed here in general order of dynamic quality.*

1. The falling fifth   (↓5)
   (or rising fourth)†

2. The falling fourth   (↓4)
   (or rising fifth)

3. The falling third   (↓3)
   (or rising sixth)

4. The rising second   (↑2)

5. The falling second   (↓2)

6. The rising third   (↑3)
   (or falling sixth)

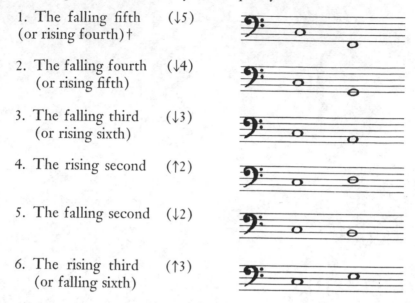

The Falling Fifth

Fundamental in traditional melody formation, the fifth also creates the strongest harmonic movement. The falling fifth V—I forms the most dynamic of all root progressions—the basis of the perfect cadence. Other falling-fifth progressions—VI—II or II—V, for example—are almost equally vigorous.

In Schumann's *Kreisleriana*, there is a passage marked *sehr aufgeregt* (very agitated), typically Schumannesque in its robust quality. A series of

* The seventh possible movement—up or down an octave—is not included in the list, for it contains no harmonic change; from the *harmonic* standpoint, it is equivalent to a repeated chord.

† Harmonically speaking, it is immaterial whether the bass moves up a fourth or down a fifth, because both movements lead to the same degree. For simplicity's sake, we shall refer to both as "falling fifths."

falling-fifth root movements adds momentum to the phrase (the circled arrow and *5* indicates a falling-fifth root movement).

Ex. 1   Schumann: *Kreisleriana*, Op. 16

The falling-fifth movement may be used effectively in a harmonic sequence called the *cycle of fifths*. It forms the strongest progression of diatonic harmony: I—IV—VII—III—VI—II—V—I.

Ex. 2   Cycle of fifths

The cycle need not be used in its entirety; even two or three falling fifths form an effective pattern. It may be written in two, four, or any number of voices; the bass may be embellished by passing or changing tones; and it may appear in a variety of rhythmic formations. Composers as diverse as Bach, Beethoven, and Wagner have employed the cycle of fifths in a wide variety of musical styles.

Ex. 3   Bach: Two-Part Invention No. 4

Dm: *falling melodic minor*

Ex. 4   Beethoven: Sonata, Op. 13 (*Pathétique*), third movement

Ex. 5   Wagner: *Die Meistersinger von Nürnberg*, Act II

Note that although the leap of a tritone was generally avoided in traditional music, the momentum engendered by the strong harmonic motion of the cycle of fifths was considered powerful enough to justify its use between IV and VII in the bass.

Ex. 6   Commonly used tritone in cycle of fifths

The Falling Fourth

Root movements down a fourth form another strong progression, second in vigor only to the fifth itself. An excellent illustration is found in the Bach chorale *Ach Gott und Herr*.

Ex. 7   Bach: *Ach Gott und Herr*

In Brahms' Third Symphony we find a tender melody supported by strong root movements of falling fourths and fifths.

Ex. 8   Brahms: Symphony No. 3, Op. 90, third movement

A series of consecutive falling-fourth root movements occurs much more rarely than the cycle of fifths; yet, when skillfully used, it forms a vigorous sequence. Haydn introduced this progression in a dramatic passage of his *Surprise* Symphony. †

Ex. 9   Haydn: Symphony No. 94 (*Surprise*), second movement

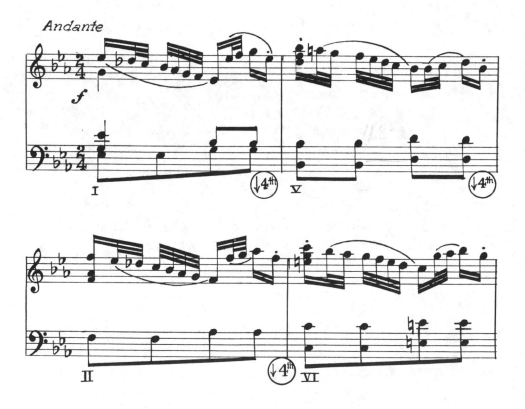

* Remember that the root movement (falling fourth) is reckoned from the *root* of I to the root of V.

† The root movements are reckoned by the first chords in each measure. (For another example of a sequence of falling fourths, see Ex. 13 in Chapter V, Volume II.)

In a familiar progression, falling fifths alternate with falling fourths in the bass. Nothing could be simpler; yet it becomes beautiful when handled with imagination.

Ex. 10   Chopin: Prelude, Op. 28, No. 7.

The Falling Third

The falling third ranks after the falling fifth and fourth among strong root movements.* I—VI—IV—II, illustrated in the male chorus from Wagner's *Tannhäuser* (Ex. 11), provides an effective progression. (Note that in reading music for chorus, the tenor parts should be played one octave lower than written.)

Ex. 11   Wagner: *Zu dir wall' ich*, from *Tannhäuser*

The quality of root movements can be demonstrated by playing Ex. 11, and then playing it backward.

Ex. 12   *Zu dir wall' ich*, in reverse

The reverse version of Wagner's phrase contains three root movements of a rising third. As we shall see, † rising-third root movements are indecisive; a

---

* An exception is the double movement V—III—I, which almost always has a weak effect. This may be due to the fact that it splits in half the strong V—I progression. Perhaps the listening mind unconsciously resents the breaking up of such an all-important progression.

† See page 235.

series of them gives the feeling that the harmony is moving in reverse (which it is, in this case).

The Rising Second

Rising seconds are counted among the strong progressions when chord roots move from IV to V, V to VI, and VII to I. In Ex. 13, the two consecutive rising seconds IV—V—VI impart forward motion to the music.

Ex. 13 Bach: *An Wasserflüssen Babylon*

When chord roots move up a second to most chords other than those named, the effect is one of moderation—neither strong nor weak. The frottola* by the Italian Renaissance composer Andrea Antico contains three consecutive seconds, I—II—III—IV (*a*). The effect is gentle and lovely.

Ex. 14 Antico: *S il focho in chui* (frottola)

*The frottola was a form of popularly inspired choral composition, which appeared in Italy around 1480. It was notable as one of the first musical forms employing block-chord harmony and a type of major-minor tonality very advanced for the period. (Note that the second full measure of Ex. 14 contains parallel fifths between alto and bass— unusual at the time.)

To observe the different effects of rising seconds when leading to II, III, and IV on the one hand, and to V and VI on the other, first play measure (*a*) of the frottola, then measure (*a*) of Ex. 13. The contrasting quality of the two progressions is unmistakable.

The Falling Second

The effect of the falling-second root movement is almost always of moderate motion.* Note, in Ex. 14, the mildness of the progressions I—VII and II—I (bars 1–3). Consider also the gentle effect of two falling seconds, I—VII—VI, in Ex. 15.

Ex. 15   Brahms: *A German Requiem*, Op. 45, third movement

* The falling second from III—II is apt to be weak unless introduced deftly.

The progression VI—V provides an exception, for it is normally a strong one. Notice (Ex. 16, *a*) how it equals the effect of the other vigorous root movements.

Ex. 16   Moussorgsky: Coronation Scene, from *Boris Godunov*

The Rising Third

The last root movement to be considered is the rising third. Its effect is gentle, undynamic, at times weak.* Avoided as a general rule in the traditional style because of its indecisiveness, the rising third is reserved for the special situations where a mild, gliding effect is desired. When Wagner, in his opera *Lohengrin*, wished to depict a swan floating on water, he used the rising-third root movement.

Ex. 17   Wagner: Swan motive, from *Lohengrin*

The gentleness of the rising-third progression also imparts its quality to the Renaissance frottola (Ex. 14, bar 2).

A quite different use of this progression is in the strong combination I—III—IV, often employed as harmony for the soprano line 8—7—6.†

* See Ex. 12 for the weak effect of a series of rising thirds.

† See also Ex. 14, page 203.

When it appears on a weak beat between I and IV, the III serves as a passing chord—part of the falling fifth movement I—IV.

Ex. 18   Bach: *Herr Gott, dich loben alle wir*

Bass Melodic Curve

Although root movements are the basic force in harmonic progression, another important element is the melodic curve of the bass. Where strong root movements already exist, a melodic bass adds to their power and effectiveness; where root movements are moderate or even weak, a well-shaped bass line can impart motion and musical meaning.* In any case, a bass line with strong directional movement furthers the momentum of a phrase. Note in Ex. 19 how the lovely, long line of the bass leads the music forward.†

Ex. 19   Beethoven: Sonata, Op. 109, third movement

---

* In Ex. 22, page 296, the root movements are far from strong; the melodic curve of the bass, however, carries the piece along.

† See also Ex. 5, page 11, and Ex. 36, page 303.

Broad Harmonic Motion

Until now we have taken a narrow view of harmonic motion, dwelling mainly on single chords or the relation between two or three chords at most. But just as the character of a melody is revealed not by two or three notes but by its entire melodic curve, so the true nature of harmonic progression stands out when we go beyond individual chords to a view of the *broad harmonic direction* of a phrase or composition.

Such a view of harmonic motion goes beyond the marking of chord symbols. Thus, Ex. 19 may be analyzed, chord by chord, as I—IV—V, etc. In a wider perspective, however (Ex. 20), its harmony consists of movement from the tonic (*a*) through various intermediate chords to a first goal, the dominant (*b*). Returning to a less emphatic form of the tonic (*c*), it moves to a second goal—a more strongly emphasized dominant (*d*). The higher intensity of this second dominant is brought about by the dark low register, plus the more vivid harmonic action of the chromatic chords immediately preceding (*d*).

Ex. 20   Broad harmonic motion of Ex. 19

Of the two broad harmonic movements in the Beethoven theme (*a—b* and *c—d*), the second is the stronger, rising to a point of even greater tension. These movements may be compared to the melodic movements of two rising waves, the second mounting higher than the first. (For such a double rising wave, see the Handel Sarabande, Ex. 53, Chapter XIV.)

Ex. 21   Melodic and harmonic movements compared

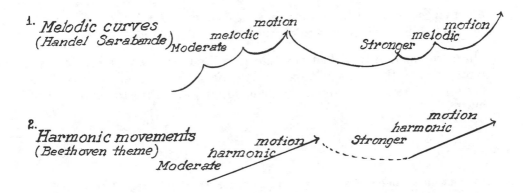

Example 21 shows patterns of mounting intensity, created in one case by melodic and in the other by harmonic motion. Obviously, melody and harmony each possess unique musical characteristics that cannot be equated. But from a comparison of the two types of movements, we learn to view chord progressions in long, sweeping lines (analogous to, but not identical with, melodic curves). Gradually, we will supplement chord-by-chord thinking with an understanding of *broad harmonic motion*. By correlating melodic and harmonic patterns, we can appreciate their interweaving and, eventually, their merging in the act of composition.*

Summary

1. The quality of a harmonic progression is determined largely by its root movements. Root movements may be classified:
   a. Strong:
      Falling fifth.
      Falling fourth.
      Falling third.
      Falling second to V.
      Rising second to V, VI, I.
   b. Medium:
      Rising second to II, III, IV.
      Falling second to IV, III, I.
   c. Gentle, gliding:
      Rising third (except I—III—IV).
      Falling second, III—II.
      Rising second, II—III.
   d. Weak:
      Rising—two or more consecutive thirds.
      Falling—two consecutive thirds, V—III—I.

2. Another factor in harmonic motion is the melodic curve of the bass. A well-shaped bass line contributes to the momentum of a phrase.

3. Harmonic motion is viewed most clearly in the broad sweep of a phrase, rather than in the connection of single chords. Like melodic curves, long harmonic lines serve to build the momentum and clarify the structure of music.

*For the interaction of melodic and harmonic motion, see page 367, especially number 5. For further discussion of patterns of harmonic intensity and movement, see "The Rhythm of Harmonic Intensities" in Volume II, Chapter IX.

More
Techniques of
Motive Variation

Eight of the most commonly used motive-variation techniques were examined in the preceding chapter; seven others remain to be studied. But first a cautionary word: although methods of variation must be studied one by one, they do not necessarily appear that way in actual music. As often as not, composers use two or more variation techniques at the same time—as in Ex. 22, (c), (e), and (g). Such simultaneous use of more than one technique is called *multiple variation.*

Ex. 22   Mozart: Rondo *alla turca,* from Sonata, K. 331

In the eight-bar phrase shown, no fewer than six motive-variation techniques are employed, singly and in combination. We find:

At (*a*) The motive (1 bar long, starting on the upbeat).
    (*b*) A sequence, a third higher.
    (*c*) A sequence of the first four notes used as a fragment, and extended to two bars (to *d*).
    (*e*) The fragment in slower time values, with a slight interval change (a half step changed to a whole step).
    (*f*) Repetition of (*e*).
    (*g*) The entire motive in slower values, with interval change.

Such a detailed analysis, it must be admitted, lends a rather formidable aspect to a light-hearted phrase. But subtle melodic techniques are revealed only through close scrutiny.

Returning now to the individual motive-variation techniques, we find seven further types:

Augmentation	Contraction
Diminution	Thinning
Interversion	Retrograde Motion
Expansion	

Augmentation

Augmentation means slowing down the time values of a motive. A very old technique, it can be illustrated by a work from the twelfth century. At that time an unknown Spanish composer based his composition on a well-known plain chant.

Ex. 23   Plain chant: *Cunctipotens genitor*

Lengthening the value of each note, he added a new phrase above it, forming a lovely two-part *organum.*

Ex. 24   Organum: *Cunctipotens genitor*

More recently, augmentation has usually implied rhythms twice as slow as in the original motive. It effects a broadening or spinning out of the rhythm.

Ex. 25   Brahms: Violin Sonata, Op. 78

Sometimes only a fragment of the motive is repeated in augmentation.

Ex. 26   Dvorak: Symphony No. 5 (*From the New World*), Op. 95, second movement

Diminution

By *diminution* we mean doubling the speed of a musical idea. Example 27 opens with a three-note motive, which then appears in diminution, twice as fast.

Ex. 27   Bach: Fugue No. 14, *The Well-Tempered Clavier*, Book I

As with augmentation, diminution may be applied to a fragment of a motive. It often produces a heightened energy.

Ex. 28   Brahms: Violin Concerto, Op. 77

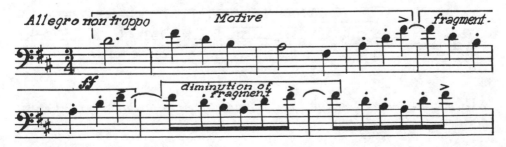

The same technique occurs in popular music.

Ex. 29   Carmichael: Stardust

*"Stardust" by Hoagy Carmichael and Mitchell Parish, copyright 1929 by Mills Music, Inc.
Copyright renewed 1957. Used by special permission of the copyright owner.*

Interversion

Interversion, a technique used for many centuries, was given its name
only recently, by the late Rudolf Reti.* It may be described as the repetition of
fragments of a motive, in different order (Ex. 30). Observe that fragments (*a*)
and (*b*) reappear in reversed order, and that (*b*) is varied.†

Ex. 30   Schubert: Symphony No. 8 (*Unfinished*)

Schubert had a fondness for this method of melody construction, employing it frequently.

Ex. 31   Schubert: *Rosamunde* Overture

Ostensibly a rather sophisticated device, interversion is found nonetheless in folk music.

Ex. 32   Traditional folk tune: The Arkansas Traveler

* Hungarian theorist, author of *The Thematic Process in Music* (New York, 1951).
† See also Ex. 43, page 160.

Expansion

Expansion lengthens a motive by adding new material in the middle; thus it differs from extension, which lengthens the motive at the end.

In the slow movement of his Fifth Symphony, Tchaikovsky started with a lovely one-bar motive, repeating it in varied form. The third statement (*a*) expands the one bar to two by the insertion of five repeated G's between the beginning and end.*

Ex. 33   Tchaikovsky: Symphony No. 5, Op. 64, second movement

Contraction

Contraction shortens the motive by deleting a fragment from the middle. The Brahms theme cited as an example of diminution also provides an excellent illustration of contraction. In the repetition of the motive at (*c*), bars (*a*) and (*b*) are omitted; the motive contracts from four to two bars.

Ex. 34   Brahms: Violin Concerto, Op. 77

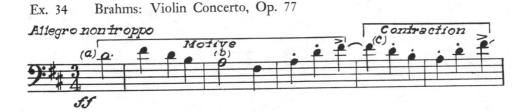

Thinning

Thinning—the opposite of ornamentation—involves deletion of certain notes of a motive, the over-all length remaining unchanged. It serves to simplify or strip a motive down to its essentials. Comparing bars 1 and 3 of Ex. 35, we find that two notes of the original have been eliminated; in bar 4, only one note of bar 2 remains.

Ex. 35   Purcell: Minuet

*See also Ex. 37, page 156.

Retrograde Motion

Used mainly in contrapuntal music of the fourteenth and fifteenth centuries, and now once again in twelve-tone music, retrograde motion is produced by writing a motive in reverse. In one of his lighter moments, Haydn wrote an entire minuet that could be played forwards and backwards with equal effect. It first appears as shown in Ex. 36.

Ex. 36   Haydn: Menuetto, *al rovescio*, from Sonata No. 4 for Piano and Violin (piano part only)

Later it is repeated, but is now played from the end back to the beginning.

Ex. 37   Haydn: Menuetto

Summary

Although studied separately, the various techniques of motive variation are often used in combination (multiple variation).

Seven additional techniques of motive variation involve repetition:

1. Augmentation lengthens the time values of a motive.

2. Diminution shortens the time values.

3. Interversion changes the order of notes or groups of notes.

4. Expansion lengthens by the addition of new material in the middle of a motive.

5. Contraction shortens by deletion of a fragment from the middle of a motive.

6. Thinning involves deleting certain notes, while the over-all length of a motive remains unchanged.

7. Retrograde motion is writing the motive backwards.

X

The
First
Inversion

We have considered the triad so far only in root position, with the root of the chord in the bass. Triads also appear in *inversion*—that is, with another tone in the bass. To change a triad to its *first inversion*, the root is *inverted*, or set an octave above its original position. The third of the triad now forms the bass of the chord.

The intervals of the first-inversion chord, counting up from the bass, are a sixth and a third. Hence the name $\frac{6}{3}$ (six-three), commonly shortened to 6, or sixth, chord.

Sixth chords have long been part of the musical language. As early as 1300, medieval composers, notably the English, wrote many passages using parallel first inversions.

Ex. 1   *Beata viscera* (English, fourteenth century)

Five hundred years later, Beethoven still took pleasure in the sound of parallel sixth chords.

Ex. 2   Beethoven: Sonata, Op. 2, No. 3, third movement

Like root-position triads, first inversions may be erected on all degrees of the scale.

Ex. 3   Sixth chords on all degrees

Functions of the Sixth Chord

Sixth chords can be substituted for root-position triads or used alternately with them for the following purposes:

1. To create greater harmonic variety.
2. To make possible a smoother bass line.
3. To produce gentler progressions.
4. To create a special harmonic color.

A good use of sixth chords will usually illustrate several of these points.

The first inversion can often be used in place of a triad having the same root. The melody in Ex. 4 could, theoretically, be harmonized by three I and V triads at (*a*) and (*b*), respectively (Ex. 5).

Ex. 4   Corelli: Concerto Grosso, Op. 6, No. 8, melody

Ex. 5   Corelli: Concerto Grosso, theoretical harmonization

Corelli, however, introduced sixth chords alternating with root position triads.

Ex. 6   Corelli: Concerto Grosso (original)

What has been gained by the inversions? The harmony is more varied, the bass line more melodic, and the accompaniment more in keeping with the light, dance-like character of Corelli's melody.

Brahms uses two sixth chords in harmonizing one of his most distinguished melodies.

Ex. 7   Brahms: Symphony No. 1, Op. 68, second movement

Note particularly the V⁶, which stands in place of the root-position triad. Its harmonic motion is gentler, and the bass gains in melodic subtlety.

In the Adagio of the Mozart Sonata K. 332, sixth chords make possible a gently falling harmonic pattern. By the same token, the bass line takes on a smooth melodic flow.

Ex. 8   Mozart: Sonata, K. 332, second movement

Various functions of the sixth chord are illustrated in two versions of the cycle of fifths.

Ex. 9   Cycle of fifths, with root-position triads and with sixth chords

Parallel Sixth Chords

A series of consecutive sixth chords produces a unique harmonic color. The following example shows parallel sixths in three voices moving over a *pedal point*, or sustained bass.

Ex. 10   Puccini: *La Bohème*, Act III

By courtesy of the publisher, G. Ricordi & C., Milan.

Sixth chords in parallel motion often create the effect of a harmonic wave. Instead of separate harmonies, the ear hears a continuous sonority, in which the first, last, and perhaps one or two intermediate chords stand out. The others form a gentle passing motion, enriching the melodic line.* The Chopin Prelude in C sharp minor, for example, can be analyzed as shown in Ex. 11.

Ex. 11   Chopin: Prelude, Op. 45

* Exs. 1, 2, and 10 can be considered in the same light.

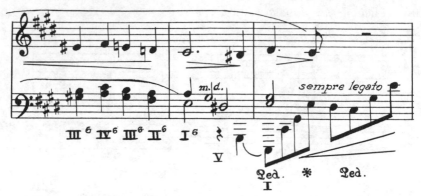

When viewed as a broad harmonic motion (Ex. 12), only essential harmonic changes stand out, passing chords being represented by sonorous lines.

Ex. 12   Chopin: Prelude, broad harmonic motion

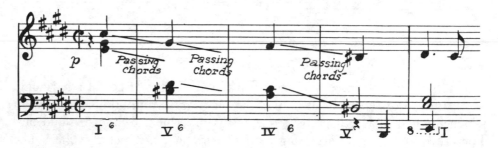

Progression of parallel sixth chords in four parts often produces voice-leading problems: parallel fifths and octaves may result. To avoid these pitfalls, one voice must not move parallel to the other three.

Mozart employed parallel sixth chords in *The Magic Flute*, three voices moving in parallel fashion (from *a* to *b* in Ex. 13).

Ex. 13   Mozart: March of the Priests, from *The Magic Flute* (one part omitted)

The fourth voice moves in contrary motion (*a*) and similar motion (*b*) to the other three (Ex. 14).

Ex. 14   Mozart: March of the Priests (original)

Special Uses of the Sixth Chord

Having examined the general functions of the sixth chord, let us turn to some of its more specific uses:

1. The role of VII⁶ as a passing chord.
2. The role of V⁶ and I⁶ as neighboring chords.
3. The role of stepwise sixth-chord progressions leading to the cadence.

Although VII—a diminished triad—appears in root position only in special circumstances,* its first inversion, VII⁶, is widely used. Serving chiefly as a *passing chord* between I and I⁶, it often contains a doubled third. To ensure the smoothest connection, all voices generally move stepwise except one of the thirds, which may leap to the fifth of the next chord.

Ex. 15   VII⁶ with resolutions

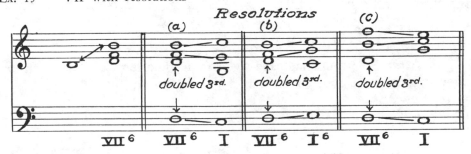

Ex. 16   Schumann: A Chorale, from *Album for the Young*, Op. 68

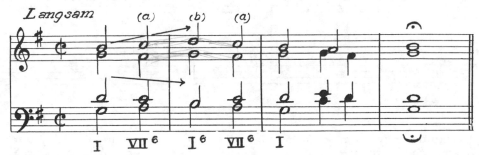

* See page 313.

In the VII⁶, the diminished fifth can be doubled when approached and left by stepwise, contrary motion, as at (a) in Ex. 16. It can also be preceded or followed by a parallel perfect fifth, as at (b).*

Ex. 17   Beethoven: Sonata, Op. 49, No. 1

A *neighboring chord* is formed when three voices of a triad move stepwise to neighboring tones, forming a second chord (a), and then back to their original positions. The fourth voice remains stationary.

Ex. 18   Neighboring sixth chords

A first-inversion triad can serve as a neighboring chord between two appearances of the root-position triad (Exs. 19, 20).

Ex. 19   Couperin: *Les coucous*

---

* When one of two fifths is diminished, the harshness of the parallelism is avoided; the progression has been freely accepted by composers writing in the traditional style. See (a) in Ex. 3, page 313.

Ex. 20   Pachelbel: Gavotte and Variations

Sixth chords form a strong rising bass line leading to the cadence. Note the substitution of II^6 for IV in Ex. 21 (*a*). This chord is widely used in the cadence formula II^6—V—I.

Ex. 21   Purcell: Shake the Cloud, from *Dido and Aeneas*

The falling stepwise progression VI^6—V^6—IV^6 provides an effective approach to the half cadence.

Ex. 22   Bach: Toccata and Fugue in D minor, for organ

Doubled Thirds in the Sixth Chord

In writing sixth chords for four voices, it is usually better to double the root or the fifth rather than the third.

Ex. 23   Sixth chords in various doublings

The doubled third is effective, however, in four different situations:

1. As part of a stepwise, contrary motion (Ex. 24, *a*).
2. As part of a minor triad (Ex. 25).
3. As part of the first inversion of a diminished triad (Ex. 15).
4. As a result of good voice-leading (Ex. 26, third chord).

Ex. 24   Doubled third in stepwise contrary motion

Ex. 25   Doubled third in minor triads

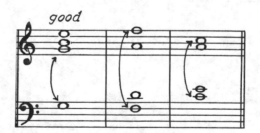

Root Movements in Sixth-Chord Progressions

In phrases containing sixth chords, the differences among strong, medium, and gentle root progressions are still evident, but with some modification. Root movements of the falling fifth, falling fourth, and falling third remain strong, and the rising third weak. But root movements up and down a second take on a more fluid character. A careful re-examination of Exs. 11 and 14 will show that the stepwise motion of first inversions softens chord-to-chord relationship, making possible the progression I⁶—II⁶—III⁶—IV⁶—VI⁶—V⁶, not practical with root-position triads.

In dealing with first inversions, *root and bass are no longer identical.* Root movements can no longer be reckoned by the bass but only by the actual roots of the chords in question.

Observe that first-inversion and root-position chords are often intermingled, varying the degree of harmonic energy in a phrase.

Ex. 26 Bach: *Aus meines Herzens Grunde*

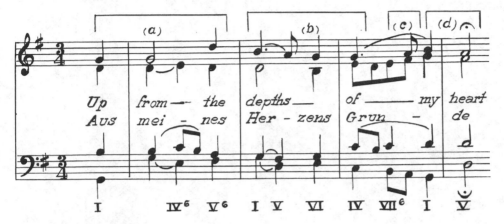

The first four chords (*a*) move gently to and from the first inversions; the four chords in (*b*) proceed in sturdier fashion from root to root; (*c*) once again introduces the milder sixth formation; and the phrase ends (*d*) with the strong root motion of the falling fourth.

Summary

1. An inversion is formed by building a triad on a tone other than the root.

2. The first inversion, with the third of the chord in the bass, is called the 6 or sixth chord.

3. The general functions of the sixth chord are:
   a. To create greater harmonic variety.
   b. To make possible a smoother bass line.
   c. To produce gentler progressions.
   d. To create a special harmonic color.

4. Parallel sixth chords often form a harmonic wave, producing a distinctive sonority.

5. Special uses of the sixth chord are:
   a. To serve as a passing chord (the VII⁶).
   b. To serve as a neighboring chord (mainly V⁶ and I⁶).
   c. To form smooth stepwise cadence progressions.

6. The best tones to double in the sixth chord are the root and the fifth, but the third may be doubled in certain circumstances.

7. With sixth chords, the quality of chord-to-chord movement is similar to that of root-position triads, except that first inversions make possible excellent stepwise bass movement between all degrees.

8. Root-position and first-inversion triads are often intermingled.

The Inner
Structure of
the Phrase

A phrase can be described as a musical thought ending in a cadence, or —in another way—as musical motion continuing until a resting point is reached. But such definitions are necessarily rather unsatisfactory. They become more meaningful only when the question is asked, "What goes to make up a phrase; what is its inner structure?"

The inner structure of a phrase can be formed in four different ways:

1. By a motive and its variations.
2. By a motive, its variations, and free material.
3. By two motives and their variations.*
4. By a free-flowing line (with *no* motive repetitions).

Phrases Based on a Motive and Its Variations

One basic type of phrase structure, dating from the Middle Ages, consists entirely of a motive with varied repetitions (Exs. 27–30).

---

* Phrases comprising more than two motives, or two motives plus free material, are quite rare.

Ex. 27   Plain chant: *Kyrie de Angelis*

Ex. 28   Beethoven: Symphony No. 5, Op. 67

Ex. 29   Chopin: Prelude in C minor, Op. 28, No. 20

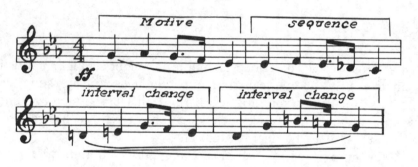

Ex. 30   Lane: Something Sort of Grandish, from *Finian's Rainbow*

In repeating a motive, composers employ different variation techniques. Note, in Exs. 27–30, repetition, sequence, inversion, interval change, contraction, and other techniques already studied. Well-defined melodic curves are important in phrases of this type.*

Phrases Based on a Motive, Its Variations, and Free Material

A second type of phrase structure consists of a motive, its variations, and free material. A composer who starts with a basic germ may repeat it in one or another form, introducing fresh material, usually near the end of a phrase.

Ex. 31   Mozart: Sonata, K. 283

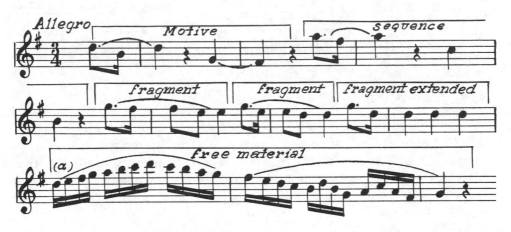

For seven bars in Ex. 31, Mozart unfolds the motive, varying it by sequence, fragmentation, and other means. At (a) he leads into a free arabesque, with a fine flourish that brings the phrase to its close.

Mozart employs the same type of phrase structure in the Minuet of his G minor Symphony.

Ex. 32   Mozart: Minuet, from Symphony No. 40, K. 550

*See also Ex. 2, page 459.

An unusual three-bar motive appears three times in succession in Ex. 32, the last time with an extension. The final four bars introduce a free touch of chromaticism as climax to the long fourteen-bar phrase.

In the Hallelujah Chorus from Handel's *Messiah*, bars 1–3 are based on the motive; bar 4 forms a free continuation.

Ex. 33   Handel: Hallelujah Chorus, from *The Messiah*

The Two-Motive Phrase

A third type of phrase structure comprises two motives. Whatever may be lost in the way of concentration is balanced by the richness and contrast of the added material. In order to establish the identity of each motive, a composer usually repeats the first before introducing the second, which is also repeated. Various ways of arranging a two-motive phrase are shown in Exs. 34–36.*

Ex. 34   Bach: *Brandenburg* Concerto No. 2, in F

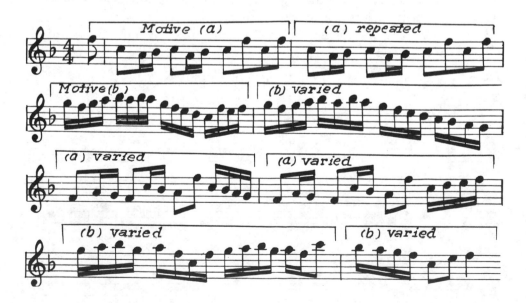

*See also Ex. 41, page 158, and Ex. 4, page 459.

Ex. 35   Bizet: Boys' chorus, from *Carmen*

Ex. 36   Dvorak: Symphony No. 5 (*From the New World*), Op. 95

Occasionally a composer employs two motives in a phrase without repeating one or the other. In such cases, the motives are sharply contrasted in character and often separated by a rest.

Ex. 37   Bach: Fugue No. 1, from *The Well-Tempered Clavier*, Book II

Free-Flowing and One-Motive Phrases

Motive repetition and variation provide a basic means of building a unified phrase, and they have figured in a great proportion of the world's melodies—indeed, of the world's music. But an equally large number of melodies have evolved from a quite different principle—that of the free-flowing, non-repetitive line. Such a line figures in two contexts:

1. *The free-flowing phrase.* Phrases of this type have already appeared in our discussion of non-repetitive rhythm.* Besides avoiding rhythmic duplications, a free-flowing melody unfolds without repeating any *intervallic* patterns. Countless Oriental and plain chant melodies, many compositions by Dunstable, Okeghem, Orlando di Lasso, and other medieval and Renaissance masters, and an equal number by such twentieth-century composers as Ives, Prokofiev, and Schönberg unfold in freely flowing lines. Unimpeded by re-

* See pages 161–162.

petitive patterns or symmetrical figures that might interrupt their development, such melodies often attain a marked freshness and distinction. Two melodies, written seven centuries apart, serve as illustration.*

Ex. 38   Plain chant: *Gloria (fons bonitatis)* (thirteenth century)

Ex. 39   Prokofiev: Symphony No. 5, Op. 100

2. *The one-motive phrase.* When a free-flowing phrase is repeated as a whole, or in part, later in the composition, the phrase itself becomes a motive: we may then speak of it as a *one-motive phrase.* Repetition of the motive forms a second phrase (Ex. 40).†

* For other examples, see Ex. 1, page 54; Exs. 45–46, page 161; Ex. 48, page 162; and Ex. 17, page 277.

† For other one-motive phrases, see Ex. 37, page 124, and Ex. 21, page 206.

Ex. 40   Haydn: Symphony No. 101 (*Clock*), last movement

Summary

The inner structure of a phrase may be formed by:

1. A motive and its variations.

2. A motive, its variations, and free material.

3. Two motives and their variations.

4. A free-flowing line.

5. One motive filling the entire phrase.

XI

The
Second
Inversion

The formation now known as the $^6_4$ chord originated from the horizontal movement of voices. Long before it was thought of as a *second inversion*, the $^6_4$ appeared in contra-puntal music. It served frequently in the works of sixteenth- and seventeenth-century composers as a *double embellishing tone* (a simultaneous embellishment of two voices), passing between one chord and another, or circling around a single chord.

Purcell's *King Arthur* contains a $^6_4$ formed by a *double neighboring tone* (Ex. 1, *a*).

Ex. 1   Purcell: Die and Reap the Fruits, from *King Arthur*

A chanson by Orlando di Lasso contains a $^6_4$ formed by a *double passing tone* (Ex. 2, *a*).

Ex. 2   Orlando di Lasso: *L'heureux amour qui s'élève*

When, in the eighteenth century, Rameau and other theorists gave names to chords, the double embellishing tone—known until that time simply as a contrapuntal device—came to be called the $^6_4$ chord, or *second inversion* triad. According to eighteenth-century theory, the second inversion is formed by inverting the two lowest tones of the root-position triad—in other words, by raising the root and third above the fifth.

Counting up from 5 (now the bass of the chord) the intervals in the second-inversion triad are a sixth and a fourth—hence the name $^6_4$ chord.

Considered thereafter as a chord structure, the $^6_4$ continued, nonetheless, to be used the same way as in the older contrapuntal style. Even in harmonic music, it has served largely as a voice-leading device, mainly in two forms: (1) the neighboring $^6_4$, and (2) the passing $^6_4$.

Neighboring $^6_4$

The *neighboring* $^6_4$ chord results from the simultaneous movement of two chord tones to their upper neighbors and back again, the two other voices remaining stationary (Ex. 3). Occurring on the weak beat (*a*), it forms a gentle harmonic embellishment. (The symbol for the $^6_4$ is placed in parentheses because it does not function as an independent chord.)

Ex. 3   The neighboring $^6_4$ chord

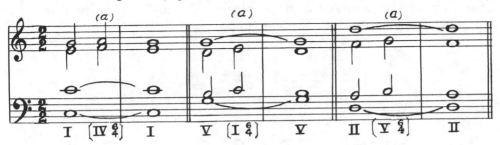

Brahms provides an example of the $^6_4$ embellishing the I, and Haydn, of the $^6_4$ embellishing the V.

Ex. 4   Brahms: Variations on a Theme of Haydn

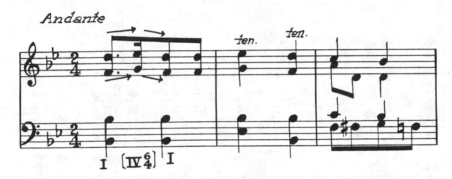

Ex. 5   Haydn: String Quartet, Op. 76, No. 3

Other familiar examples of the neighboring $^6_4$ are found in the first measures of "Silent Night" and in the Thanksgiving Hymn "We Gather Together."

Unaccented Passing $^6_4$

The most important function of the $^6_4$ is that of a double passing tone between two chords. The passing $^6_4$ occurs in two forms: unaccented and accented.

The *unaccented passing* $^6_4$, appearing on a weak beat, often results from a stepwise movement of the bass between a triad and its first inversion. The V$^6_4$, for example, acts as a link between I and I^6.

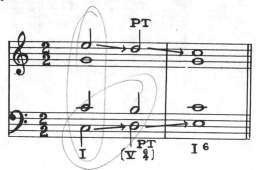

In such progressions, the bass moves up or down through three steps; another voice moves stepwise in contrary motion, while a third voice sustains the common tone.

Ex. 6   Beethoven: Sonata, Op. 10, No. 3

In another use of the unaccented passing $^6_4$ chord, the upper voices serve as passing tones (Ex. 7, *a*).

Ex. 7   Beethoven: String Quartet, Op. 59, No. 1, second movement

Other examples of the unaccented passing $^6_4$ chords are shown in Ex. 8; note the stepwise approach to and resolution of the passing tones. In (*b*), (*c*), and (*d*) the passing $^6_4$ leads from a sixth chord on one degree to a sixth chord on another.

Ex. 8   Further examples, unaccented passing $^6_4$

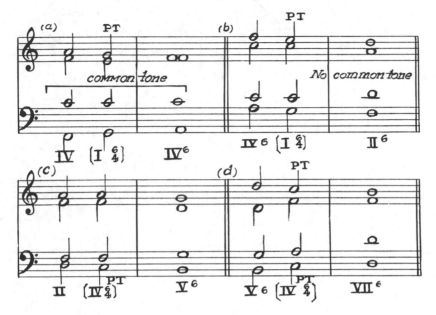

Accented Passing $^6_4$

The *accented passing* $^6_4$ chord occurs on the strong beat, to which it adds emphasis. Used mainly in the perfect cadence, it is known as the *cadential* I $^6_4$. An unstable chord, it has an obligatory drive to the V, which in turn possesses a drive to the final tonic. So effective is this double movement to the last chord that it forms an almost essential feature of the traditional style. In a sense, this I $^6_4$ is not really a tonic chord, but a V, whose two upper tones gain special emphasis through being delayed.

Ex. 9   Cadential I $^6_4$

The accented I$^6_4$ serves to add breadth and emphasis to cadences already studied; thus IV—V—I is expanded to IV—I$^6_4$—V—I.

Ex. 10   Handel: Sinfonia, from *The Messiah*

Similarly, II⁶—V—I becomes II⁶—I$_4^6$—V—I (Ex. 11, *b*). In addition to its role in the perfect cadence, the accented passing I$_4^6$ also serves in the half cadence (*a*).

Ex. 11   Mozart: Sonata, K. 331

Examining Ex. 11 (*b*), we note that when the accented passing $_4^6$ is written in four voices:

1. The passing sixth and fourth are approached and resolved in stepwise manner.

2. The outer voices approach the chord in contrary motion.
3. The bass of the $\frac{6}{4}$ is doubled (not the sixth or fourth*).
4. The bass remains on the same degree (in this case simply exchanging a lower for an upper octave), while the upper voices resolve.

We have discussed the main functions of the $\frac{6}{4}$ (the only ones the student will use for the present). Three secondary functions appear, chiefly in instrumental music: (1) the appoggiatura $\frac{6}{4}$, (2) the bass arpeggio $\frac{6}{4}$, and (3) the alternating bass $\frac{6}{4}$.

Appoggiatura $\frac{6}{4}$ Chord

The *appoggiatura* $\frac{6}{4}$ resembles the accented passing $\frac{6}{4}$, except that one or both sensitive tones, the sixth and the fourth, are approached by leap instead of by step. Because of its more disjunct quality as compared with the passing chord, the appoggiatura $\frac{6}{4}$ occurs rarely, mainly when special emphasis is desired. The sixth and fourth resolve to adjacent tones of the following chord.

Ex. 12   Beethoven: Sonata, Op. 2, No. 1, Menuetto

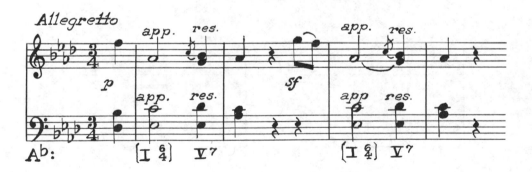

* Since the regular resolutions of the passing sixth and fourth are downward, doubling either of these tones may result in parallel octaves.

Ex. 13   Schumann: *O wie lieblich ist das Mädchen*

Oh, how love-ly   is   the maid-en,
O wie lieb-lich ist das Mäd-chen

[IV ⁶₄] I

Bass Arpeggio ⁶₄

In the Minuet from Mozart's *Don Giovanni*, the bass moves up through all three tones of the tonic triad, reaching the tonic again in the next bar. If we analyze each beat as a separate chord, the result is I—I⁶—I⁶₄—I. But, listening to the Minuet, we tend to hear simply a bass line passing through various tones of the tonic triad.

Ex. 14   Mozart: Minuet, from *Don Giovanni*

I   I⁶   [I⁶₄]

Further examples of bass arpeggio ⁶₄ are the chorus of "America" and the opening of Beethoven's Minuet in G.

Alternating Bass ⁶₄

In many marches, waltzes, folk song arrangements, and the like, in which one chord sometimes extends through several bars, the bass alternately sounds the root and fifth of the chord.

Ex. 15   Alternating bass $^6_4$

The alternate bass tone does not represent a change of chord in such cases; it simply provides a rhythmic pattern that adds variety to what might otherwise be a tiresome chord repetition. Not a $^6_4$ chord in the traditional sense, such a tone is called an *alternating bass* $^6_4$.

Ex. 16   Brahms: Hungarian Dance No. 5

Summary

1. The second-inversion triad, or $^6_4$ chord, can be formed by raising the root and third of the chord above the fifth.

2. The $^6_4$ chord functions primarily as:
   (a) A neighboring chord.
   (b) An unaccented passing chord.
   (c) An accented passing chord.

3. It also functions as:
   (a) An appoggiatura chord.
   (b) Part of a bass arpeggio.
   (c) An alternating bass tone.

4. It is best to double the bass of the $^6_4$, rather than the sixth or the fourth.

5. The sixth and fourth are most smoothly approached by step, in contrary motion to the bass.

6. The sixth and the fourth normally resolve by step, downward.

The Outer
Structure of
the Phrase

Sometimes the question arises, "How long should a phrase be?" The simplest answer is, "As long as the music demands." Formerly, some theorists found a special virtue in foursquare, or symmetrical, patterns: phrases of four or eight bars were termed "normal" or "regular." But modern musicians discover no magic in the number four, being aware that asymmetrical as well as symmetrical patterns occur in the music of many nations and ages.

The Free-Form Phrase

Phrases vary enormously in pattern and length. In music without meter or bar lines (plain chants, certain folk songs, cadenzas, and recitatives), they are completely irregular or *free-form*.

Ex. 17   Plain chant: *Salve Regina*

277

Ex. 18   Menotti: Recitative, from *The Medium*

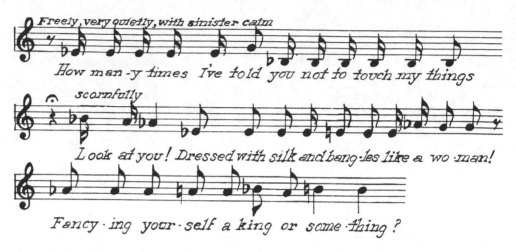

Freely, very quietly, with sinister calm

How man-y times I've told you not to touch my things

scornfully

Look at you! Dressed with silk and bang-les like a wo-man!

Fancy-ing your-self a king or some-thing?

Copyright 1947 by G. Schirmer, Inc. International copyright secured. Used by permission.

The Asymmetrical Phrase

Asymmetrical, or uneven, phrases occur in music with meter and bar lines. The shortest are three-bar phrases, which often have a fresh, intriguing quality.

Ex. 19   Schubert: *Der stürmische Morgen*

Ziemlich geschwind, doch kräftig

Five-bar phrases, more common than those of three bars, have been used with telling effect by such composers as Haydn and Bartók.

Ex. 20   Haydn: String Quartet No. 41, Menuetto (Peters ed.)

Ex. 21   Bartók: Tale, from *Mikrokosmos*, Vol. III

Seven- and nine-bar phrases occur more rarely.*

Ex. 22   Mendelssohn: Songs Without Words, Op. 30, No. 6

Ex. 23   Schubert: Symphony No. 8 (*Unfinished*)

Six- and ten-bar phrases are on the borderline between symmetrical and asymmetrical construction.

Ex. 24   Moussorgsky: Coronation Scene, from *Boris Godunov*

*See also Ex. 4, page 372.

Ex. 25   Beethoven: Sonata, Op. 2, No. 1, last movement

The Symmetrical Phrase

Curt Sachs, the noted scholar, pointed to the dance as the probable origin of musical symmetry.* In the dances of many primitive and peasant cultures, evenly balanced movements—so many steps forward, so many back, or so many to the left, so many to the right—are accompanied by similar musical patterns. Thus the balance of 4 + 4 or 8 + 8 measures is found in early medieval dance music.

Ex. 26   Ductia, thirteenth-century dance

Reprinted by permission of the publishers from Archibald T. Davison and Willi Apel, Historical Anthology of Music, Vol. I. Cambridge, Mass.: Harvard University Press, copyright 1949, 1950 by the President and Fellows of Harvard College.

Note that the difference between 4 + 4 and 8 + 8 may be merely a matter of notation, as in the Troubadour melody Bele Yolanz.

* Curt Sachs: World History of the Dance (New York, 1937), pages 195–197.

Ex. 27   Troubadour song: *Bele Yolanz*

Symmetrical phrases have long been characteristic of Western dance music and of popular songs associated with the dance. Serious composers, however, used a great variety of phrase lengths well into the eighteenth century.

But around 1750, when art tended to be governed by the formal designs of the Age of Reason, foursquare patterns—felt then to be more "rational"—became the norm for serious as well as popular music. Since that time, evenly balanced construction has characterized the themes of many sonatas, symphonies, and concertos. Almost any Classical or Romantic work offers examples of the familiar four- or eight-bar phrase, the basis of symmetrical form.

Ex. 28   Beethoven: Sonata, Op. 27, No. 1 (*Moonlight*), second movement

Ex. 29   Haydn: *The Creation*

The notation of a symmetrical phrase varies according to its tempo. If slow, the phrase may be written as two bars (Ex. 30); if fast, as eight or sometimes sixteen bars (Ex. 31). The ear, however, detects little difference between these and four- and eight-bar phrases, respectively.

Ex. 30   Bach: *Wachet auf, ruft uns die Stimme*

Ex. 31   Porter: Begin the Beguine

The Repeated Phrase

As we have seen, a motive is firmly established by repetition. The same holds true for a phrase; countless compositions emphasize symmetry by repeating the opening phrase immediately after the perfect cadence.* (A phrase ending in a perfect cadence is known as an *independent phrase*.) Repetition can be indicated by a double bar and repeat marks, or by writing out the same music twice.

* See also Ex. 26.

Ex. 32   Schubert: *Du bist die Ruh'*

In other compositions, the repetition may be varied by:

1. Embellishing the melody (Ex. 33).
2. Changing the register (Ex. 34, page 284).
3. Changing the style of accompaniment (Ex. 34, page 284).
4. Changing the instrumental color (Ex. 34, page 284).
5. Changing the harmony, except at the cadences (Ex. 26, page 280).

Ex. 33   Chopin: Mazurka, Op. 6, No. 2

Ex. 34   Beethoven: Violin Sonata, Op. 24, last movement

Although a repeated phrase may be varied even more extensively than in Exs. 33 and 34, two elements that may *not* be altered without changing the basic form are (1) the general contour of the melody, and (2) the final cadence. If either of these is altered, we enter the domain of the parallel period, to be examined in Volume II.*

Summary

1. The outer structure of the phrase refers to its shape as a whole, its length, and its free-form or symmetrical design.

2. An independent phrase ends in a perfect cadence.

*See Volume II, Chapters I–III.

3. Free-form phrases are those without meter or bar lines.

4. Asymmetrical phrases are those of uneven length (3, 5, 7, 9 bars and the like) with meter and bar lines.

5. Symmetrical phrases include:
   a. Those of four and eight bars.
   b. Less commonly, those of two and sixteen bars.

6. A repeated phrase is one in which statement and repetition have the same general contour and the same final cadence.

7. A repeated phrase may be:
   a. Repeated exactly.
   b. Varied by embellishment, change of register, accompaniment style, instrumental color, or harmony (except at the cadences).

XII

Harmony in Minor

The rich, flexible character of the minor mode springs from the diversity of its scale patterns and chord structures. Whereas major has one scale form, minor boasts three; major has one chord series, while minor produces two different triads on every degree (except the tonic). Each of the three minor scales, moreover—*natural*, *harmonic*, and *melodic*—possesses distinctive characteristics. Since different forms of minor are frequently intermingled (in ways to be discussed later), the mode as a whole embraces a wide range of color and expressive possibilities.

All forms of minor share the same lower tetrachord. They differ in the position and direction of the *variable tones*, 6 and 7 (Ex. 1), which may be either *raised* (R) or *lowered* (L).

Ex. 1   Lower and upper tetrachords in minor

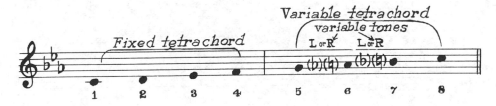

The different combinations of raised and lowered variable tones in the upper tetrachord produce the natural, harmonic, and melodic forms of minor scales (Ex. 2). (Note that natural and falling melodic minor share the same pattern.)

Ex. 2   Upper tetrachord, different forms in minor

Natural Minor

Natural minor is the oldest form of the mode. Identical with Aeolian, it was widely used in Renaissance music but fell out of favor after 1600. When it returned again in the late nineteenth century, it appeared mainly in compositions suggesting a folk-like or archaic quality.

Lacking the half step between 7 and 8, natural minor possesses no decisive drive to the tonic. Its cadential activity and, hence, its feeling of tonality are less definite than those of the harmonic and melodic forms. It is this tonal vagueness that imparts much of the charm to pieces in natural minor.

Ex. 3   Carol: Oh Come, Immanuel

Ex. 4   American white spiritual: Wondrous Love

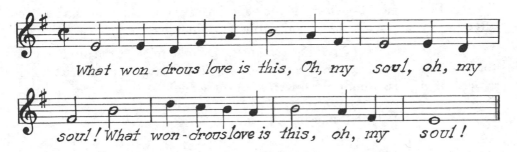

What won-drous love is this, Oh, my   soul, oh, my
soul! What won-drous love is this, oh, my   soul!

As the oldest of the three forms, natural minor provides the key signature for all. Accidentals needed in the other two forms must be added during the course of a composition.

Ex. 5   Beethoven: String Quartet, Op. 95

Natural minor   *Accidentals added to produce melodic minor*

Harmonic and Melodic Minor

Harmonic and melodic differ from natural minor in possessing a true leading tone, which resolves upward by a half step. As compared with natural minor, their cadences have a more decisive drive to the tonic.

Ex. 6   Natural, harmonic, and melodic minor cadences

Natural minor cadence   Harmonic minor cadence   Melodic minor cadence

Although they share the same type of cadence, harmonic and melodic minor differ in the activity of the variable sixth and seventh tones *during the course of the phrase.* These differences distinguish the two scales from each other.

Variable Tones

Two principles determine the behavior of the variable tones, the first affecting melodic and the second harmonic minor.

1. *When 6 and 7 follow each other* (melodic minor), the direction of the last tone determines the behavior of both: if 7 is last, both are raised and ascend; if 6 is last, both are lowered and descend.

Ex. 7   Variable tones following each other

Ex. 8   Vivaldi: Violin Concerto in A minor

2. *When 6 and 7 appear apart from each other* (harmonic minor), 7 is raised and ascends, while 6 is lowered and descends.

Ex. 9   Variable tones appearing apart from each other

Ex. 10   Mozart: Violin Sonata, K. 304

Melodic and harmonic minor can be distinguished as follows:
1. In melodic minor, the variable tones agree in form and direction. When the melody changes direction, both tones change together.

Ex. 11   Bach: Italian Concerto, second movement

2. In harmonic minor, the variable tones disagree in direction: 7 strives upward, 6 pulls downward. The contrast of these two tendencies produces much of the expressive quality of the mode.

Ex. 12   Beethoven: String Quartet, Op. 131

Raised and Lowered Chord Forms

Like the variable sixth and seventh tones, chords in minor are also variable. Each triad in minor (except the tonic) can appear in *raised* or *lowered* form.

Ex. 13   Chord forms in minor

The direction of 6 and 7 determines the form of the chords to which they belong. *When 6 and 7 are raised, they produce raised chord forms; when lowered, lowered chord forms result.*

Ex. 14   Harmonic results of melodic direction

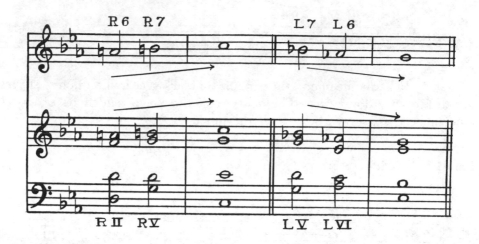

Generally, the upper melody line determines the chord forms, but sometimes the bass melody—or even one in an inner voice—becomes the governing factor.

Ex. 15   Bass melody determining chord forms

In the chorale *Herr, ich habe misgehandelt*, the raised 6 and 7 cause IV and V to appear as raised chords. Being part of an ascending bass line, the raised 6 and 7 produce a raised IV⁶ at (*a*) and V⁶ at (*b*).

Ex. 16   Bach: *Herr, ich habe misgehandelt*

Lord, I have sinned most grievously,
Herr, ich habe misgehandelt,

Conversely, in the chorale *Herzlich tut mich verlangen* the lowered 7 and 6 determine lowered forms of V and VI⁶.

Ex. 17   Bach: *Herzlich tut mich verlangen*

Oh, Lord Forgive this sinner
Ach, Herr mich erbarmen Sünder

The falling soprano and bass lines alternate in determining lowered chord forms—the soprano causing lowered V and VI⁶ at (*a*), the bass, lowered V⁶ and IV⁶ at (*b*). Note that the V on which the half cadence (*c*) rests is, as always, a major chord. Although the tension relaxes at such a cadence, the leading tone gives it an active quality pointing forward to the next phrase.

Example 16 presented only raised chords, and Ex. 17, only lowered ones. Such separation of raised and lowered forms occurs frequently in melodic minor. In harmonic minor, however, the two are usually intermingled —lowered IV, for example, being quickly followed by raised V, or vice versa.

Ex. 18   Intermingling of lowered and raised forms in harmonic minor

Ex. 19   Mozart: Violin Sonata, K. 304, second movement

In the Mozart Sonata, raised V (*a*) is followed in the next bar by lowered IV.

Consonant and Dissonant Triads

The chords produced by the variable tones may be divided into two categories: *consonant* and *dissonant*. The major and minor triads are considered consonant, the diminished and augmented ones, dissonant.

A *diminished triad* consists of two minor thirds superposed; an *augmented triad* consists of two major thirds.

Ex. 20   Diminished and augmented triads

Dissonant triads play an important role in the minor mode, as can be seen in the two series of raised and lowered chord forms (Ex. 21; C = consonant, D = dissonant).*

Ex. 21   Raised and lowered triads in minor

Let us compare the two series:

Raised Forms

4 consonant triads
3 dissonant triads
Primary triads: 2 major (IV, V), 1 minor (I)
V contains the leading tone

Lowered Forms

6 consonant triads
1 dissonant triad
Primary triads: all minor
V has no leading tone

The raised-chord series, which contains the leading tone and a greater number of dissonant and major triads, is active and energetic; the lowered series, with more consonant triads and no leading tone, is more stable and restful. Let us explore this distinction a little further.

Harmony in Various Types of Minor

Natural minor, possessing only lowered chord forms, tends toward darker, more tranquil progressions than do other forms of minor. As in other minor and major scales, the tonic triad is central to the tonality. Neither V

* For a detailed discussion of the dissonant triads, see Chapter XIII.

nor IV, however, have the same importance as in other scales; they bear scarcely more weight than the secondary III, VI, and VII. Chord progressions in natural minor seem to flow rather than to stride vigorously forward; in the absence of a leading tone, chords move gently into the cadence.

Written during the Renaissance by a Flemish composer who lived in Venice, the *Ricercar* by Adrian Willaert provides a lovely example of gliding harmony. It also illustrates the relative equivalence of all chords in natural minor, the tonic excepted.

Ex. 22   Willaert: *Ricercar*

Four centuries after the Willaert composition, Maurice Ravel rediscovered the poetry and grace of the older type of harmony, making use of natural minor in his *Mother Goose* Suite.

Ex. 23   Ravel: *La belle au bois dormant,* from *Ma mère l'Oye*

In melodic minor, as we have seen, the quality of chords and progressions depends almost entirely on the direction of the phrase. The falling forms, all lowered, have the tranquil, dark character of natural-minor harmony —with which, indeed, they are identical.

Ex. 24   Brahms: *Schnitter Tod*

The rising melodic-minor forms could scarcely stand in sharper contrast; their quality is far more active. Compare the lift and energy of the raised major IV and V (Ex. 25) to the darkness of Brahms' lowered minor IV and V.

Ex. 25   Bach: *Herr, ich habe misgehandelt*

In melodic minor, opposing harmonic tendencies can be separated; one may write several measures of lowered chords before changing to raised chords, and vice versa. Alternating appearances of the two types of chords create a contrast of dark and bright areas—a contrast characteristic of the mode.

In harmonic minor, however, tones and chords of opposing tendencies are so closely interwoven that it would be difficult to write more than one or two chord changes without shifting from dark to bright forms, or the reverse.

Ex. 26   Lowered and raised chords in harmonic minor

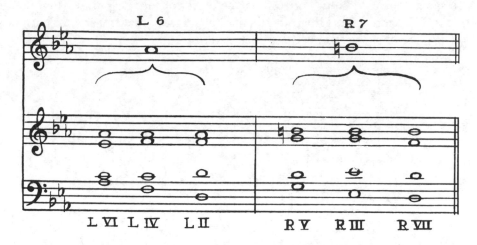

The intermingled tendencies of these two groups—one striving downward and the other up—produce a tension deeply embedded in the harmonic minor form. It is not surprising, then, that this form has proved suitable for music of an expressive and dynamic character. Two excerpts from Gluck's opera *Orfeo*, the one violent and the other brooding and oppressive, illustrate the dramatic extremes possible in harmonic minor.

Ex. 27   Gluck: *Dance of the Furies*, from *Orfeo*, Act II

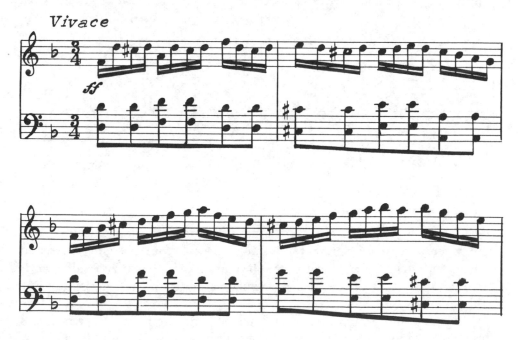

Ex. 28   Gluck: *Ah! dans ce bois*, from *Orfeo*, Act I

Root Positions and Inversions

Root-position triads create a certain vigor and solidity in minor, as in major.

Ex. 29   Purcell: When Monarchs Unite, from *Dido and Aeneas*

When mon-archs u-nite, how

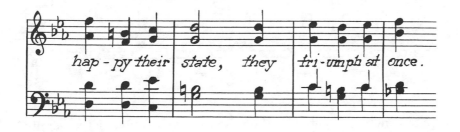

hap-py their state, they tri-umph at once.

Ex. 30   Handel: Variation V, from Suite No. 3

Sixth chords also play the same roles in minor as in major. The varied harmonic possibilities of the mode permit the use of both raised and lowered forms in the same phrase.

Ex. 31   Bach: *Als vierzig Tag' nach Ostern war'n*

As for-ty days, and Eas- - - - -ter past
Als vier-zig Tag nach Os- - - - -tern war'n

Note the contrasting sound of the raised IV⁶ at (*a*) and the lowered IV⁶ at (*d*), and also between the raised and lowered V⁶ at (*b*) and (*c*), respectively.

Ex. 32   Gavotte (eighteenth century)

At (a) and (d) in Ex. 32, the introduction of V⁶ adds harmonic variety; from (b) to (c), a series of consecutive sixth chords produces a smooth bass line, a series of gentle progressions, and the color of first-inversion triads.

The lighter quality of sixth chords when used as part of a cycle of fifths is apparent in minor as in major.*

Ex. 33   Vivaldi: Concerto Grosso, Op. 3, No. 6

* The special characteristics of the II⁶ and VII⁶ in minor are discussed in Chapter XIII.

The $^6_4$ chord, like the sixth chord, serves the same functions in minor as in major. At (*a*) in Ex. 34, we have a passing chord, and at (*b*) a cadential I $^6_4$ leading to the half cadence.

Ex. 34   Mozart: Symphony No. 40, K. 550, last movement

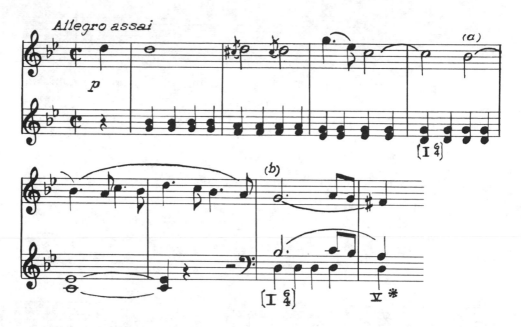

In Ex. 35 (*a*) and (*b*), the $^6_4$ acts twice as a neighboring chord.

Ex. 35   Schumann: *Album for the Young*, Op. 68, No. 8

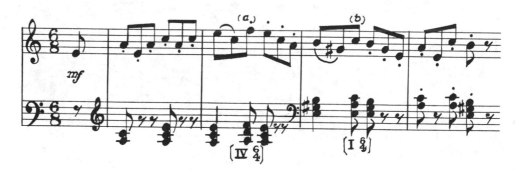

Examples of the $^6_4$ used in a bass arpeggio and as an alternating bass tone likewise occur in minor as in major.

Embellishing Tones and Cadences

Passing tones, escaped tones, anticipations, neighboring tones, and appoggiaturas are also very effective in the minor mode. The first three are illustrated in Ex. 36.

Ex. 36   Corelli: Sonata for Violin, Op. 5, No. 8

Example 13 in Chapter VI illustrates the neighboring tone in minor, and Ex. 20 in Chapter VI, the appoggiatura. Note the more intense quality of these half-step embellishments as compared with the whole-step embellishments in major (Ex. 37).

Ex. 37   Comparison of half- and whole-step embellishments

Perfect, imperfect, plagal, half, and deceptive cadences also function in minor much the same as in major. One important difference is created by the lowered 6. It adds a greater urgency to chords leading to the half cadence, in progressions such as I—V⁶—IV⁶—V and I⁶—II⁶—V.

Ex. 38   Half-cadence patterns in minor

The downward, stepwise approach to the half cadence is further illustrated in Exs. 15, 17, and 31 in this chapter, as well as Ex. 22 in Chapter X; the rising stepwise approach is shown in Ex. 21, Chapter X.

Summary

1. The expressive variety of the minor mode is made possible by its three scale forms. In all three, the first tetrachord has a half step in the middle. The differences in the second tetrachord are:
   a. Natural minor: L6, L7 (half step at bottom).
   b. Harmonic minor: L6, R7 (one and a half steps in middle).
   c. Melodic minor, rising: R6, R7 (half step at top).
      Melodic minor, falling: L7, L6 (half step at bottom).

2. Natural minor was widely used before 1600, and also after 1850 in music of an archaic or folk-like character.
   a. It lacks a true leading tone.
   b. Its harmonic feeling is gentler and its tonal feeling vaguer than in other types of minor.

3. Both melodic and harmonic minor have a raised 7 and strong harmonic motion at the cadence.

4. During the course of a phrase,
   a. When 6 and 7 follow each other, if 7 is last, both are raised and ascend; if 6 is last, both are lowered and descend; the melodic minor scale is formed.
   b. When 6 or 7 appear apart from each other, the 7 is raised and ascends; the 6 is lowered and descends; the harmonic minor scale is formed.

5. Wherever the variable tones appear, their form determines the form of the chords that accompany them.
   a. Raised 6 and 7 determine raised chord forms.
   b. Lowered 7 and 6 determine lowered chord forms.

6. All chords except the tonic have two different forms in minor.

7. Natural minor, using lowered chord forms only, tends toward a flowing, gentle type of harmony.

8. Melodic minor, containing a contrast of raised and lowered forms, produces an opposition of light and dark harmonic colors. Often these appear alternately.

9. Harmonic minor, containing raised and lowered chord forms intermingled, often produces dynamic harmonic activity.

10. Triads in root position and in first and second inversion serve the same functions as in major.

11. Embellishing tones play the same roles as in major, except that those involving half-step progression are more intense than those including the whole step.

12. All cadences are used, as in major. The descent to the half cadence by half step in the bass has special urgency.

Melody
in Minor

The minor mode, with its three types of scales, offers rich opportunity for varied melodic movement. During the course of a composition—sometimes even during a single phrase—a melody may utilize (a) the raised 6 and 7, (b) the lowered 7 and 6, and (c) the lowered 6 and raised 7.

The varied directional drives of these patterns grant to minor melody a special suppleness and expressive variety. Yet despite this wide range of expression, popular myth has it that "minor melodies are sad." No doubt many are, but it is not difficult to find brisk, gay minor melodies as well, as Exs. 39 and 40 show.

Ex. 39   Beethoven: Symphony No. 9, Op. 125, second movement

Ex. 40   Scotch folk song: Charlie Is My Darlin'

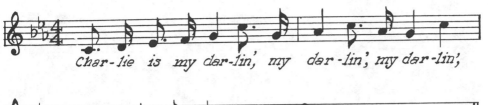

Char-lie is my dar-lin', my dar-lin', my dar-lin',

Char-lie is my dar-lin', the gay ca-va-lier.

Natural-Minor Melody

Each scale form presents special melodic possibilities. Natural minor, as we have seen, suggests the archaic and folk-like. This description should not be taken, however, to imply a pallid or precious kind of music—as witness the Scotch tune of Ex. 40.

The melodic possibilities of natural minor have been richly exploited by nineteenth- and twentieth-century composers, including Dvorak, Borodin, Stravinsky, Milhaud, and Kodaly.

Ex. 41   Kodaly: Song, from *Hary Janos*

p espress

Harmonic-Minor Melody

Harmonic minor was used little if at all before the eighteenth century. The *augmented second*, or step-and-a-half, between its sixth and seventh degrees was considered an unacceptable irregularity in melodic movement. Even after 1700, composers treated this interval with circumspection, observing in general the melodic tendencies already described.* When they ignored the traditional proscription of the augmented second, it was usually for a specific, expressive purpose. Bach, for example, introduced the interval in passages of a dramatic nature (Ex. 42), and Beethoven employed it in a highly personal way (Ex. 43).

* See pages 290, 291.

Ex. 42   Bach: Chromatic Fantasy

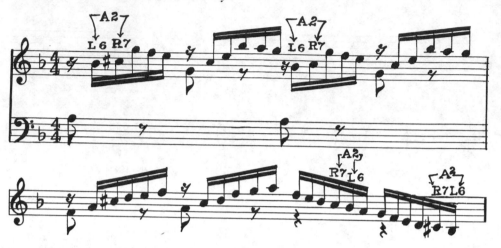

Ex. 43   Beethoven: String Quartet, Op. 131, seventh movement

When a stepwise melody reaches one of the tones forming the augmented second and, instead of making the traditional alterations to "smooth the crossing," leaps boldly across the gap, the result is an increase in energy. Passages that cross the augmented second in harmonic minor are often found in music of vigorous character.*

Ex. 44   Schumann: Symphony No. 1, Op. 38, last movement

Melodic-Minor Melody

In both natural and harmonic minor, scale structure is fixed. Melodic minor, on the other hand, permits a more variable melodic line. Bach often made sensitive use of the color possibilities inherent in the alternation of raised and lowered tones.

* See also Ex. 27.

Ex. 45   Bach: Sarabande, from Partita No. 2

Other examples of rapid shift between raised and lowered forms can be found in Bach's Chromatic Fantasy (Ex. 3, Chapter VI), and Beethoven's String Quartet, Op. 95 (Ex. 5 in this chapter).

Summary

1. Minor melodies often possess a wide range of color and expression.

2. Natural-minor melody often expresses the folk-like and the archaic.

3. Harmonic minor is characterized by the augmented second between 6 and 7.
   a. Before 1700, this interval was generally avoided as a melodic step.
   b. Since 1700, it has been frequently used, especially in dramatic or expressive melodies.

4. In melodic minor, the alternate use of raised and lowered forms of 6 and 7 is characteristic of expressive and dramatic melodies.

XIII

More
about Minor
Harmony

Continuing our study of the minor mode, we turn now to certain special problems: (1) the role of the augmented and diminished triads, (2) the major region of the minor mode, (3) the harmonization of melodies in minor, (4) mixtures of various types of minor, and (5) free forms of melodic movement in minor.

Dissonant Triads in Minor

Whereas the major mode contains only one dissonant triad (VII), the minor mode, as we have seen, gives rise to four such chords: three diminished triads (II, VI, and VII), and one augmented triad (III). These dissonant chords contribute to the greater intensity and complication of harmonic movement in minor as compared with major.

Triads possessing an unstable fifth need careful *preparation* and *resolution* to ensure smooth continuity. A dissonant tone of a chord is prepared by having it form part of a consonant chord immediately preceding. It is resolved by moving one step down from a diminished fifth, and one step up from an augmented fifth (Ex. 1).

311

Ex. 1   Preparation and resolution of dissonant tones

The Diminished Triad

Because of the ungainly sound of its dissonant fifth, the diminished triad occurs rather rarely in root position. First-inversion diminished triads, on the other hand, especially II⁶ and VII⁶, are quite freely used in minor. The II⁶ forms an effective preparation for V, especially in the cadence, the instability of its diminished fifth driving it strongly toward the dominant.

Ex. 2   Mozart: Quintet, K. 516, second movement

(a)

The VII⁶ serves largely as a passing and neighboring chord centered around the I, the bass always moving stepwise (Ex. 3). A passing VII⁶ occurs at (a).

Ex. 3   Bach: *Vater unser in Himmelreich*

The VII⁶ serves as a neighboring chord at (*a*) in Ex. 4.

Ex. 4   Bach: Little Preludes and Fugues for organ

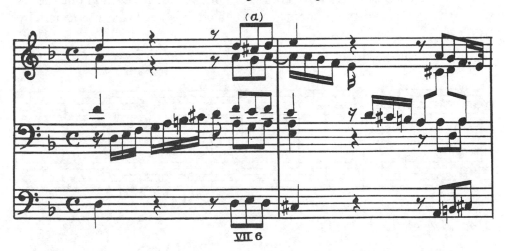

On those infrequent occasions when the diminished triad appears in root position, it hardly exists as a separate entity, serving almost entirely as (1) a neighboring chord (Ex. 5), or (2) a passing chord (Ex. 6). In both cases,

Ex. 5   Beethoven: Sonatina in G

the bass is usually approached and always left by stepwise motion. In Ex. 6, the VII appears briefly, at (*a*), passing between the IV⁶ and I chords.

Ex. 6   Bach: *Ach wie flüchtig, ach wie nichtig*

The diminished triad functions as an independent chord in one special case—the cycle-of-fifths progression, in which it is approached and left by the leap of a fifth.*

Ex. 7   Diminished triad in the cycle of fifths

The Augmented Triad

The augmented triad on III was rarely used by composers of the traditional period, for whom it was too dissonant. It is found occasionally in rising harmonic sequences (Ex. 8). Note that the augmented fifth (*a*) is prepared in the preceding chord and resolved in the following one.

Ex. 8   Augmented triad in rising sequence

* For further examples of the dissonant triad in sequences, see Ex. 2, page 227, and Ex. 6, page 229.

An extraordinarily bold use of *two successive* augmented chords occurs in a work written in 1691 by Henry Purcell. In the English composer's *King Arthur*, augmented triads help to create the unearthly mood of a dramatic scene in which the Cold Genius (the spirit of winter) and the people are frozen and quivering with intense cold.

Ex. 9   Purcell: *King Arthur*

The Major Region of the Minor Mode

In the discussion of secondary triads in major (Chapter VIII), we saw that they often create a modal region in a major key. The reverse is also true: secondary triads in minor may form *a major region* of a minor key.

The key signature of a minor key is the same as that of the major key a minor third above. C major, for example, is known as the *relative major* of A minor, which in turn is known as C major's *relative minor*. The tones and chords of natural and falling melodic minor are exactly the same as those of their relative major.

Ex. 10   Minor and relative major

Since a minor key and its relative major share many chords in common, how can one tell to which key a given progression belongs—for example, the one shown in Ex. 11?

Ex. 11   Ambiguous chord progression

When a progression does not emphasize a specific tonal center, it is impossible to identify its key. The chords in Ex. 11 possess a double identity: they belong to both the minor key and its relative major.

But when the key is established by a cadence, the tonality of the entire progression becomes clear. One of the most important roles of the cadence is precisely this: to define the tonality. Thus, if we add a perfect cadence in A minor to the end of Ex. 11, the whole phrase is heard in that key.

Ex. 12   Chord progression in A minor

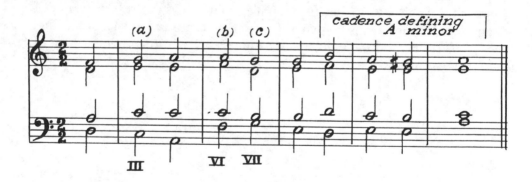

The three major chords at (a), (b), and (c), which might have formed the I, IV, and V of C major, turn out now to be the III, VI, and VII of A minor. These three triads (all lowered forms of the secondary chords in minor) are widely used in both natural and falling melodic minor.

The major III, VI, and VII, if given sufficient weight, can form a *major region of the minor mode.* Such a region becomes an important means of achieving harmonic variety in minor.*

* If the major region is stressed strongly enough, it becomes a modulation to the relative major key. See Chapter IV, Volume II.

Ex. 13   Major region of the minor mode

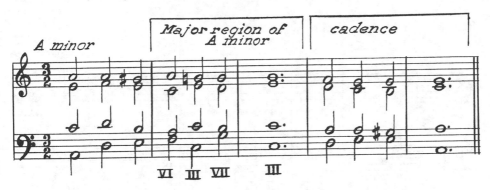

Another function of the major region is to form a special type of half cadence resting on III. In a piece by the English Renaissance composer Peerson, the major III serves at the half cadence in place of the usual V.

Ex. 14   Peerson: The Fall of the Leaf

Secondary triads are stressed in bars 3–6, forming a major region in contrast to the opening minor region. When the tonic minor triad returns again (at *a* and *b*), the reversion to minor feeling is welcome.

The half cadence on III also appears in a Schubert Waltz.

Ex. 15   Schubert: Waltz, Op. 77, No. 9

Another function of the major triad is to serve as a conclusion to a minor composition. Containing a major third, known as the *tierce de Picardie*, this device was frequently employed by Bach (Ex. 16, *a*).*

Ex. 16   Bach: *Vater unser in Himmelreich*

* See also Ex. 14.

Harmonization of Melodies in Minor

Once the variable tones are clearly understood, harmonization of melodies in minor presents few problems different from those of major melodies. For example, let us look at the lovely "Coventry Carol"—traditionally harmonized in block chords.

Ex. 17   The Coventry Carol (1520)

Proceeding as before, we plan the cadences. It soon becomes apparent that half cadences occur at (*a*) and a perfect cadence at (*b*). The final measure may be something of a puzzle until we remember that the melody dates from 1520, when the *tierce de Picardie* was in vogue—hence a major triad for the last bar. Harmonizing the cadences, we arrive at the sketch shown in Ex. 18.

Ex. 18   Coventry Carol, Sketch 1

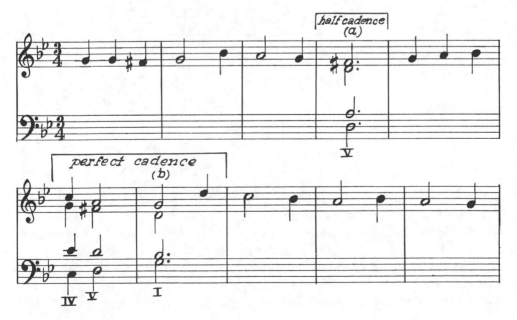

As the next step, we fill in the bass line. Bars 1 and 2 present no problems, but bar 3 raises an interesting question, because there are three possible ways of harmonizing it.

Ex. 19   Coventry Carol, Sketch 2

Which is best? We can quickly rule out (b), for the use of the V⁶ chord in this bar would produce a certain monotony—we have already heard the V in bar 1, and it is shortly to appear as the half cadence chord in bar 4.

The chords in (a) seem to present an excellent solution. Looking ahead, however, to the third phrase of the melody (Ex. 18), we find the half cadence there approached by the same notes as in the first phrase. Since it would be tiresome to approach the half cadence twice with exactly the same harmonies, let us save (*a*)—a strong progression—to add vigor to the half cadence in the third phrase. We can then use (*c*) in the first phrase. Our sketch will now appear as in Ex. 20.

Ex. 20   Coventry Carol, Sketch 3

The largest open area remains in the third phrase. Since the other phrases contain many tonic and dominant chords, emphasizing the minor tonality, a little harmonic diversion in this one may be interesting. As it happens, the melody permits us to enter the major region of the minor key, making use of the major III and VII chords for a refreshing contrast.

Ex. 21   Coventry Carol, Sketch 4

Two remaining bars of harmony as well as the inner voices remain to be filled in. With this task accomplished, the harmonization is complete.

Ex. 22   Coventry Carol, harmonization

Three further observations can be made:

1. The sequence of work—marking the cadences, the approaches to the cadence, then the bass line, and finally the inner voices—is a practical one, for we establish the broad harmonic structure before taking care of the less important details. But don't adhere to such a procedure rigidly. If, in the course of harmonizing a melody, you have an idea for particularly felicitous voice leading in a given area, don't hesitate to sketch it in.

2. An important aspect of harmonization, as suggested above, consists of planning ahead. It is better to move forward and backward from the end to the beginning than simply to start at the first note and fill in chords bar by bar. Sometimes an idea that seems suitable in a given spot will be still more effective later on.

3. The harmonization we have arrived at for the "Coventry Carol," traditional and tasteful, *is not the only possible one*.

Let us examine two further problems in the harmonization of minor melodies. First, an old German song.

Ex. 23   Zuccalmaglio: *Verstohlen geht der Mond auf**

Like the "Coventry Carol," this melody lends itself to a variety of harmonic rhythms. After establishing the cadences, as in previous harmonizations, we note in Ex. 24 that bars 1 and 2 suggest one chord per bar (more than this would create a ponderous effect); bar 3 suggests two chords per bar, and bar 4 suggests three chords.

Ex. 24   *Verstohlen*, Sketch 1

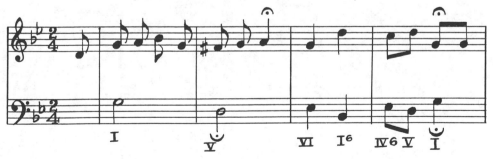

In Ex. 23, bar 5 once again suggests a single chord, and bar 6, three. In bars 7 and 8, we arrive at a little refrain. Marked *mf* after the preceding *p*, it implies a contrast of mood. Rapid harmonic change—four chords in a bar—will sharpen this contrast. Finally, the last two bars call for a broader harmonic rhythm.

* Zuccalmaglio, a little-known nineteenth-century poet, passed this off as a genuine German folk song; it was used by Brahms in the second movement of his Piano Sonata No. 1, Opus 1.

Ex. 25   *Verstohlen*, Sketch 2

As noted before, clues to harmonization may be suggested by tempo (*ruhig, zart** = quiet, delicate), dynamics, and of course the text, if any. The tender mood of this song has led us to a gentle harmonic motion—hence the liberal use of sixth chords (too many root-position triads would have weighed the melody down). In our search for delicacy, note, at (*a*) in Ex. 26, the gentle sonority of parallel sixths; at (*b*), parallel thirds; and at (*c*), the soft effect of the lowered III chord.

Ex. 26   *Verstohlen*, harmonization

* Always look up such indications in a musical dictionary.

One additional essay in minor harmonization remains: the setting of a piano accompaniment to a Chopin melody. The jumping-bass style of the first two beats is given in Ex. 27.

Ex. 27   Chopin: Nocturne, Op. 48, No 1

As with every melody, there are several (not unlimited) possibilities. One is shown in Ex. 28.

Ex. 28   Chopin: Nocturne, theoretical harmonization

Following the long phrase mark starting at (*a*), an attempt is made in the second bar to create a broad harmonic movement by sustaining the V for a whole bar. At (*d*), the phrase is rounded out by a rolled chord in the left hand.

Although it is idle to try to match the harmonic genius of a master, much can be learned by comparing one's own efforts with Chopin's original harmonization.

Ex. 29   Chopin: Nocturne, original harmonization

It is apparent at (*a*) that our holding the V for a whole bar was not a happy idea. In view of the free melodic rhythm, an interruption of the steady pulsation of the bass robs the phrase of its forward-moving impulse. In Chopin's original, at (*f*), the regular march of the harmony lends strength to the passage.

Furthermore, the introduction of the tonic chord at (*b*), forming a perfect cadence right in the middle of the phrase, halts the movement of the harmony, and creates a dead spot at this point. Compare, at (*h*), the superior effect of VI in the same place.

Note also how much more gracious are the sixth chords at (*e*) and (*f*) than the heavy root-position triads on the corresponding beats of Ex. 28. At (*h*) observe Chopin's subtlety in thinning out the left-hand chords from five voices to four, and then, at (*i*), to three, as the melody descends, relaxing gracefully at the end of the phrase. (The rolled chord at *d* produced the opposite effect, thickening the chord inopportunely.)

Such trial harmonizations followed by careful comparison with the original are invaluable. They reveal in detail the craftsmanship of the great composers, with a vividness that extends the meaning of theoretical discussion and generalizations about chord behavior.

Summary

1. Four dissonant triads that contribute to the harmonic richness and intensity of the minor mode are:
   a. The diminished triads on VII, II and VI.
   b. The augmented triad on III.

2. The fifth of the diminished triad must be prepared as a tone of the preceding chord, or by stepwise motion. It resolves one step down.

3. Diminished triads—especially II and VII—are used more often in first inversion than in root position. They serve mainly as passing and neighboring chords.

4. When the diminished VII appears in root position, its bass is usually approached and always resolved by stepwise motion, except when the chord forms part of a cycle-of-fifths progression.

5. The fifth of the augmented triad must be prepared as a tone of the preceding chord. It resolves one step up.

6. The lowered VI, III, and VII, when used together, form a major region of the minor mode. This major region:
   a. Produces harmonic variety.
   b. May serve as a half cadence on III.

7. The third of a major triad ending a minor composition is known as a *tierce de Picardie*.

8. A useful procedure in harmonizing minor melodies is to:
   a. Play or sing the melody over, studying its character.
   b. Plan for a variety of harmonic rhythms whenever the melody permits.
   c. Take cues for the character of the harmonization from the mood of the melodic line, from the dynamics, and from the text, if any.
   d. Plan the cadences, and then the approach to each.
   e. Sketch the bass line.
   f. Fill in the cadence chords.
   g. Complete the entire harmonization.
   h. Compare your work, when finished, with the original score, if you are harmonizing a melody from the works of a master.

More
about Minor
Melody

Mixtures of Various Types of Minor

In order to distinguish their characteristics, we have discussed the three forms of minor separately—as though they were different scales. In actual practice, however, the various forms of minor, especially melodic and harmonic, are often intermingled, sometimes even in one phrase.

Ex. 30   Bach: *Italian* Concerto, second movement

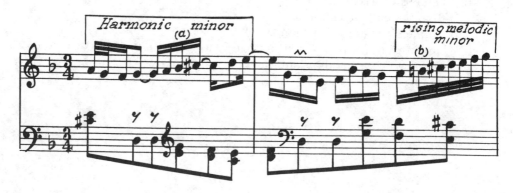

In Ex. 30, the melody rises along harmonic minor lines at (*a*); at (*b*) it rises once again—this time, however, in melodic minor form, descending at (*c*) through the falling melodic minor.

From many examples of this kind, it becomes apparent that *harmonic and melodic minor are not two different scales, but two different varieties of melodic and harmonic motion through the upper tetrachord of the same scale.* Their alternation produces much of the richness of the minor mode.

Natural minor is also combined with other forms of the mode. For some time before and during the Renaissance, it was traditional to end natural minor (Aeolian) melodies with the raised-seventh cadence.* For instance, the carol "Greensleeves," is in natural minor throughout, except for the two cadences (*a*) and (*b*), the first of which uses the harmonic minor and the second the rising melodic minor.

Ex. 31   English carol: Greensleeves

* In this practice, known as *musica ficta*, the accidental forming the raised 7 was not written into the music, but was added by singers and instrumentalists during performance.

The mixture of natural and melodic minor also occurs in a Bach Partita.

Ex. 32   Bach: Air, from Partita No. 6

Although the falling bass line may have determined the use of natural minor at (*a*), the pattern is unusual in Bach, to say the least—especially when followed by the *rising* melodic minor for a descending line at (*b*).

Free Melodic Movement in Minor

At the outset of Chapter XII, it was stated that when 6 and 7 are used apart from each other, 7 rises and 6 falls. This principle holds true largely for melodies harmonized in choral, block-chord style. But it has two important exceptions, which mainly concern instrumental music.

1. When the chord accompanying a melody (or implied by it) is clearly a major V, the *raised* forms of 7 and 6 are used, even though a melody falls.

Ex. 33   Ph. Em. Bach: Solfeggietto

At (*a*), where the V is clearly the implied harmony, the raised 7 leaps downward; at (*b*) the raised 7 and 6 move down in a scale line outlining the same chord.

2. When the chord accompanying or outlined by a melody is a minor IV, the lowered 6 may rise, as part of a broken chord figure (Ex. 34, *a*).

Ex. 34   Mozart: Sonata, K. 457

Finally, we note two further examples of free movement in minor.

1. When the melody rises from 6 to 7 but then drops back again through 6 to 5, lowered forms are used.

Ex. 35   Melodic patterns L6—L7—L6—5

Bach uses this pattern in a lovely example.

Ex. 36   Bach: *Gott hat das Evangelium*

2. Schubert provides an unusually beautiful example of a *cross-relation*—a harmonic pattern containing *both the raised and lowered forms* of a tone. This device is used only rarely in traditional practice—generally to depict emotions of pain, depression, and the like. Note at (*a*) the raised 7 in the bass, and at (*b*) the lightly stressed lowered 7 in the melody—the dissonant cross-relation suggesting the "cold sun."*

* Widely cultivated by composers of the English Renaissance, the cross-relation was infrequently used in the Classical period, but returned in Romantic compositions, in the blues, and in works of such composers as Stravinsky, Gershwin, and Ravel.

Ex. 37   Schubert: *Der Wanderer*

The cross-relation—whether sounded by two voices at the same time or one immediately following the other—should be avoided by the student for the time being.

Intervals in Harmonic Minor

Distances between various degrees in harmonic minor form several diminished and augmented intervals that are characteristic of the mode.

Ex. 38   Augmented intervals

The *augmented second* (between 6 and 7)

The *diminished fourth* (between 7 and 3 above)

The *augmented fifth* (between 3 and 7 above)

The *diminished seventh* (between 7 and 6 above)

Composers of the Middle Ages and early Renaissance generally avoided diminished and augmented intervals, considering them strange and illogical. Later composers, searching for more intense means of expression, began to use the hitherto forbidden intervals more and more freely, especially in music of a coloristic or highly emotional character. In the nineteenth century, these dramatic intervals became the hallmark of Romantic music.

We have already seen examples of the augmented second,* as well as the augmented fourth and diminished fifth.† The *diminished fourth* occurs in one of Beethoven's last quartets. The interval, which plays an important role in the work, bears the enigmatic inscription *Muss es sein?* ("Must it be?").

Ex. 39   Beethoven: String Quartet, Op. 135, last movement

Diminished and augmented fourths and diminished fifths are used most impressively in Bach's Suite No. 5 for solo cello.

Ex. 40   Bach: Sarabande, from Suite No. 5 for Solo Cello

The *diminished seventh* served to underline dramatic surprises in opera for so long that it became a cliché, and was abandoned by later composers. Employed by the great masters, though, it had telling power. Note two very different examples of the interval: a dramatic, sorrowful chorus from Handel's *Messiah,* and the stormy theme of Beethoven's Sonata, Op. 111.

* Exs. 42–44, page 308.

† Exs. 26–34, pages 42–45.

Ex. 41   Handel: And with His Stripes, from *The Messiah*

Ex. 42   Beethoven: Sonata, Op. 111

Diminished intervals can be formed by contracting minor or perfect ones a half step; augmented intervals, by expanding major or perfect ones a half step. Examples 43 and 44 show all diminished and augmented intervals within the range of an octave (some of them rarely used) and their relation to the corresponding perfect, major, and minor intervals.

Ex. 43   Diminished intervals

Diminished - by lowering the top note

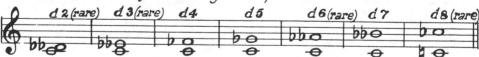

Diminished - by raising the lower note

Ex. 44   Augmented intervals

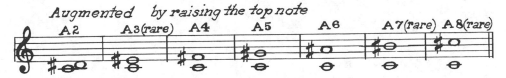

Augmented   by raising the top note

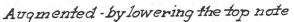

Augmented - by lowering the top note

Summary

1. Harmonic- and melodic-minor melody are often intermingled, sometimes even in the same phrase.

2. Harmonic and melodic minor are not two different scales, but two different pathways through the upper tetrachord in minor.

3. Natural minor may also be intermingled with harmonic or melodic minor.

4. When the chord is clearly a major V:
   a. The raised 7 and 6 may be used as part of a falling line.
   b. The raised 7 may leap downward as part of a broken chord.

5. When the chord is clearly a minor IV, the lowered 6 may rise as part of a broken chord.

6. The lowered 6 may rise as part of the grouping L6—L7—L6—5.

7. A cross-relation is a simultaneous or successive appearance in two voices of raised and lowered forms of a single tone; it is used only for a special poetic or dramatic purpose.

8. Several diminished or augmented intervals are characteristic of the harmonic minor scale. Among them are:
   a. The augmented second (between 6 and 7).
   b. The diminished fourth (between 7 and 3 above).
   c. The augmented fifth (between 3 and 7 above).
   d. The diminished seventh (between 7 and 6 above).

9. Diminished intervals are one half step smaller than minor or perfect ones; augmented intervals, one half step larger than major or perfect ones.

XIV

The Dominant Seventh

For a long time, the triad proved entirely adequate for the harmonic needs of composers. But in the late Renaissance and early Baroque periods, the search for a more personal and dramatic means of expression awakened a desire for an expanded harmonic language. A new chord began to be widely used: the *dominant seventh*, or V^7, containing four different tones. Appearing most prominently in the madrigals and operas of Monteverdi (1567–1643), it struck musicians as an intensely active harmony.

The V^7 can be formed by the addition of a minor third to the dominant triad.

The clash between the seventh and the root of the chord creates a tension that is relaxed when the seventh resolves one step down to the sixth.

An even greater tension is produced by the interval between the seventh and third of the V^7—the famous *diabolus in musica* (augmented fourth or diminished fifth, depending on the position of the voices).

This dissonance, like a coiled spring, has a strong drive to push outward:

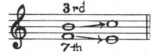

or pull inward:

The tense intervals embedded in the dominant seventh lend their energies to the chord structure, making V^7 the most dynamic harmony we have studied so far.

The V^7 may be formed, as we have seen, by the addition of a third above the triad; but it did not originate in this way. The first appearance of the seventh as part of a chord evolved from its use as a passing tone descending from 5. An early example occurs in the works of Josquin des Prés (1445-1521).

Ex. 1   Josquin des Prés: *Benedicite opera omnia Domine*

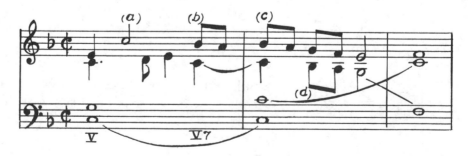

From Edward E. Lowinsky, Tonality and Atonality in Sixteenth-Century Music (*Berkeley, California, 1962*). *Reprinted by permission.*

The soprano sounds 5 (the root of the V) at (*a*). Passing downward, it dwells on the chord seventh at (*b*) and stresses it once more at (*c*); the seventh also occurs as a passing tone in the alto, at (*d*). Approach to this interval by falling stepwise movement introduces it gently into the phrase, softening its dissonant quality.

Regular Resolution of the V⁷

When the V⁷ resolves, its most active tones progress by half steps to tones of the I: its third moves up to the tonic, and its seventh down to 3 (Ex. 2). The direction of these tones governs that of the chord as a whole; V⁷ resolves almost inevitably to I.*

Ex. 2   V⁷ in various positions, with resolutions to I

Functions of the V⁷

The joining of a seventh to the V enhances its active qualities already noted; the V⁷, in addition, develops special functions of its own. It serves:

1. To intensify harmonic movement.
2. To increase the drive toward the cadence.
3. To add richness to the V.
4. To define a key quickly.
5. Together with I, to harmonize melodies containing all tones except 6.

Beethoven is one of the composers who extended the V⁷ over several measures in a typical "gathering-of-tension" effect. Note the dynamic quality of this chord in a passage from the Fifth Symphony. †

* These tendencies may be disregarded only for very special reasons; see pages 348–349.

† For another example of insistence on the V⁷, see Ex. 24 of Chapter IX, Volume II.

Ex. 3   Beethoven: Symphony No. 5, Op. 67, last movement

The strong drive of the V⁷ toward the cadence plays so important a role in Classical and Romantic music that it would be difficult to find a piece without it.

Ex. 4   Schubert: Symphony No. 8 (*Unfinished*)

The addition of the seventh brings a new richness of color and sonority to the V, as revealed by a comparison of the two chords (Exs. 5–7). In each example, (*a*) shows chords from which the sevenths have been deleted, and (*b*) shows the original music containing the V⁷.

Ex. 5   Chopin: Prelude, Op. 28, No. 7

Ex. 6   Chopin: Waltz, Op. 34, No. 3

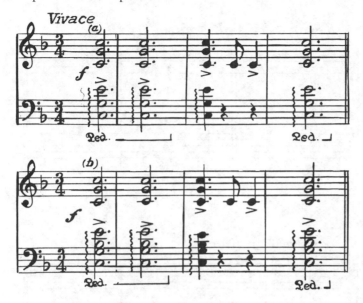

Ex. 7   Schubert: *Ecossaise*

The V and I can establish a given key; the V⁷ and I do so more decisively. For example, the triad on G may belong to several keys; even the progression G triad—C triad does not in itself define a single key—it forms part of progressions in various tonalities: among them C major, G major, and E minor.

Ex. 8   Different interpretations of G—C progression

But a dominant *seventh* on G belongs to one major key only—that of the tone a fifth below. The progression G[7]—C unequivocally establishes the key of C.

Ex. 9   V[7]—I defining key of C

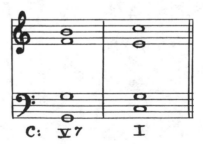

The power of V[7] to define a key quickly and precisely is one reason why many compositions employing elementary harmony contain this chord rather than the V.

Ex. 10   Mozart: Symphony No. 41, K. 551 (*Jupiter*), third movement

Ex. 11   Haydn: Symphony No. 94 (*Surprise*), third movement

Role of the V⁷ in Harmonization

Finally, the V^7 serves in the harmonization of melodies, especially those containing intervals of the chord. Schubert's *Ständchen* starts with the leaps shown in Ex. 12.

Ex. 12   Schubert: *Ständchen*, melody alone

It would be awkward, indeed, to introduce any other chord than the V^7, clearly outlined by the leap 7—4.

Ex. 13   Schubert: *Ständchen*, with harmony

Many folk songs and classical compositions written in popular style suggest the use of V^7 in the accompaniment.

Ex. 14   American folk song: The Foggy, Foggy Dew

Ex. 15   Schubert: *Die Forelle*

Ex. 16   Czerny: *Two Austrian Folk Themes*, No. 1

Note the precision with which Czerny distributed the voices of the V⁷ to achieve a well-balanced sonority. At (*a*) in Ex. 16, where the third of the chord appears in the right hand, the accompanying chord omits that tone. At (*b*) and (*c*), where the melody sounds the fifth of the chord, the left hand omits the fifth, sounding the third. At (*d*), the melody moves up the scale toward 7; the left hand carefully avoids doubling that sensitive tone, waiting for it to arrive on the last beat of the measure.

Preparation of the V⁷

We have noted the preparation of the chord seventh by stepwise motion from above. Equally smooth is its introduction as a note tied over from the preceding chord. Any chord containing the 4 can serve.

Ex. 17   Preparation of the seventh by 4

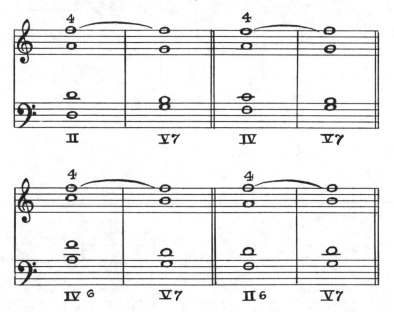

The same preparation is effected when the seventh repeats a tone of the preceding chord, rather than sustaining it.

Ex. 18   Preparation of the seventh as a repeated note

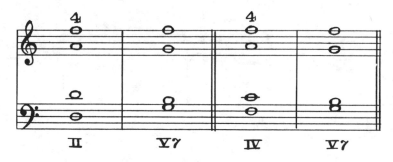

Classical masters adopted two different approaches to the seventh of the V⁷. In the earlier period of traditional harmony, they considered it too harsh an interval to be introduced without careful preparation, as outlined above. (For the time being, you should follow this earlier method, always preparing the entry of the V⁷ chord.) At a later period, the V⁷ was often sounded without preparation. Sometimes a leap to the seventh (Ex. 19, *a*) produces a striking harmonic accent.

Ex. 19   Bach: Prelude No. 7, from *The Well-Tempered Clavier*, Book I

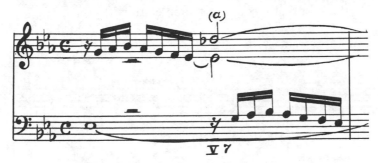

At other times, such a leap to the seventh (Ex. 20, *a*) may create a light, playful effect.

Ex. 20   Schumann: *Arlequin*, from *Carnaval*, Op. 9

Note, in Exs. 19 and 20, that when one voice leaps to a seventh, the other voice forming the interval remains stationary. In general, the seventh is best approached by oblique or contrary motion; approach by similar motion produces a harshness out of keeping with the traditional style.

Ex. 21   Approaches to the V⁷ by oblique and similar motion

Irregular Resolutions

We have referred to the "almost inevitable" quality of the resolution V⁷ to I—a quality so basic that other resolutions seem surprising and irregular.

Example 22 shows the most common irregular resolution: to VI.* (In this progression, the VI usually contains a doubled third.)

Ex. 22   Mozart: Fantasy, K. 397

Progression of the V^7 to other chords is quite rare, and for that reason is interesting when it does occur. In the irregular resolution to IV^6 (most common) and IV (quite unusual), the seventh does not resolve downward, but remains stationary, forming a common tone between the two chords.

Ex. 23   Irregular resolutions, V—IV^6, V—IV

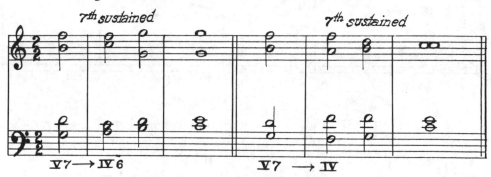

Such progressions are generally the result of a melodic movement, as in the passages from Brahms and Chopin shown in Exs. 24 and 25.

Ex. 24   Brahms: Sonata No. 3, Op. 5, second movement

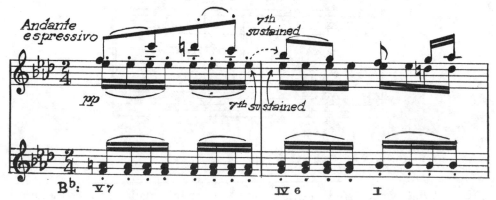

* See also Ex. 17, page 204.

Ex. 25   Chopin: Prelude, Op. 28, No. 17

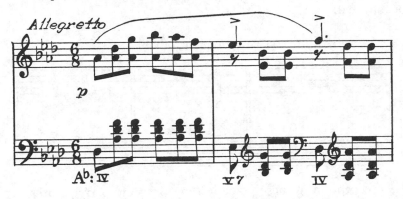

Problems of Voice Leading

In the resolution of the V^7, the tone to which the seventh resolves should not be doubled by similar motion. Such doubling gives this tone undue emphasis, throwing the chord out of balance.

Ex. 26   Doubled note of resolution

Note that when the V^7 is complete (all four tones of the chord being sounded), the following I will of necessity lack a fifth, having in most cases a tripled root (Ex. 27, a). Resolution to the complete tonic triad would create awkward voice leading (Ex. 27, b, c).

Ex. 27 V^7—I

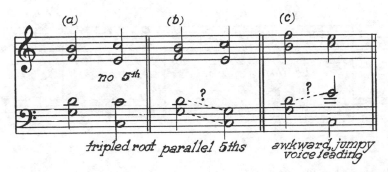

Should a complete I be desired, one tone of the V⁷—usually the fifth—must be omitted.

Ex. 28   V⁷ with fifth omitted; complete I triad

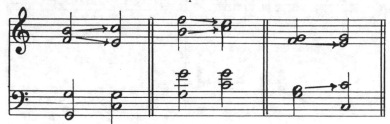

An exception to these voice-leading procedures frequently occurs in the perfect cadence, when the soprano moves from 2 to 1.

Ex. 29   Bach: *Ich dank' dir, lieber Herre*

At (*a*), the leading tone in the inner voice drops down to 5 instead of resolving in the usual way to the tonic.* This makes possible the use of both the complete V⁷ and I, producing a full sound at the cadence.

Another voice-leading procedure involves exchange of voices and delayed resolution of the active tones of the V⁷. The third and seventh in certain voices of the chord can move to other voices before resolving to I; the resolution will then follow from the new positions.

Ex. 30   Mozart: *Es lebe Sarastro*, from *The Magic Flute*

* A similar voice leading between V and I was noted in Ex. 16, page 180.

In Ex. 30, the third and seventh of the V⁷ are exchanged between the voices, resolving from their new positions. The chord seventh in the soprano at (*a*) shifts to the tenor at (*b*), resolving at (*c*). Likewise, the third of the V⁷, in the bass at (*d*), shifts to the soprano at (*e*), resolving at (*f*).

Inversions of the V⁷

Like the triad, the dominant seventh chord appears in various inversions, each identified by the intervals between the bass and the other tones of the chord.

Ex. 31   V⁷ Inversions

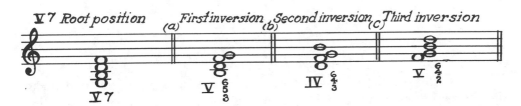

The *first inversion*, (*a*), with the third in the bass, is known as the $\frac{6}{5}$ chord, commonly shortened to $\frac{6}{5}$.

The *second inversion*, (*b*), with the fifth in the bass, is called the $\frac{6}{4}$ chord, usually shortened to $\frac{4}{3}$.

The *third inversion*, (*c*), with the seventh in the bass, is the $\frac{6}{4}$, or $\frac{4}{2}$ chord.

Functions of the V⁷ Inversions

The inversions of the V⁷ possess a variety of functions, partly identical with those of triad inversions, and partly unique. The V⁷ inversions serve:

1. To add increased tension and greater movement to the harmony.
2. To add richness and color.
3. To make possible gentler harmonic progression, avoiding the force of the root-position V⁷.
4. To form a more varied, smoothly flowing bass line.
5. As neighboring chords.
6. As passing chords.
7. As part of bass arpeggios.

Inversions of the V⁷, containing intervals in more unstable relationships, add to the momentum of the chord.

Ex. 32   Mozart: Sonata, K. 332, third movement

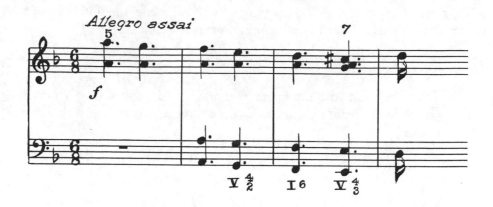

In this phrase from Mozart, the top line descends from 5 to 7, cadencing on the tonic. Imitating the falling line, the bass passes through the third inversion (V_2^4) and the second inversion (V_3^4) before reaching the tonic. By sounding the two inversions, the bass generates more energy than would have been produced by mere repetition of the V^7.

The third inversion is especially active, because the bass forms two dissonances with the chord tones above: a second and an augmented fourth (Exs. 31, *c*; 33).

Ex. 33   Bach: Toccata and Fugue in D minor, for Organ

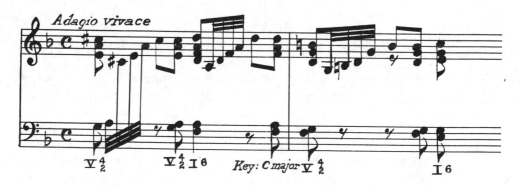

In the Bach Toccata, V_2^4 is stressed on the first beat of both measures. The downward pull of the chord seventh is emphasized, strongly impelling the chords to move and adding vigor to the passage.

Inversions of the V^7 also add to the color possibilities of the chord.

Ex. 34   Beethoven: Sonata, Op. 57 (*Appassionata*), second movement

Note the care with which Beethoven avoids doubling the sensitive seventh of the chord. The bass and the voice next to the top effect an exchange of tones between (*a*) and (*b*) and again between (*b*) and (*c*). The close position and low register produce a rich, resonant sonority.

Like inversions of the triad, those of the V^7 also make for gentler harmonic progressions by avoiding the heavy repetitions of the root-position chord. Compare the lightness of the bass in Mozart's Sonata, K. 283 (Ex. 35) with a version in which repeated root-position chords are substituted for the inversions (Ex. 36).

Ex. 35   Mozart: Sonata, K. 283

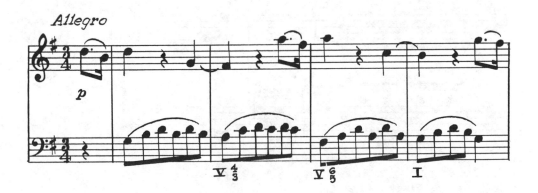

Ex. 36   Mozart: Sonata, K. 283, with root-position V⁷ chords

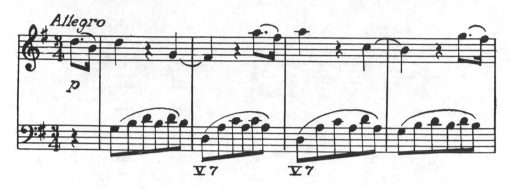

The use of V⁷ inversions also makes possible a smoothly flowing bass line.

Ex. 37   Mozart: Sonata, K. 283, second movement

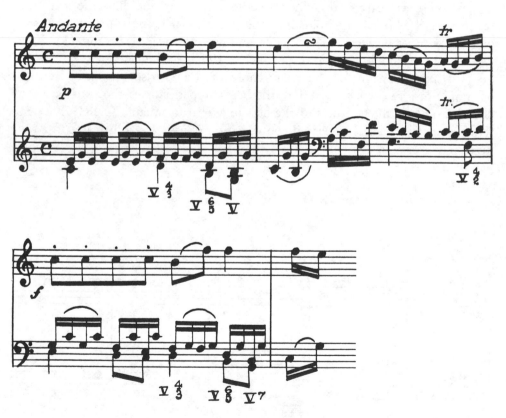

V⁷ Inversions as Passing, Neighboring, and Bass-Arpeggio Chords

The roles of the V⁶ and V$_4^6$ as passing and neighboring chords have already been noted. The addition of a seventh to such chords increases their richness, as shown in a comparison of progressions containing (*a*) inverted triads and (*b*) inverted seventh chords.

Ex. 38   V and V⁷ inversions in passing and neighboring chords

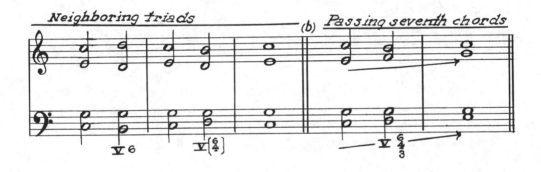

Note, in (*b*), the rising movement of the chord seventh in the alto to 5—instead of its usual falling resolution to 3. Such a resolution is common to progressions of this kind, in which the seventh acts as a passing tone, paralleling the movement of the bass. This is further illustrated in Ex. 39 (*a*).

Ex. 39   Beethoven: Sonata, Op. 31, No. 3, third movement

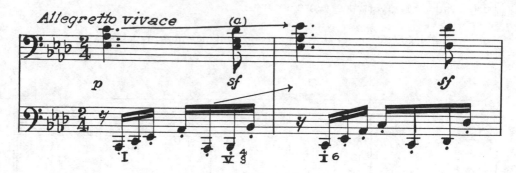

In Ex. 40 (*a*), the V$_5^6$ serves as a neighboring chord.

Ex. 40   Mozart: Six Viennese Sonatinas, No. 1, third movement

A final function of V^7 inversions consists of their roles in a bass arpeggio. When the lowest voice outlines a broken chord, each tone need not be considered as the bass of a separate chord block; it is enough to think of the arpeggio as a movement passing through various phases of the V^7.

Ex. 41   Mozart: Sonata for Violin and Piano, K. 547, second movement

Preparation of V⁷ Inversions

As with root-position V⁷ chords, V⁷ inversions were always carefully prepared by early classical masters. V⁷ inversions are most smoothly prepared in one of two ways:

1. By letting the V⁷ inversion follow a chord which contains the fourth degree. Consonant in the first chord, the 4 remains in the same voice, becoming the dissonant seventh of the second.

Ex. 42   Preparation of V⁷ inversion by fourth degree

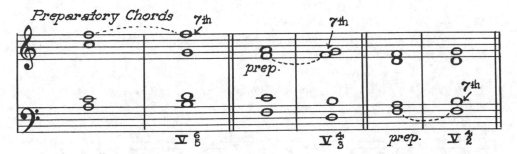

2. By approaching the seventh stepwise from above or below.

Ex. 43   Stepwise approach to the seventh

In Ex. 44 and 45, the bass tones at (*a*) are repeated at (*b*), forming the seventh of the ⁴₂ chord.

Ex. 44   Bach: Prelude No. 1, from *The Well-Tempered Clavier*, Book I

Ex. 45   Bach: Sarabande, from English Suite No. 4

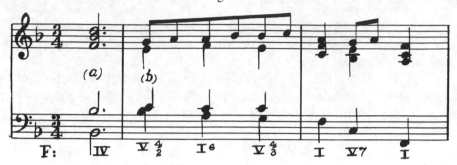

Stepwise movement through various inversions of the V⁷ occurs in a well-known chorus from Haydn's *Creation*.

Ex. 46   Haydn: The Heavens Are Telling, from *The Creation*

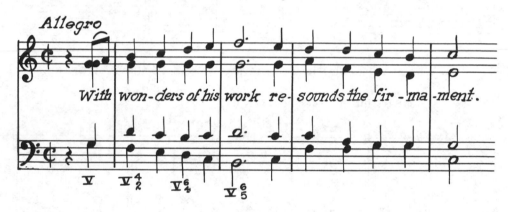

When writing V⁷ inversions, the student should follow the methods of the earlier composers for the present, always preparing the seventh.

In the works of later masters, the seventh of the V⁷ inversions—like that of the root-position chord—is often approached by leap. At times, the dissonance receives deliberate emphasis (Ex. 47, *a*)—in this case by being placed on a syncopated beat.

Ex. 47   March, from *The Notebook of Anna Magdalena Bach*

At other times, as in the slow movement of Beethoven's Sonata *Pathétique*, the unprepared seventh is so smoothly introduced (*a*) that it is difficult today to appreciate its former effect as a dissonance.

Ex. 48   Beethoven: Sonata, Op. 13 (*Pathétique*), second movement

Resolution of the V⁷ Inversions

The inversions of the V⁷, like those of the root-position chord, generally resolve to the nearest position of the I or I⁶. No matter in which voices they occur, the chord third and seventh resolve in the same way—the third rising, the seventh falling.*

Ex. 49   Resolutions of V⁷ inversions

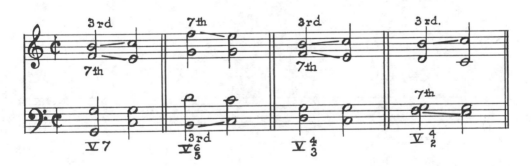

The root of the chord generally stays in place as a common tone, and the fifth usually moves to the tonic. For melodic reasons, however, the fifth may sometimes leap to the fifth of the I (see the second bar of Ex. 48).

Irregular resolutions of the V⁷ inversions are quite rare. Substitute or delayed resolutions, on the other hand, in which various tones of the chord exchange positions, or in which one inversion moves to another before proceeding to the I, are quite common.

---

* The rising resolution of the seventh in the passing V ⁴/₃ forms an exception. See Exs. 38 and 39.

Ex. 50   Bach: *Nun freut euch, Gottes Kinder all*

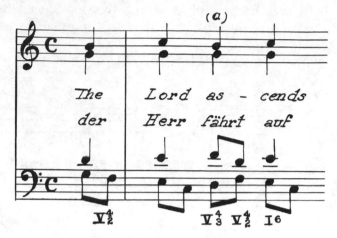

In Ex. 50, the V_3^4 is sounded at (*a*). Before resolving, however, the tenor and bass exchange parts, forming the V_2^4 briefly on the second half of the beat; the resolution follows.

The VII and V_5^6

The V_5^6 serves as a neighboring chord to the I, in a role similar to that of the VII[6] (discussed on page 313.)

Ex. 51 V_5^6 and VII as neighboring chords

The progressions in Ex. 51 show three voices moving stepwise away from and back to the I. In (*a*), the common tone, G, is sustained, forming the V_5^6; in (*b*) and (*c*), the omission of G from the middle chord forms the VII. Thus both chords have the same function. The neighboring-chord role of the VII is further illustrated in Ex. 52 (*a*).

Ex. 52   Mozart: Six Viennese Sonatinas, No. 4, last movement

The V $\frac{6}{5}$ appears in a comparable role in the second bar of Ex. 46.

Summary

1. The V⁷ chord consists of a major triad plus a minor third.
   a. Its active quality derives from the dissonant intervals it contains: the minor seventh and the diminished fifth (or augmented fourth).

2. V⁷ generally resolves to I.
   a. The chord seventh resolves downward.
   b. The chord third resolves upward.

3. The functions of the V⁷ chord are:
   a. To intensify harmonic movement.
   b. To increase the drive toward the cadence.
   c. To add richness and color to the harmony.
   d. To define a key quickly.
   e. Together with I, to harmonize all tones but 6.

4. The seventh of the V⁷ is prepared in three ways:
   a. By a chord containing 4.
   b. By stepwise approach.
   c. By leap (rougher preparation than the other two ways).

5. Irregular resolutions of the V⁷ are to VI, IV⁶, and IV.

6. Active tones (the third and seventh of the V⁷) may be exchanged among the voices, with resolution following from the new positions.
   a. Resolutions may also be delayed.
   b. Neither the third nor the seventh may be doubled.

7. In the progression V⁷—I, the fifth of one or the other chord is usually omitted.

8. Inversions of the V⁷ are numbered as follows:

a. First inversion: $\frac{6}{5}$

b. Second inversion: $\frac{4}{3}$

c. Third inversion: $\frac{4}{2}$

9. Functions of the V^7 inversions are:
   a. To add greater tension and forward movement.
   b. To add richness and color.
   c. To make possible gentler progression than the V^7 itself.
   d. To make possible a more varied, smoothly flowing bass line.
   e. To serve as embellishing chords.
   f. To serve as passing chords.
   g. To form bass arpeggio movements.

10. The seventh is prepared in the inversions in the same manner as in the V^7 itself.

11. Resolution of V^7 inversions is regularly to the I or I⁶.
    a. Resolution to other chords is rare.
    b. Delayed or substitute resolution of sensitive tones is common.

12. The VII and $V\frac{6}{5}$ serve the same function as neighboring chords.

Musical Analysis

Together with perceptive listening, musical analysis provides insight into the structure of music. By focusing on subtleties of construction, on the fine details of a composer's craftsmanship, and above all on interrelationships of the constituent elements, analysis reveals aspects of a composition not apparent to the casual listener. Distinguishing the individual roles of melody, harmony, and rhythm, it reveals their organic interplay in the creation of musical structure.

Analysis of short pieces can proceed in four stages: (1) an over-all view of the form, (2) a study of melodic and rhythmic patterns, (3) a study of harmonic structures, and (4) a synthesis of all elements forming the whole.

As an example, we shall analyze the Sarabande from Handel's Suite No. 11 (Ex. 53).

Ex. 53   Handel: Sarabande, from Suite No. 11

The Over-all Form

Looking over the composition as a whole, we find two phrases of equal length and balanced construction (8 + 8 = 16 bars). The opening phrase reaches a climax at (c), cadencing on V; the second phrase rises to a greater climax at (f), cadencing on I shortly thereafter. Order and symmetry are expressed through the parallelism of phrases and the contrast of cadences, one producing a sense of expectation and the other of fulfillment. Together, the two phrases form a parallel period.

Melodic and Rhythmic Patterns

Moving at a slow, measured pace, the melody evolves entirely from a well-defined two-bar motive. Marked chiefly by an insistent rhythm, the motive repeats almost literally six times in succession, breaking into a short, flowing melisma only near the end (*e*).

Melodically, the motive is very restricted, containing the narrowest of intervals. Repeated in sequence, the pattern rises in a long, sweeping wave; falls back to the original pitch; and mounts again to a strong climax at the end. The over-all curve forms a double rising wave. Among its small intervals, the fourth becomes a vivid leap—especially near the peak of both phrases (*b* and *e*).

The motive-variation techniques used are of the simplest: sequence, and (at *a*, *b*, and *d*) a slight rhythmic alteration. At the very end, however, an interesting expansion of the motive occurs.

Ex. 54   Handel: Sarabande, bars 1 and 2 compared with 12–16

The original motive is expanded in Ex. 54 to four bars by the insertion of new material between the original bars 1 and 2. Besides promoting rhythmic life, the new material doubles the length of the motive, lending weight to the final climax.

As to the mode of the composition, falling melodic minor predominates; its sober, mellow quality adds to the dignity of the Sarabande.

One final characteristic merits attention—the continuation of the movement by the bass each time the melody pauses. Three quarter notes in the left hand in bar 2 bridge the rhythmic gap between the end of the motive in that bar and its restatement in bar 3. The left-hand figure recurs so consistently that it might be regarded as a *countermotive*, playing an essential part in the rhythmic life of the piece.

Harmonic Structures

Before examining the broad harmonic structure of a work, it is important to analyze each chord. Then follows an identification of the root movements and embellishing tones (Ex. 55).

Ex. 55   Handel: Sarabande: Identification of chords, root movements, and
embellishing tones

As the next step, we study the general character of the chord structures and patterns of harmonic motion. Example 55 reveals the following:

1. Consisting almost entirely of triads in root position, the harmony possesses a sturdy, elemental character. One $^6_4$ chord, at (g), adds movement to the final climax.*

2. Tonality receives strong emphasis in this very stable music. Both phrases start with I and V and end with either IV—V or V—I. In the middle of each phrase, the lowered III and VII (at a, b, d, and e) suggest the major region of the minor mode, creating a welcome variation in harmonic color.

3. The sturdy nature of the music is further emphasized by the prevailingly strong root movements. Unusually predominant are the falling fourths, which occur no fewer than seven times; falling fifths and thirds also move the music forward.

4. Harmonic rhythm remains remarkably constant—one chord per bar for the first twelve bars. Acceleration to two and then three chords per bar at the end provides another factor in building the final climax.

5. The last conclusion concerning harmony is perhaps the most important, for it concerns the *broad direction of harmonic motion*. Each phrase moves from an area of stability and low harmonic tension to an area of instability and higher tension, returning then to the starting point. Phrase 1 leads from the tonic through secondary chords to a temporary rest on V (relatively stable, but still demanding to push onward). Phrase 2 begins once more on the tonic, leading now to harmonies of greater tension (from f to g), which form the climax of the piece. The strong perfect cadence reaffirms the return to the tonic, bringing the necessary release of tension at the end.

Seen in perspective, the two harmonic movements away from the tonic to areas of complication and tension parallel the two phrases and the two rising melodic curves (in Ex. 56, the letters refer to Ex. 53). The second movement is the boldest; it leads, as we shall see, to the most important point of the composition.

Ex. 56   Lines of melodic and harmonic intensity †

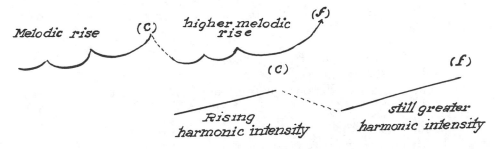

* Other unstable harmonic structures include two formations not yet studied: a suspension, at (c), and a VII$^6_5$ chord, at (f). (See Chapters XVI and XVII.)

† Compare Ex. 21, page 237.

Synthesis of All Elements Forming the Whole

In Handel's Sarabande, melody, harmony, and rhythm unite to form a perfectly balanced, symmetrical form. The slow, stately dance grows from a single motive whose narrow-range melody and incisive rhythm are repeated almost obsessively. The repetitive motive and rhythm, the slow ascent of the line in a double rising wave, and the vigorous root movements of the harmony combine to produce a strong forward motion.

The form, a period of two symmetrical phrases, is articulated by the two climaxes, one at the end of each phrase. The constant reiteration of rhythmic, melodic, and harmonic patterns for twelve consecutive bars makes the free movement at the end all the more striking. At the final climax, six factors combine to create the feeling of "arrival at a goal":

1. The motive, hitherto restricted to two bars, expands to four bars.
2. The rhythmic lockstep is broken, with a rush of faster notes.
3. Interrupted hitherto by rests in every bar, the melody becomes a flowing line.
4. The over-all melodic curve reaches its highest point (F).
5. The harmonic rhythm, one chord per bar, is doubled and tripled.
6. After a preponderance of root-position triads, the last four bars contain more complex chords: a VII$^6_5$ and a I$^6_4$.

The synthesis of these elements reveals the masterly way in which the composer has marshalled his forces to achieve the desired form.

Summary

Musical analysis follows four broad stages, each subdivided into smaller steps:

A. An over-all view of the form, including:
   1. The number of phrases.
   2. The length and relationship of phrases.

B. Melodic and rhythmic patterns:
   1. Melodic motion: steps, jumps.
   2. Range: narrow, medium, or wide over-all compass.
   3. Melodic curve or curves.
   4. Motive or motives: number, character, and length.

5. Characteristic intervals.
6. Rhythmic structure.
7. Types of motive variation used.
8. Climaxes: partial and over-all.
9. Mode.
10. Inner structure of the phrase.
11. Outer structure of the phrase.

C. Harmonic structures:
   1. Analysis of individual chords.
   2. Analysis of root movements.
   3. Analysis of embellishing tones.
   4. Summary of chord types.
   5. Means of affirming or negating the tonality.
   6. Harmonic rhythm.
   7. Cadences.
   8. Broad harmonic motion.

D. Synthesis of elements forming the whole: a summary of the basic features of A, B, and C, and the way they unite to form the character and structure of the entire composition.

XV

Piano-Style Harmony

Having acquired various techniques of harmony, melody, and rhythm, let us see how they interweave in the actual process of composition. To expand the possibilities, we shall write simple pieces for the instrument most readily available, the piano.

Block-Chord Style

Choral writing in harmonic idiom tends to emphasize the block-chord style.

Ex. 1   Haydn: The Heavens Are Telling, from *The Creation*

371

In one of the simplest methods of writing for the piano, the choral block-chord technique is simply transferred to the keyboard.

Ex. 2   Schumann: Chorale, from *Album for the Young*, Op. 68, No. 4

One advantage of the piano is its wide range—more than seven octaves, as compared with the choral range of a little more than three. On the piano it is easy to vary the sonority by shifting from one register to another.

Ex. 3   Beethoven: Sonata, Op. 31, No. 3, Menuetto

The keyboard offers two other advantages in writing block chords: (1) the possibility of enriching the sonority by increasing the number of voices; and (2) the possibility of varying the sonority by changing the number of voices from measure to measure. Such variations in the thickness or thinness of sound are called alterations of musical *texture*.

Ex. 4   Schubert: Piano Sonata, Op. 120

In the Piano Sonata, Op. 120, Schubert achieves considerable interest by constant variations in texture. The sonata opens with chords in six voices (note that the voices in the left hand simply double the corresponding right-hand voices). In bar 2, the number of parts is reduced to four, then three. This textural change of the first two bars is repeated in bars 3 and 4 (except that the first chord of bar 3 has seven voices). Bar 5 presents six voices again, and in bar 6 the number is once more reduced to four. These constant alterations in the number of voices add to the charm of the music.

As long as the block-chord style is retained, the change from choral to piano writing remains relatively minor. A more characteristically pianistic sound occurs in music featuring melody and accompaniment. Here the possibilities are numerous. Let us start with four simple pianistic techniques: jumping bass, broken-chord bass, rolling bass, and alternating bass.

Jumping Bass

In the so-called *jumping-bass* style of accompaniment, a single bass tone is sounded on the downbeat, with two or three voices completing the chord on the afterbeats. A block-chord progression can be changed into a melody with jumping-bass accompaniment as shown in Ex. 5.

Ex. 5   Block-chord progression changed to melody with jumping bass

Since the bass notes of a broken chord are usually sustained by the pedal, they are often notated simply as quarter notes. Such broken chords, it is understood, are played one pedal to the bar.

Ex. 6   Common notation of jumping bass

Note the characteristic open position of jumping-bass chords. With the root in the bass (Ex. 6), the afterbeat (a) usually has the third on top; when the third is in the bass, the fifth often appears on top (b).

To obtain a complete harmony in the accompaniment, a third voice is frequently added to the left-hand afterbeats.

Ex. 7   Schubert: Waltz, Op. 18a, No. 5

Jumping-bass patterns of this type have been widely used in pieces of a dance-like character ever since the eighteenth century. In such music, the chords often change once in a bar (Ex. 7).

It is by no means uncommon, however, for a composer to vary the harmonic rhythm by changing twice in a bar; he may further vary the pattern by omitting an afterbeat here or there—as at (a) and (b) in Ex. 8.

Ex. 8   Chopin: Mazurka, Op. 17, No. 1

Still another means of varying a jumping-bass pattern is to insert an occasional block chord embellished by passing tones, as at (*a*) in Ex. 9.

Ex. 9   Chopin: Mazurka, Op. 24, No. 3

The shift from block- to broken-chord writing does not change the basic principles of good voice leading. The same care must be taken with jumping-bass patterns as with block chords to ensure the preparation and resolution of dissonances. In bars 1 and 2 of Ex. 10, the voices resolve exactly as they would in block chords.

Ex. 10   Resolution of dissonances in broken and block chords

Alberti and Rolling Bass

Another type of accompaniment figure was widely favored in the eighteenth century—a triad or V⁷ in close position played as a broken chord. Called *Alberti bass*, this pattern appeared in various forms.

Ex. 11   Mozart: Sonata, K. 284

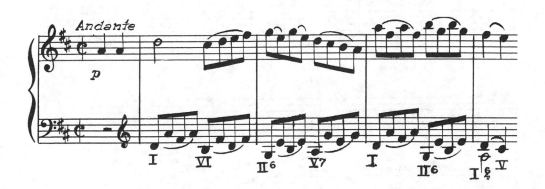

Ex. 12   Haydn: Piano Sonata

After the pedal came into general use in the nineteenth century, composers achieved richer sonorities by expanding the left-hand movement beyond the range of an octave.

The wide broken-chord pattern called *rolling bass* is a hallmark of Romantic piano music.

Ex. 13   Schubert: *Moment Musicale*, Op. 94, No. 2

When extended into an arpeggio covering several octaves, this rolling-bass accompaniment develops a rich sonority.

Ex. 14   Schumann: *Chopin*, from *Carnaval*, Op. 9

Alternating Bass

Mentioned in Chapter XI, an *alternating tone* forms a pseudo-$^6_4$—that is, a chord that sounds like a second inversion but does not function as such. The alternating bass serves merely to produce rhythmic motion when one harmony is repeated for several bars.

Ex. 15   Chopin: Waltz, Op. 64, No. 3

To observe the value of the alternating bass, play Ex. 15, repeating the left hand of bar 1 four times.

Variations in Texture

When writing for the piano, it is important to bear in mind the different sonorities of various registers. The lower you descend into the bass range, the heavier become the strings of the piano and the thicker the sound; the higher you go, the lighter the strings and the thinner the sound. It follows that the same chord does not sound equally well in all registers. A triad in close position, perfectly satisfactory in the middle or upper range, tends to be muddy in the lower reaches of the instrument.

Ex. 16   Chords in various registers

For this reason, composers generally write open-position chords in the lower register (unless they deliberately wish a thick, heavy effect).

The poor effect of close-position chords in the lower register can be seen in Ex. 17.

Ex. 17   Schubert: *Moment Musicale*, Op. 94, No. 2 (bass altered)

Compare the superiority of Schubert's original (Ex. 13). Also, note in Ex. 18 how Chopin leaves one or two empty chord tones between the downbeat and the afterbeat when the left hand is in low register.

Variations of texture in accompanied-melody style can be achieved in four ways:

1. By changing the thickness of the accompanying chords.
2. By changing their register.
3. By changing their rhythm.
4. By reversing the roles: writing melody in the left hand and accompanying chords in the right.

Ex. 18   Chopin: Mazurka, Op. 24, No. 1

Example 18 illustrates three ways of varying the texture. At (*a*), the chords in the left hand lie higher than in the preceding bars, and the bass tone on the downbeat is omitted, lending variety to the rhythm. At (*b*), the chords return to the original register, but now with only two voices. Such variations in texture, register, and rhythm add freshness and subtlety to an accompaniment pattern, and are characteristic of piano writing.

Melody in the left hand with accompanying chords in the right occurs frequently in Chopin.

Ex. 19   Chopin: Waltz, Op. 34, No. 2

In Ex. 20, the right hand has alternately a repeated tone and a chord.

Ex. 20   Chopin: Prelude, Op. 28, No. 6

Summary

1. Among the techniques of writing a simple piano accompaniment for a melody are:
   a. Block-chord style (similar to choral style).
      (i) This may be in four or more voices.
      (ii) The number of voices may be varied from bar to bar.
   b. Jumping-bass style: the bass alone on the downbeat, two or three voices on afterbeats.
   c. Alberti bass: broken chords in close position.
   d. Rolling bass: broken chords in open position, extending over an octave.
   e. Alternating bass: the fifth of the chord as the low tone of a jumping bass, on alternate beats or in alternate bars.

2. Chords can be set in close position in middle or high register; open position is preferable in low register.

3. Variety of texture can be attained by:
   a. Changing the thickness of the accompanying chords.
   b. Changing their register.
   c. Changing the rhythm of the accompaniment.
   d. Placing the melody in the left hand and the accompanying chords in the right.

Piano-Style Melody

For many centuries, chords evolved from older melodic processes. By the eighteenth century, however, when harmony had matured as an art, the influence began to act in reverse: now melodies were derived from harmonic patterns. Between 1700 and 1900, many themes of sonatas, concertos, and symphonies and many songs and operatic arias were conceived in chordal terms.

Since the piano was a favored instrument during this period, most piano melodies from Philip Emanuel Bach to Debussy were based on harmonic progressions.

Harmonic Generation of Melody

The I and V^7 chords, played alone, are a commonplace in music.

Ex. 21   I and V^7 chords

But when various rhythmic and melodic ideas are developed from these chords, distinctive musical thoughts emerge.

Ex. 22   Haydn: Symphony No. 94 (*Surprise*), second movement

Ex. 23   American folk song: Skip to My Lou

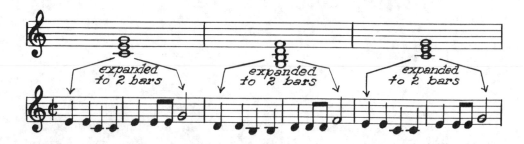

Ex. 24   Johann Strauss: *The Beautiful Blue Danube*

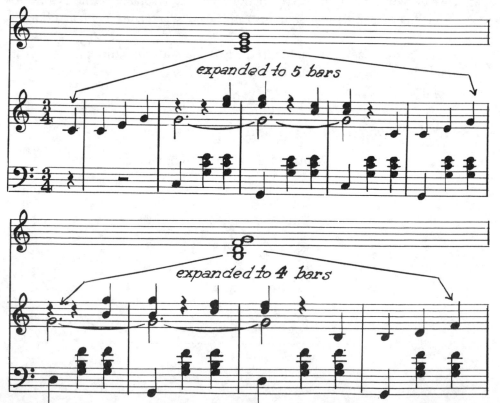

A more complex chord progression can give rise to a more highly developed melody.

Ex. 25   Beethoven: Sonata, Op. 2, No. 1

In addition to leaping along chord lines, melody may also evolve from scale passages based on harmonic patterns.

Ex. 26   Schubert: Impromptu, Op. 90, No. 2

Pianistic Elaboration of Progressions

Melodies consisting of embellishing tones circling around well-defined chord patterns constitute another type of harmony-engendered phrase.

Ex. 27   Beethoven: Rondo, Op. 51, No. 1

In still another type of harmony-centered melody, embellished arpeggios extend over several octaves.

Ex. 28   Schumann: *Vogel als Prophet*, from *Waldscenen*

From a rather elementary chord progression (Ex. 29), Philip Emanuel Bach derived a distinctly pianistic melody, combining arpeggios, scales, and turning figures (Ex. 30).

Ex. 29   Chord progression

Ex. 30   Ph. Em. Bach: *Solfeggietto*

The keyboard lends itself to virtuoso passages developed from chord patterns. Note, in Ex. 31, the characteristically pianistic combination of turning figures, scale passages, arpeggios, and block chords in one four-measure phrase.

Ex. 31   Chopin: Prelude, Op. 28, No. 10

The preceding pages have presented several techniques by which pianistic melody evolves from harmonic progressions. Further examples in endless variety can be found in the piano works of Beethoven, Schubert, Mendelssohn, Chopin, Schumann, and Brahms among nineteenth-century composers, and in the music of Debussy, Ravel, Bartók, and Prokofiev among twentieth-century masters.

Summary

Pianistic melody may be evolved from basic chord progressions in several ways, by the use of:

1. Simple or embellished broken chords.

2. Scale passages.

3. Turning figures.

4. Embellished arpeggios extending over several octaves.

5. A combination of these techniques.

XVI

Suspension and Pedal Point

In the chapter on embellishing tones (Chapter VI), it was indicated that more were to follow. Suspensions and pedal points complete the list.

Suspension

A *suspension* is created by a tone held over when the chord changes. The clash of the held-over tone with the new chord produces a tension in the harmony and a rhythmic delay in the melody. The tension is eased when the delayed tone resolves to the nearest step, usually downward. Rhythmically speaking, the point of suspense occurs on a strong beat, the resolution on a weak one.

One of the most useful embellishing tones, the suspension has a variety of functions, from delaying rhythmic movement to heightening expressive intensity.

Every suspension has three stages:

1. Preparation: the note to be held over forms part of the preceding chord.
2. Suspension: the note is held over while the chord changes on the strong beat.
3. Resolution: the note moves one step, usually downward.

Ex. 1   Suspension: the three stages

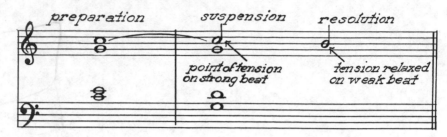

The techniques of preparing and resolving suspensions are older than harmony itself, having been well known in the early Renaissance.

Ex. 2   Obrecht: *Parce Domine*

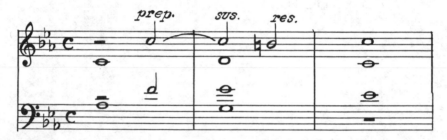

The soprano forms part of the first chord (*prep.*); becomes a dissonant suspension (*sus.*) when the chord changes on the strong beat in bar 2; and resolves downward (*res.*), becoming a consonance on the following weak beat.

Suspensions are not limited to the soprano; they can occur in any voice. Example 3 shows a suspension in the alto.

Ex. 3   Josquin des Prés: *Ave verum corpus Christi*

A suspension is most effective when it creates a tension with the other voices of the chord. A lovely example occurs at the beginning of "Dido's Lament" in Purcell's opera *Dido and Aeneas*.

Ex. 4   Purcell: Dido's Lament, from *Dido and Aeneas*

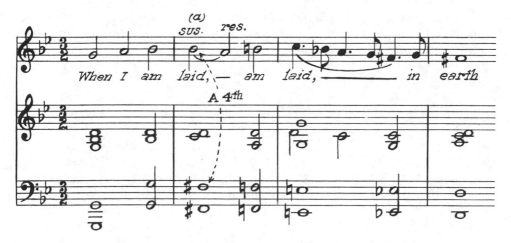

When I am laid,— am laid,———— in earth

The suspension at (*a*), forming the interval of a diminished fourth between soprano and bass, produces a harmonic clash that underscores Dido's anguish.

Even in the twentieth century, the suspension retains its power to reinforce an expressive moment.

Ex. 5   Hindemith: *Die Darstellung Maria in Tempel*, from *Das Marienleben*

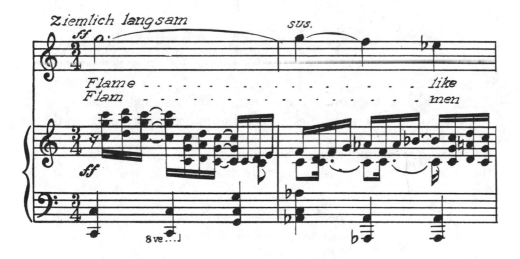

A suspension can be either a tied or a repeated note. The former is the earlier type, but since the Baroque period both types have been widely used.

Suspension in Upper Voice

Suspensions in the upper voices are named according to the interval formed with the bass. The four main possibilities are the ninth, seventh, sixth, and fourth above a bass tone, which resolve as follows: 9—8, 7—6, 6—5, and 4—3.

Ex. 6   Suspensions in an upper voice

Although they are prepared and resolved in similar manner, not all suspensions have the same effect. Their impact varies according to the dissonance of the intervals formed with the other tones of the chord; the more dissonant the interval, the more striking the suspension. In the following list, the most dissonant suspensions are near the top, the least dissonant near the bottom:

> Minor ninth and major seventh
> Major ninth and minor seventh
> Perfect fourth*
> Sixth (consonant)

In Ex. 7, the minor ninth in the soprano (*a*) clashes sharply with the bass. Compare the intensity of (*a*) with the blandness of the fourth and sixth suspensions at (*b*).

* The diminished fourth, however, is quite dissonant (see Ex. 4).

Ex. 7   Bach: Prelude No. 12, from *The Well-Tempered Clavier*, Book II

The major ninth is a milder suspension than the minor one.

Ex. 8   Chopin: Mazurka, Op. 41, No. 2

The major seventh suspension often serves to strengthen the drive to the cadence.

Ex. 9   Josquin des Prés: *Pleni sunt coeli*

Compare the effect of the minor sevenths in Ex. 10 with that of the major seventh in Ex. 9.

Ex. 10   Orlando di Lasso: *Psalm of Penitence*, No. 2

The lack of tension in the 6—5 suspension, already mentioned, is illustrated in Ex. 11.

Ex. 11   Orlando di Lasso: *Expectatio justorum*

The fourth, when used solely in relation to the bass in a two-voice setting, has almost as little tension as the sixth.

Ex. 12   Bach: Two-Part Invention No. 9

When, on the other hand, a suspension forming a fourth with the bass occurs in a three- or four-voice chord in which it creates a dissonant interval with *another voice of the chord*, the effect is strong.

Ex. 13   Vittoria: *O magnum mysterium*

Ad - mi - ra - bi - le - sa - cra   -   men   -   tum,

At the cadence, the soprano forms a fourth with the bass—a gentle relationship. The interval of the seventh between soprano and tenor gives the chord its heightened quality.

Suspension in Lowest Voice

Suspensions in the lowest voice are those forming intervals of a second, fourth, fifth, and ninth with an upper voice above. The normal resolutions are downward, to the step below: 2—3, 4—5, 5—6, and 9—10.

Ex. 14   Suspensions in the lowest voice

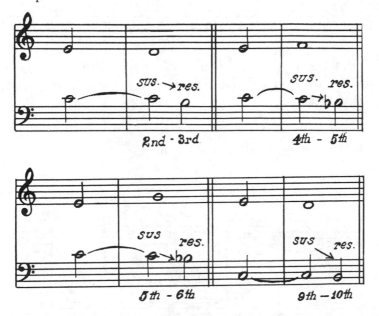

As with suspensions in an upper voice, those in the lowest voice are most telling when they produce dissonances—in this case, seconds or ninths. Minor seconds are the sharpest, minor ninths nearly as harsh.

Ex. 15   Bach: Prelude 22, from *The Well-Tempered Clavier*, Book I

Compare the effect of the major and minor seconds in Ex. 15 with the minor ninth in Ex. 16.

Ex. 16   Gluck: Overture to *Iphigenia in Aulis*

When the lowest voice suspends a fourth or fifth with only one voice above it, the effect is extremely mild. For this reason it was rarely used, except in early Renaissance music.

Ex. 17   Josquin des Prés: *Pleni sunt coeli*

Ex. 18   Josquin des Prés: *Agnus dei*

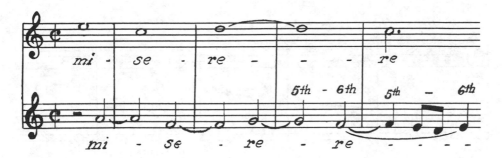

Doubling of the Suspension

The old contrapuntal masters, aware of the effect of the suspension, were careful to avoid any move in other voices that might detract from it. To this end they observed the principle: *when a note is suspended, the note of resolution is not sounded in another voice at the same time.* Simultaneous sounding of the suspension and the note of resolution destroys the feeling of suspense, vitiating the entire effect.

Ex. 19   Simultaneous sound of suspension and note of resolution

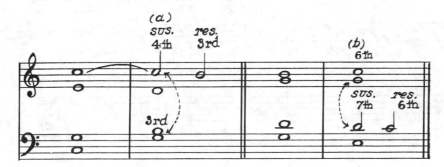

At (*a*) the soprano suspends the fourth; it will resolve to the third presently. But the tenor, sounding the third simultaneously, destroys the effect of suspense. The same muddled result occurs at (*b*) where the suspension (D) in the tenor loses its value because the note of resolution (C) is sounded at the same time by the soprano.

At a later period, an exception was made to the rule of non-simultaneity. Composers felt that a note of resolution could be sounded *in the bass* at a distance of a ninth or more away from the suspension. Due to the wide space in between, the sonority was considered pleasing and effective (Ex. 20, *a*).

Ex. 20   Beethoven: Sonata, Op. 27, No. 2, second movement

When several suspensions follow each other so that a note of resolution immediately becomes another suspension, we speak of a *chain of suspensions*. Such a chain of dissonances and rhythmic displacements creates a strong forward drive. This device was used from Orlando di Lasso to Mozart (and after) to develop climactic tension.

Ex. 21   Orlando di Lasso: *Expectatio justorum*, from *Cantiones duarem vocem*

Ex. 22   Mozart: Sonata, K. 533

Another structure worthy of mention is the *multiple suspension. Double suspensions* (two tones held over) have already been quoted (Exs. 7 and 20). A triple suspension, sometimes called a *suspension chord*, can produce a rich harmonic color (Ex. 23, *a*).

Ex. 23   Beethoven: Sonata, Op. 22, second movement

Strict and Free Suspensions

In the Renaissance and early Baroque periods, suspensions were always prepared and resolved according to strict rules. The rule governing the preparation of the suspension provided that *the note of preparation shall be as long as or longer than the suspended note.* (If, for example, the suspension is a half note, the preparation must be a half note or longer.) Re-examination of the examples in this chapter will show that most suspensions follow this rule.

Starting in the later Baroque, however, composers adopted a freer approach to the preparation of suspensions. Examples 23 and 24 show suspended tones prepared by tones of shorter duration.

Ex. 24   Schumann: *Chiarina*, from· *Carnaval*, Op. 9

Another relaxation of the rules regarding suspensions occurred when composers began to *resolve them upward* as well as downward. Such upward resolutions were already known to Bach (Ex. 25, *a*).

Ex. 25   Bach: Sarabande, from English Suite No. 2

Upward resolution of suspensions became common among the composers in the late eighteenth and nineteenth centuries. Brahms was fond of the practice, using it with characteristic delicacy (Ex. 26, *a*).

Ex. 26   Brahms: Intermezzo, Op. 76, No. 7

Sometimes a suspended note may move to another note before resolving. Such a detour is called an *embellished resolution.*

Ex. 27   Beethoven: Sonata, Op. 14, No. 1, second movement

Ex. 28   Bach: Fugue No. 4, from *The Well-Tempered Clavier*, Book I

In Ex. 27 (*a*), the suspended B arrives at A only after passing through A's lower neighbor, G sharp—an embellished resolution. In Ex. 28, F sharp in the tenor (*a*) makes a detour involving three embellishing tones before arriving at its goal, E sharp (*b*).

Example 29 is a list of various embellishments used in the resolution of suspensions.

Ex. 29   Embellishments in resolution of suspensions

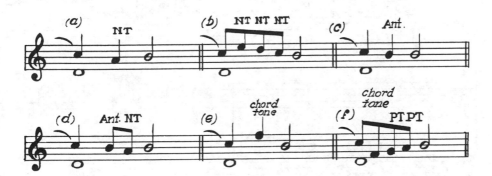

(*a*) A neighboring tone.
(*b*) Three neighboring tones.
(*c*) An anticipation of the resolution.
(*d*) An anticipation and its neighboring tone.
(*e*) A leap to another tone of the chord.
(*f*) The same, with the space between the chord tone and the tone of resolution filled in by passing tones.

Pedal Point

A *pedal point* is a single pitch held as a sustained tone or as a series of repeated tones while the chords change over, under, or around it. Found most often in the bass (it originated in the organist's practice of holding a low pedal tone while improvising), it occurs also in middle and top voices.

The most effective pedal points generally start and end as chord tones, but soon after starting become dissonant in relation to the chords accompanying them. The persistent retention of one tone (usually the tonic or dominant) affirming the key permits the composer to move harmonies in a free and at times quite dissonant manner without endangering the sense of tonality. The conflict between the tonally fixed pedal and the wandering harmonies can be a valuable dramatic device, as Bach so often demonstrated.

Ex. 30   Bach: Prelude No. 2, from *The Well-Tempered Clavier*, Book I

Not all pedal points are quite so elaborate. Mozart used the device simply—as a repeated note, over which tonic and dominant chords alternate.

Ex. 31   Mozart: Sonata, K. 310

In *Boris Godunov*, Moussorgsky wrote an upper pedal—an octave tremolo high in the orchestra—above the choral voices in middle register.

Ex. 32   Moussorgsky: Coronation Scene, from *Boris Godunov*

star - that   bright-ens the   Hea - vens,

A striking example of an inner pedal point is found in Chopin's *Rain-drop* Prelude: G sharp, repeated obsessively, persists with minor interruptions from one end of the composition to the other. Example 33 shows a few bars from the middle section.

Ex. 33   Chopin: Prelude, Op. 28, No. 15

Consonance and Dissonance

The use of changing chords over a fixed pedal point brings up once more the question of consonance and dissonance, already touched on several times. A fixed definition has not been attempted here, for the two terms are purely relative, changing with the changing tastes of a culture. What seems dissonant at one historical period often becomes consonant at a later one; the same experience occurs in the musical development of an individual.

About 1600, as we have seen, the dominant seventh chord was considered a harsh dissonance; critics bitterly denounced Monteverdi for introducing such a violent combination of sounds without preparation. Later, of course, the former harshness changed to sweetness, and the chord became a commonplace. A similar process occurred in other centuries: Mozart, Beethoven, Wagner, Stravinsky, and Ives were assailed as madmen for "dissonant" chords that fifty years after their time were freely accepted as consonant.

The distinction, however, has not lost all validity. Relative though it may be, the difference between consonance and dissonance remains important, indicating degrees of greater and lesser tension *within any given style*. As long as music remains an expressive art, variations in levels of harmonic intensity will lend meaning to the contrast of the two terms.

Summary

1. A suspension is a tone held over when the chord changes, producing:
   a. A rhythmic delay in the melody.
   b. A tension in the harmony.

2. The point of tension occurs on the strong beat, the resolution on a weak beat.

3. The suspended note is prepared by forming part of the preceding chord.

4. In traditional suspensions the suspended note:
   a. Is tied over from the preceding tone.
   b. Resolves downward.

5. In free suspensions the suspended note:
   a. Is a repeated note.
   b. Resolves up or down.

6. Suspensions in an upper voice include the ninth, seventh, sixth, and fourth above a bass tone. Their resolutions are:

$$9—8$$
$$7—6$$
$$6—5$$
$$4—3$$

7. Suspensions in the lowest voice include the second, fourth, fifth, and ninth below an upper voice. Their resolutions are:

$$2—3$$
$$4—5$$
$$5—6$$
$$9—10$$

8. Simultaneous sounding of a suspended note and its note of resolution is to be avoided, except for the suspension of a ninth above a bass tone.

9. A series of consecutive suspensions is called a chain of suspensions.

10. Suspensions can occur in two or three voices simultaneously.

11. In strict suspensions, the note of preparation is at least as long as the suspension: in free suspensions, it may be shorter.

12. An embellished resolution is one that passes through other tones before arriving at the note of resolution.

13. A pedal point is a single pitch sustained while chords change (usually forming dissonances) over, under, or around it.

14. Concepts of consonance and dissonance have changed in various periods. The distinction has validity, nonetheless, as a description of greater or lesser degrees of tension within a given style.

Embellishing Tones: A Résumé

Embellishing tones can be grouped into two categories:

1. Those that occur on weak beats, or between the beats, are mainly *decorative* in character and do not affect the harmonic structure. They include:

   a. The passing tone.
   b. The neighboring tone.
   c. The anticipation.
   d. The escaped tone.

Ex. 34   Decorative embellishing tones

2. Those that occur on strong beats are *expressive* in character, and affect the harmonic structure by displacing chord tones or clashing with them. They include:

   a. The appoggiatura.
   b. The suspension.
   c. The accented passing and neighboring tones.
   d. The pedal point.

When an embellishing tone occurs on the beat, if approached by leap it is an appoggiatura; if by step, an accented passing or neighboring tone; and if prepared by the same tone, a suspension.

Ex. 35   Approaches to appoggiatura, accented passing tone, accented neighboring tone, and suspension

Words,
Melody, and
Harmony

The human voice is the basic melody instrument. First and most universal of all instruments (we each bear it with us wherever we go), the voice has the unique capacity to utter words and music at the same time. With this virtue comes an obligation for the composer of vocal music: unlike the musician concerned only with instrumental writing, he must understand the value of words and their relationship to music.

Although song is a basic expression of the child, the untrained person, and the folk musician, the joining of words and music may not be so simple as it appears. A number of composers, even great ones, failed at times to understand its essential character. Chopin wrote very little for the voice; Mendelssohn, except for his oratorio, *Elijah*, had little success with it; and even Beethoven, who created many glorious vocal works, was occasionally ill at ease in writing for the voice.

The mating of text and sound is an art that demands special skill and aptitude. Words tend to impose their rhythm, inflection, and meaning on the music, guiding the composer in molding the melodic line and even the harmonic direction. Music adds new implications to a text, often strengthening, sometimes changing its emotional qualities, and imposing its formal patterns on those of prose and verse alike.

410

Influence of Words on Melodic Rhythm

The prime influence of the text falls on melody: words offer many suggestions for melodic rhythms and inflections. In religious chants and operatic recitatives, the rhythm of the words is transferred intact to the music. Sometimes it becomes unnecessary to notate rhythmic values; they are obviously those of the text.

Ex. 36   Plain chant: *Laus Deo Patri*

From Masterpieces of Music before 1750, *compiled and edited by Carl Parrish and John F. Ohl. Copyright 1951 by W. W. Norton & Company, Inc., New York, New York. Reprinted by permission of the publisher.*

When poetry is metrical, the accents of the words tend to be impressed on the melody. Folk music gives us countless examples.

> When Ísrael wás in Égypt lánd,
> Lét my péople gó.

Ex. 37   Negro spiritual: Go Down Moses

Such perfect matching of poetic and musical rhythms marks the work of the authentic folk musician. Less happy were the efforts of those poetasters in colonial America who set new words to traditional melodies with little concern for agreement between the meters of text and tune.

> Confésse Jehóvah thánkfully,
> For Hé is góod; for His mércie
> Contínuéth foréver.

For this grand old "Strassburg tune," an early New Englander contrived a text setting that is a masterpiece of ineptitude. Not only did he misplace accents; he gave the strongest notes, at the end of the first two lines, to weak syllables: "thankfulLY" and "merCIE."

Ex. 38   Bay Psalm Book: Confesse Jehovah

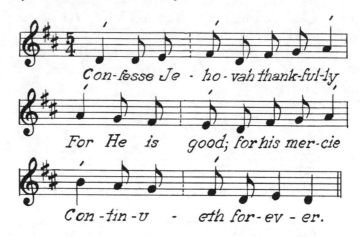

Prosody

Prosody is the correct musical setting of word accents (illustrated in both good and bad examples in Exs. 37 and 38–39, respectively). The special characteristics of every language affect the prosody of its vocal music. English, as compared with French, is a more strongly accented tongue. A two-syllable word often bears a strong accent on the first syllable—a trait alien to French.

Ex. 39   Go Down Moses, French words

Thus, French words added to "Go Down Moses" sound awkward. The rhythm in bar 2, not native to the French language, is characteristic of English; from common speech it has passed over into English and American song. (This rhythm, marked with an asterisk, has been called, in unduly restrictive fashion, the "Scotch snap.")

Ex. 40   Purcell: The Frost Scene, from *King Arthur* (1691)

Ex. 41   Scotch song: Comin' thro' the Rye

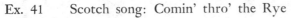

If a bo-dy   meet a bo-dy   com-in' thro' the rye.

Ex. 42   Negro spiritual: All God's Chillun Got Wings

Heab'n,——   Hea-b'n,——   Hea-b'n,——   Ev'ry bo-dy talk-in' 'bout

The joining of Negro syncopation to its older English counterpart has led to the further development of English prosody. Traditionally, the word Jericho might normally be inflected "Jéricho," and set to music as in bar 1 below; how much livelier is the American Negro version (bar 2):

Je – ri - cho   *Je – ri - cho*

The subject of American prosody is a long one, and would involve a detailed study of folk and popular music, whose matching of poetic and musical rhythm is generally exemplary.

Influence of Words on Melodic Line

Every language has its own speech melody. The foreigner with a perfect schoolbook command of English often betrays his inability to master the subtle curves of inflection that are second nature to the native. Recitative appropriate for Italian does not sit well in German; nor French recitative in English: the speech melody requires subtle and painstaking translation.

Because of the inflected character of English, it is quite normal to mark stressed syllables with wide intervals:

No - bo - dy knows de trou -ble I   seen,

Rhythmic stress, a higher pitch, or both generally emphasize important words in a phrase. Thus, "NObody knows de TROUB-le I seen." We should find ludicrous "NoboDY knows DE trouBLE I seen."

The composers of Shakespeare's England had a fine ear for the matching of words and melody. Example 43 shows a remarkably vivid setting by Thomas Morley of a colloquial Elizabethan text.

Ex. 43   Morley: Whither Away So Fast?*

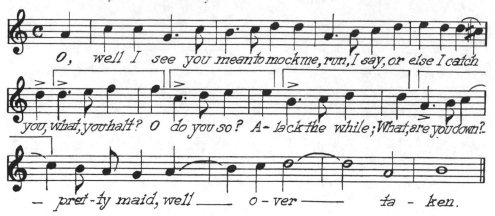

In addition to their rhythm and inflection, words have influenced melody in a broader sense through their meanings and associations. On a naïve level, one finds the imitation of natural and man-made sounds: the tolling of bells (*Din, don, din*) in *Frère Jacques*, the street cries of London in Elizabethan rounds, the song of the cuckoo in many madrigals and folk songs.

Ex. 44   German folk song: *Kuckuck, Kuckuck, ruft's aus dem Wald*

On a more developed level, there is the suggestion of imagery through musical symbolism. For centuries, composers used a rising line on the words "ascending," "climbing," "Heaven," and the like; and a falling one for the opposite. Darkness was suggested by the use of flats or low tones, and flowing waters by gently murmuring figures. In the oratorio *Israel in Egypt*, Handel suggested rain, lightning, the jumping of frogs, even the splitting of the Red Sea by appropriate melodic figures. The following excerpt from *The Messiah* speaks for itself.

Ex. 45   Handel: Thus Saith the Lord, from *The Messiah*

* From Morris: *Contrapuntal Techniques in the Sixteenth Century* (Oxford, 1922). The brackets and accents are by Mr. Morris.

Influence of Words on Harmony

Harmony, too, is often colored by verbal meanings. We have noted Purcell's use of the augmented triad to depict a weird scene (Ex. 9, Chapter XIII) and of dissonant suspensions to portray Dido's anguish (Ex. 4 in this chapter). Volume II shows modulations, the diminished seventh chord, and other harmonic phenomena introduced into a phrase to underscore expressive and dramatic implications of a text.*

The evolution of the relationship between harmonic motion and verbal meanings forms a large part of the history of music from the sixteenth through the nineteenth centuries. Expressive imagery may reflect more than a word or a phrase; it often illustrates the basic idea of a text. In one of the most dramatic moments of Bach's *St. Matthew Passion*, words, rhythm, melody, and harmony unite in depicting an awesome scene.

Ex. 46   Bach: *St. Matthew Passion*

* See especially "Dramatic Sources of Harmony and Melody" in Chapter X, Volume II.

Song Accompaniments

Starting in the late eighteenth century, a great literature of solo songs with piano accompaniment grew up. One of the more personal forms of expression, the song (German: *Lied*) is characterized by a rich and varied interplay between the voice and piano parts. Many different forms of accompaniment have been developed by such masters of the song as Schubert, Schumann, Brahms, Moussorgsky, Debussy, Ravel, and Ives. A few of the many diverse styles of piano accompaniment should be mentioned here.

The simplest of all has the right hand of the piano supporting the vocal line throughout, while a jumping-bass figure appears in the left hand. Ives' "Old Home Day" (1920) contains early reflections of jazz syncopation.

Ex. 47   Ives: Old Home Day

In another type of accompaniment, the piano part supports only certain tones of the melody, without duplicating its line.

Ex. 48   Moussorgsky: The Orphan

A third kind of accompaniment has the piano sustaining background harmonies over which the melody moves freely. In Schubert's *Morgengruss*, the entry of the voice is preceded by four bars of piano introduction.

Ex. 49   Schubert: *Morgengruss*

Repeated chords form another type of background accompaniment. Note Brahms' use of syncopation in Ex. 50.

Ex. 50   Brahms: *Sapphische Ode*

Still another accompaniment figure consists of broken-chord patterns flowing up and down beneath an independent vocal line.

Ex. 51   Schumann: *Widmung*

Arpeggios frequently occur in a harmonic background. Note the use of a repeated I^9 chord in Ex. 52. Note also the polyrhythmic pattern of the accompaniment: a 7/8 grouping within a meter of 4/4.

Ex. 52   Ives: Two Little Flowers

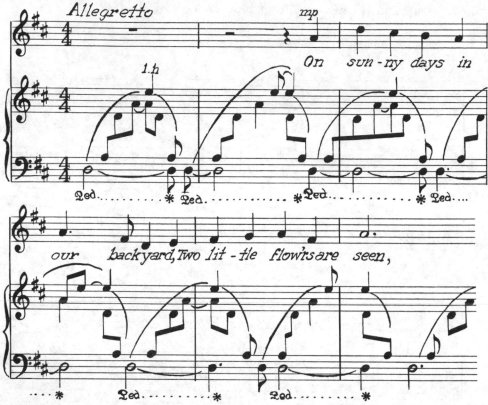

In an imaginative approach to song writing, the piano part suggests a specific mood, setting the scene before the voice enters. Thus, in Hugo Wolf's *Das verlassene Mägdlein*, the first four bars, with their thin, empty sound, convey the bleakness of early morning.

Ex. 53   Wolf: *Das verlassene Mägdlein*

Early the rooster crows, Tiny stars scarce disappeared,
Früh wann die Hähne krähn, eh' die Sternlein schwinden,

Then must I tend the hearth, set the fire burning.
muss ich am Herde stehn, muss Feuer zünden.

Finally, a most interesting type of song is one in which the piano has an independent melody. Alternating with that of the voice, it plays a special role in depicting the action or scene indicated by the poem. In Schubert's *Der Leiermann* ("The Organ-Grinder"—Ex. 54), the piano suggests the unchanging drone of the hand organ; and in bars 3–4 and 7–8, the impoverished melody played on it.

Ex. 54   Schubert: *Der Leiermann*

Organ grinder's playing just outside the town,
Drüben hinter'm Dorfe steht ein Leiermann,

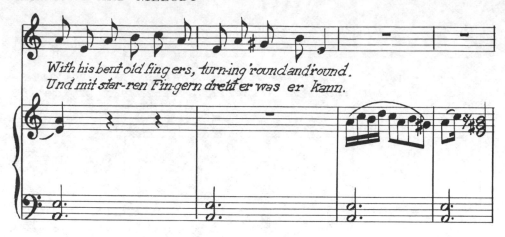

With his bent old fingers, turn-ing 'round and 'round.
Und mit star-ren Fingern dreht er was er kann.

Musical Forces Governing Vocal Music

So much stress has been laid on the power of words to shape the course of music that a mistaken conclusion might be drawn: that the text governs completely, and music has no necessities of its own. Nothing could be further from the truth. Joined to words, music remains nonetheless music, with its own requirements, directions, powers, and forms.

Musical form does not depend solely on the text. With the possible exception of recitative, whose function is to transmit the words as directly as possible, other types of vocal composition have their own special musical structures and characteristics. Rarely is there anything in the words of a song to suggest the return of a phrase or the choice of a specific musical pattern.* These are musical necessities and requirements; often they impose themselves on the words by a process of reverse influence.†

Even in folk music, lines of text have often apparently been added for the sole purpose of providing a musical balance.

> I'll give to you a paper of pins
> And that's the way our love begins,
> If you will marry me.

The idea is complete in these three lines; the repeated words (Ex. 55, *a* to *b*) serve to round out the *musical* form.

Ex. 55   American folk song: Paper of Pins

I'll give to you a   pa-per of pins, and that's the way our

---

* For a complex musical pattern set to an elementary verbal one, see Ex. 33, page 442, and the text accompanying it.

† In popular music, a lyric writer, knowing the demands of composers, will often construct his verses to fit the pattern of an A—A—B—A tune as yet unwritten.

love be gins, If you will mar-ry me, me, me, if
you will mar-ry   me.

Just as in the folk song, so in many other types of vocal composition, purely musical demands often govern the development of words as well as of melody, harmony, and structure. In the operas of Mozart, the *Lieder* of Schubert, and the tunes of Gershwin, music—inspired as it may be by words— nevertheless attains its own fullest development.

Summary

1. In writing vocal music, an understanding of the relation of words and music is essential.

2. Words influence the rhythmic patterns of melody.
   a. In religious chant and operatic recitative, the rhythm of the words is transmitted intact to the music.
   b. The meter of the melody tends to agree with that of the words.
   c. Accented words or syllables tend to receive musical accents.
   d. Prosody is the correct musical setting of the words.
   e. The strong inflections of the English language have led to musical settings often strongly inflected, as in the "Scotch snap."

3. Words also influence the pitch contour of a melody.
   a. Patterns of verbal inflection suggest melodic inflections.
   b. On the simplest level, melodic imagery can imitate natural sounds.
   c. On another level, melodic imagery may enhance the effect of words expressing human emotions or portraying natural phenomena.

4. Words can also influence harmonic procedures. Dissonant chords or embellishing tones can be used to emphasize words that depict strange or dramatic events or strong emotions.

5. Seven simple types of song accompaniments are those in which:
   a. The right hand of the piano duplicates the vocal line, the left hand forming a chordal background.
   b. The piano part supports only certain tones of the melody.
   c. The piano sustains chords while the melody moves freely.
   d. The piano part contains repeated chords.
   e. The piano part consists of broken-chord patterns.
   f. The piano part consists of arpeggios.
   g. The piano part sets the mood of the song.
   h. The piano has its independent melody, alternating with that of the voice.

XVII

Seventh Chords

Our study of seventh chords has thus far covered only one type, the dominant seventh, found on V of the diatonic scale. Seventh chords of various types, however, are found on all degrees of the major and minor scales (Exs. 1, 2). The sevenths they contain have been considered traditionally as dissonant tones.

Ex. 1   Seventh chords in major

Ex. 2   Seventh chords in minor

Functions of the Seventh Chord

To some extent, the functions of the seventh chord are similar to those of the dominant seventh.* They serve (1) to add richness and color to the harmony; (2) to intensify harmonic movement, by providing active chords on all degrees of the scale; and (3) to add drive to the cadence.

Seventh chords in a Brahms Intermezzo produce a full, sweet sound.

Ex. 3   Brahms: Intermezzo, Op. 119, No. 3

In a Vivaldi Sonata, they add force to the harmony by providing dissonances on the downbeat of the second and following bars.

Ex. 4   Vivaldi: Violin Sonata, Op. 2, No. 4

* See Chapter XIV.

IV⁷   V(⁴₂)   VI⁷   V(⁴₂)

A most imaginative use of seventh chords to produce color and harmonic tension is found in a Chopin Prelude (Ex. 5, Chapter I).

In a Handel aria, the dissonance in IV⁷ (*a*) serves a particularly valuable function in sharpening the drive to the cadence.

Ex. 5   Handel: *Lascia ch'io pianga*, from *Rinaldo*

and that I should sigh for   my li - - ber - ty.
e   che so · · spi · ri   la   li - - ber - tà.

IV⁷

The II⁷ preceding V in the perfect cadence frequently appears in first inversion (Ex. 6, *a*).*

Ex. 6   Brahms: *A German Requiem*, Op. 45

Andante moderato

that   I   must   per_____ - ish

Dm: II⁶₅ V   I

* See also page 438.

At times there is little difference between a 7—6 suspension and a seventh chord carefully prepared and resolved.

Ex. 7   Mozart: String Quartet, K. 387

Is the chord at (*a*), for example, a II[7], or a VII[6] with the high G suspended from the preceding beat? The musical effect remains the same, whichever way one reads the chord.

Preparation

Seventh chords are best prepared in the same manner as suspensions. The dissonant seventh arrives most smoothly when tied over from a consonant tone, or when that tone is repeated.

Ex. 8   Preparation of seventh chord

The seventh in Ex. 9 (*a*) enters so smoothly that its "dissonant" quality is scarcely noticed as such.

Ex. 9   Bach: Passacaglia in C minor for Organ

The appearance of the seventh in Ex. 10 (*a*) as a repeated note is nearly as smooth as that of Ex. 9.

Ex. 10   Dvorak: Symphony No. 4, Op. 88

A slightly freer preparation of the seventh—by stepwise movement from a voice of the preceding chord—also softens its dissonant quality. The seventh chords at (*a*) and (*b*) in Exs. 11 and 12 emerge from a stepwise contrary motion of the preceding notes.

Ex. 11   Beethoven: Symphony No. 3, second movement, Op. 55

Ex. 12   André Campra: *L'Europe galante* (1697)

From Charles Koechlin: Traité de l'Harmonie, Vol. II (*Paris, 1930*).

On the other hand, the approach to the seventh of a chord by leap emphasizes its dissonant quality.

Ex. 13   Monteverdi: *Lasciate mi morire*

This early seventeenth-century example of a leap to the seventh emphasizes the intensity of the text. A similar leap, used by Bach to stress high emotion, appears in the *Crucifixus* from the B minor Mass.

Ex. 14   Bach: *Crucifixus*, from the Mass in B minor

Resolution

Like the V^7, other seventh chords usually resolve to the chord a fifth below; the dissonant seventh tone moves one step down. Resolution may be to a triad or another seventh chord.

Ex. 15   Resolution of seventh chord (a) to triad, and (b) to seventh chord*

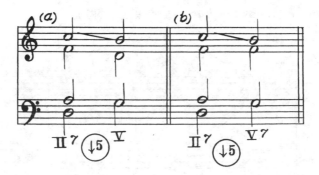

* For other examples of the falling-fifth resolution, see Exs. 12 (*b*) and 20.

In less common types of resolution, the bass moves up a second, or remains in place.

Ex. 16   Resolution by rising bass *

Ex. 17   Resolution with bass remaining in place

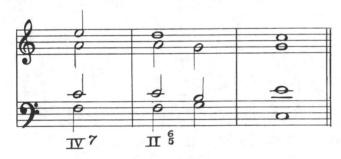

Beethoven uses such a resolution effectively in his first string quartet.

Ex. 18   Beethoven: String Quartet, Op. 18, No. 1, second movement

* For the resolution IV⁷—V, see Ex. 13.

The resolution of the seventh, like that of the suspension it resembles, can be embellished (Ex. 19).* The seventh of the IV⁷ at (a) passes through three other tones before resolving to the step below, at (b).

Ex. 19   Bach: Prelude No. 16, from *The Well-Tempered Clavier*, Book I

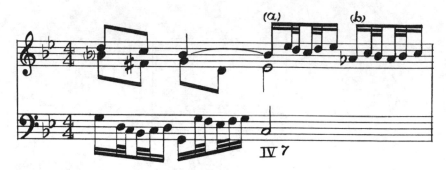

In general, voice-leading principles governing the V⁷ apply with equal force to other seventh chords. It would be a good idea to review those principles at this point.†

The Cycle of Seventh Chords

A series of resolutions from seventh chord to seventh chord, called *the cycle of seventh chords*, forms a variant of the cycle of fifths.

Ex. 20   Vivaldi-Bach: Concerto in D minor for Organ

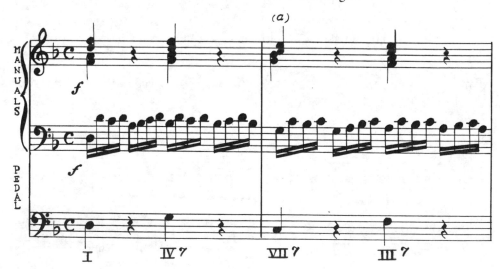

* Compare pages 403–404.

† See pages 349–351.

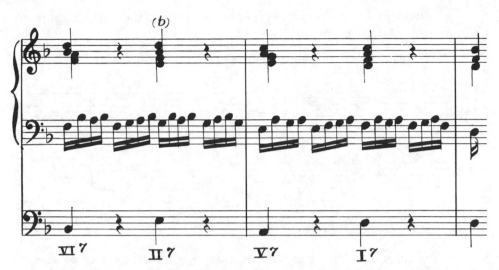

The addition of a seventh to each chord of the cycle enhances the forward movement inherent in falling-fifth root progressions. In Schumann's *Kreisleriana*, we find a rich pianistic setting of the cycle.

Ex. 21   Schumann: *Kreisleriana*, Op. 16

When the cycle receives a four-voice setting, the fifth is generally omitted from alternate chords.

Ex. 22   Cycle of seventh chords in four voices

$$IV^7 \quad VII^7 \quad III^7 \quad VI^7 \quad II^7 \quad V^7 \quad I$$

Types of Seventh Chords

Re-examining Exs. 1 and 2, we note six different types of seventh chords found on various steps of the major and minor scales:

1. The *major seventh*

is the most aggressive of all seventh chords. Found on I and IV in the major scale and on VI and III in minor, its dissonant outer interval adds bite to phrases in which it occurs. (See Exs. 3, *b*, and 5, *a*.)

2. The *minor seventh*

found in major on II, III, and VI, and in minor on IV and sometimes on other degrees, has a warm, mellow sonority. (See Exs. 4, 10, *a*, and 12.)

3. The *dominant seventh*

needs little further discussion here. In addition to its appearance on V, it also occurs on VII in melodic minor, falling. (See Ex. 20, *a*.)

4. The *half-diminished seventh*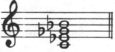

appears on the VII in major and II in minor. Quite unstable because of its diminished fifth, this chord has a strong forward-moving impulse. (See Exs. 20, *b* and 21, *a*.)

5. The *diminished seventh*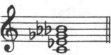

is dealt with in detail in Volume II, Chapter VII. Suffice it to say that its structure, containing both the diminished seventh and the diminished fifth, is extremely unstable. (See Ex. 11, *a*.)

6. The *minor-major seventh*

extremely rare, appears occasionally on the l in minor. The seventh acts as an appoggiatura, resolving upward to the tonic. (See Ex. 23 here and Ex. 22, last bar, in Chapter VI.)

Ex. 23   Minor-major seventh

Seventh-Chord Inversions

Seventh-chord inversions are similar in structure (except for the exact size of the intervals involved) to corresponding inversions of the dominant seventh. Like the latter, each seventh chord has three inversions.

Ex. 24   Seventh-chord inversions

Voice-leading principles are also similar. The seventh of the chord, no matter in which voice it appears, must be prepared by the same step in the preceding chord. The second note may be tied to the first, or may repeat it.*

Ex. 25   Preparation of the seventh

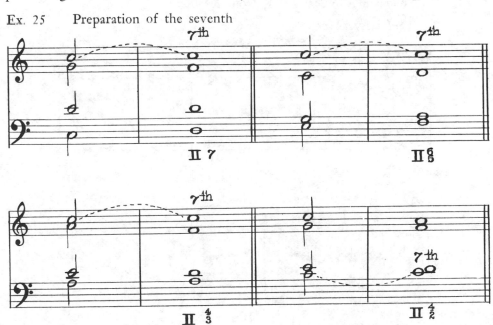

* For the $\frac{6}{5}$ chord, see Exs. 6 (a) and 31; the $\frac{4}{3}$, Ex. 25; and the $\frac{4}{2}$, Ex. 28.

Concerning resolution, the seventh—no matter in which voice it appears—usually moves downward one step. Less commonly, it remains in place while the other voices move to a triad.

Ex. 26   Resolution of seventh chord

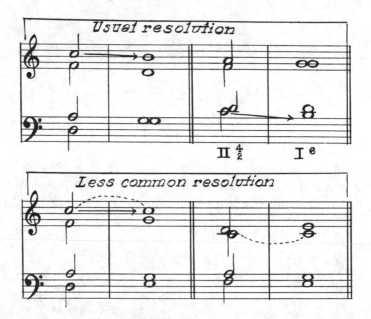

In Ex. 27, the sevenths of the IV$^6_5$(a) and II$^6_5$(b) are prepared by tones of the preceding chords. They resolve one step down.

Ex. 27   Schumann: Intermezzo I, from *Kreisleriana*

At (*a*) in Ex. 28, the seventh, lying in the bass, is prepared in the preceding bar, and then resolves downward (*b*).

Ex. 28   Bach: Prelude No. 1, from *The Well-Tempered Clavier*, Book I

Cadential Role of the II $\frac{6}{5}$

The II⁷ is the most important of all seventh chords (except the V⁷) because of its role in the cadence. Including the three tones of the IV triad, one of which has become a dissonant seventh, II⁷ produces a more energetic subdominant effect than the triad itself.

Ex. 29   Cadential function of II⁷

Still more effective is the first inversion II $\frac{6}{5}$. Combining the power of 4 in the bass with the dissonant strength of the seventh chord, it creates an intense drive to the dominant.

Ex. 30   Subdominant cadential function of II

$$\text{II} \, {}^{6}_{5} \quad \text{V} \qquad \text{I}$$

The combination II$^{6}_{5}$—V—I forms a standard cadential progression in the Bach chorales.

Ex. 31   Bach: *Jesu, meine Freude*

Summary

1. Seventh chords, of various types, are found on all degrees of the major and minor scales.

2. Seventh chords serve:
   a. To add richness and color to the harmony.
   b. To intensify harmonic movement, by providing active chords on all scale degrees.
   c. To add drive to the cadence.

3. The dissonant seventh of the chord is:
   a. Prepared, traditionally, by a consonant tone of the preceding chord, or by stepwise movement; freely, by leap.
   b. Resolved stepwise downward, or by remaining in place while the other voices move. The resolution may be ornamented or delayed, in the same manner as a suspension.

4. The seventh chord usually resolves to a fifth below. Less commonly, the bass moves stepwise upward or remains in place.

5. When seventh chords succeed each other consecutively in a cycle of fifths, they are said to form a cycle of seventh chords.
   a. The addition of the seventh increases the harmonic drive.
   b. The fifth is generally omitted in alternate chords.

6. The six different types of seventh chords are:
   a. Major (M. triad + M. third)
   b. Minor (m. triad + m. third)
   c. Dominant (M. triad + m. third)
   d. Half-diminished (Dim. triad + M. third)
   e. Diminished (Dim. triad + m. third)
   f. Minor-major (m. triad + M. third)

7. Seventh-chord inversions are prepared and resolved like those of the V^7.

8. The II^6_5 plays an important role at the cadence—analogous to, but with more drive than, the subdominant triad.

Dissonant Tones: a Résumé

Looking back over the various types of dissonant tones discussed in the foregoing chapters, we can draw certain conclusions. Broadly speaking, dissonances are of two types: (1) those created by the melodic motion of embellishing tones; and (2) those forming the dissonant element in chords such as diminished and augmented triads, and seventh chords.

Seen in perspective, dissonances have served to give variety and tension to a composition. Dissonant chords, unstable in their nature, seek to contract or expand into consonant chords. This need to resolve chordal tension has been a basic source of harmonic drive. During the Renaissance, composers led into and away from dissonances with the greatest care, to avoid any sudden irregularity or bumpiness in a phrase (Ex. 32, a). Starting in the Baroque and increasing in the Classical period, dissonant tones and chords were treated with somewhat greater freedom (Ex. 32, b). In the Romantic age, they were often introduced very freely into the phrase, as expressive or dramatic enhancement (Ex. 32, c). In the twentieth century, as we shall see in Volume II, they frequently form the basic texture of a composition, and are used with the utmost liberty.

Ex. 32   Varying treatments of dissonance

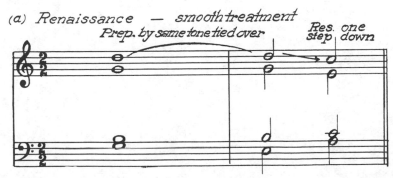

(b) Baroque and Classical — somewhat freer treatment

(c) Romantic — free treatment

Melodic Styles

Style is more than a collection of techniques or a manner of assembling musical elements. No formula exists for the melodic style of any composer—a Purcell, a Bach, a Puccini, or a sensitive jazz musician. An artist's idiom derives from his background and training, and evolves through his experience and imagination.

The variety of melodic styles seems almost endless. If we consider twentieth-century melody alone, the possibilities are vast: the personal melodic languages of Ives, Prokofiev, Bartók, Revueltas, Berg, Webern, Hindemith, Ravel, Milhaud, Honegger, and a dozen other composers in as many countries; the styles of American folk music—Negro spirituals, blues, cowboy songs, mountain ballads, and fiddle tunes; the styles of popular music—gospel songs, rhythm-and-blues, show tunes, and Calypso; the styles of jazz melody, from Dixieland to cool and avant-garde; the innumerable folk and popular music styles of other countries—Mexico, Bulgaria, Spain, Italy, and India (itself a wilderness of melodic styles). In addition to all these, there are, of course, the countless musical styles of the past.

We can discuss only a few of these styles here. The following melodies from widely separated historical periods include (1) a plain chant, (2) a section of an early Renaissance motet, (3) a passage by Bach, (4) a theme by Mozart, (5) a Schubert song, (6) a Tchaikovsky melody, and (7) an American folk tune.

Plain Chant

Several brief excerpts from the rich literature of plain chant have appeared in earlier chapters. Medieval church song evolved for almost a thousand years, and is still being used today. Composed chiefly for ritual purposes, the chant developed one-line melody into a highly formal and sophisticated art. Free of harmonic constraints, plain chant and folk music offer the richest fields for the study of pure melody.

The eleventh-century *Kyrie Alme Pater* provides a beautiful example.

Ex. 33   *Kyrie Alme Pater*

The *Kyrie* is a work of noble architectural proportions—a melody that flows in long, rounded curves. Its motion, mainly stepwise with a few small skips of thirds and fourths, is characteristically vocal, and its range—an eleventh—makes use of the full compass of the bass-baritone voice.

The first line establishes the Dorian mode on D—a tonality emphasized throughout by the repetition of 1 or 5 at the beginning and end of almost every phrase.

The modal character, free-flowing rhythm, and unequal phrase lengths produce a fluid, asymmetrical motion. The design of the phrases forms a well-balanced structure based on the number three—sacred in the middle ages as the symbol of the Trinity. There is mysticism in the three-times-three repetition, derived from the ancient text of the Mass:

> *Kyrie eleison, kyrie eleison, kyrie eleison* (God have mercy)
> *Christe eleison, Christe eleison, Christe eleison* (Christ have mercy)
> *Kyrie eleison, kyrie eleison, kyrie eleison* (God have mercy)

The unknown composer, or composers (for it is probable that such a melody evolved at the hands of more than one musician), derived from the elementary symmetry of the words a subtly proportioned musical design. Where the words follow the simple pattern

$$
\begin{array}{ll}
A & (a\ a\ a) \\
B & (b\ b\ b) \\
A & (a\ a\ a)
\end{array}
$$

the music forms the more elaborate triptych

$$
\begin{array}{ll}
A & (a\ a^2\ a) \\
B & (b\ a'\ b) \\
A' & (c\ a'\ c\ c\ a')
\end{array}
$$

Each part of the large symbol of the Trinity (ABA') is subdivided into three smaller parts, creating forms within forms. The last section (A'), however, is expanded into a five-part pattern (c, a', c, c, a'), the additional repetition of (c) lending oratorical emphasis to the melodic climax (high D), which appears six times. Through this expansion of the form, an interesting asymmetry is created within the broadly symmetrical design.*

Besides the organized relationship of its phrases, the *Kyrie Alme Pater* suggests the character of a litany in the constant return of its opening section. The repetitions, however, are neither literal nor regular. Particularly noteworthy is the long vocalise on the last reiteration of "Kyrie." The repetitions, set apart by various contrasting phrases, establish the formal unity of the work.

---

* A parallel to this musical example of *irregularity within a larger symmetry* is found in the medieval architecture of Chartres Cathedral, whose two balancing towers are of different heights and bear different styles of ornamentation.

Josquin des Prés

Some four centuries after the notation of the *Kyrie Alme Pater*, medieval religious music evolved into the music of the early Renaissance, one of whose greatest composers was Josquin des Prés. In addition to his other gifts, Josquin was a supreme melodist. Example 34 shows the soprano line of one of his motets for two and three voices.

Ex. 34   Josquin des Prés: *Ave verum corpus Christi**

Written for the church, Josquin's motet continues the medieval tradition of free, asymmetrical melody without bar lines. But unlike plain chant, it is in the major mode and has a metric unit, the half note. The four phrases are all of different lengths (12, 5, 10, and 15 beats, respectively); the rhythmic structure, moreover, changes constantly. Thus, phrase (*a*) consists largely of whole and half notes, (*b*) introduces a syncopated half note (D) after the second beat, (*c*) develops the syncopated idea in a lovely turning figure of quarters and eighths (the notes over *vir* and *gi* both emphasize off-beats), and (*d*) expands the values once more to conclude in a long, sweeping curve.

Melodically, the *Ave verum* moves in smooth, flowing lines; the skips, however, are wider and more emphatic than those of a previous age. Three leaps of a fourth, two of a fifth, and one of an octave form part of the composition. The motive, a pattern of three rising notes, recurs throughout in inver-

* In the notation of this period the half note was the basic unit of beat; it should be performed at the speed of a quarter note in modern notation.

sion. It is also varied rhythmically, with graceful embellishments. Although some upward movement appears, the general tenor of the line tends downward in gentle slopes, steadily becoming slower and longer.

The high point of the piece (F) appears five times; the low point, twice. The over-all curve, therefore, is a wave. Despite a tender, hovering mood, the melodic direction is distinctly forward, as shown by the following characteristics:

1. The important melodic leaps grow larger as the melody develops. The fourths occur near the beginning, the fifths toward the middle, and the all-important octave leap before the last phrase.

2. The slow rhythm of phrase (a) quickens in phrase (b), grows still more lively in phrase (c), and broadens impressively when the motive is repeated in phrase (d) to form an emphatic conclusion.

3. The peak tone (F) always follows leaps of a third or a fourth, occurring once each in phrases (a), (b), and (c). To start the climactic final phrase, however, the high tone enters after an octave leap, is stressed by appearing twice in succession, and forms the over-all climax when it is sustained for a whole note (five notes after d).

While full appreciation of Josquin des Prés' motet requires a hearing of all the voices, the soprano line alone reveals the sensitive craftsmanship of the composer.

Bach

Confronted with the extraordinary variety of melodic types found in the works of Bach, it is impossible to select *the* typical Bach melody. His styles range from the precision of a gavotte in one of the English Suites to the flamboyant arabesques of the G minor Prelude for Organ, from the nobility of Jesus' recitatives in *The St. Matthew Passion* to the passionate chromaticism of the cantata *Weinen, Klagen*. An excerpt from the Second Partita for Clavier illustrates, therefore, *a* Bach style, not *the* Bach style.

Ex. 35   Bach: Sinfonia, from the Partita No. 2 for Clavier

So much has been written about Bach's counterpoint that we are apt to forget his magnificent melodic powers. One of his special gifts was the ability to take a single motive and from it spin a long melodic line in ever-fluctuating shapes and rhythms. In Ex. 35 we find a lovely arabesque deriving from such a melodic kernel (bar 1). Each measure contains a slightly different rhythmic pattern, whose freedom makes the listener forget the solid harmonic bass underneath.

Yet this is distinctly harmonic music. The chords, clearly outlined in the opening bars, are embellished by passing and neighboring tones, appoggia-turas, and scale passages, in the decorative style of the eighteenth century. Bach's melody, however, cannot be divided into "essential" and "embellishing" tones; all are essential. Not one note could be omitted from the melody without destroying its perfection.

Rhythmically, the values are the rapid ones of Baroque instrumental music: eighths, sixteenths, and thirty-second notes, in ever-changing combina-tions. Note that the faster values tend to occur in the first half of the bar (bars 1 and 2) or on the first half of the beat (bars 3 and 4), adding forward motion to the rhythm. The syncopated notes (especially in bars 3–6) are an abrupt check to the racing thirty-second notes; they provide rhythmic contrast and suspense.

The motive, stated at the outset, is reiterated constantly but never twice in the same form. Variation appears already in bar 2. Bar 3 is virtually a transformation: the opening moves down instead of up, the fast notes occur on the first instead of the second beat, and the motive forms a bowl instead of an arch. Bar 4 repeats bar 3 in sequence. From here on, the motive grows progressively shorter and tighter, until in bar 7 the five F's hammer away in preparation for the climactic G in bar 8. This is the only bar in which the first beat has broader values, preparing the final downward rush of fourteen consecutive thirty-second notes to the cadence.

In this melody the climax is produced not by a high point (A flat appears five times in eight bars) but by the intensification of the melodic rhythm, and through a device often employed by Bach—the splitting up of one line to give the impression of two separate voices. In bar 7, Bach arranges the melody in such a manner that while the upper part reiterates high F, the lower portion of the line, acting as a second voice, descends from C to F. This outlining of two voices by one produces the effect shown in Ex. 36.

Ex. 36   Splitting of one voice into two

Although only the melody has been discussed here, you should by all means look at the original score of the Partita, noting the beautiful contrast between the rhythmically varied melody and the steady marching bass, insistent in its eighth-note rhythm.

Mozart

The time differential between Bach and Mozart is much smaller than between the composers of the preceding examples; only six years separated the death of one from the birth of the other. The differences between their two styles, however, were considerable. Even within Mozart's brief lifetime, his own music underwent considerable evolution; we must remember that Ex. 37 presents but one of Mozart's different styles.

Ex. 37　　Mozart: String Quintet in G minor, K. 516

This superb melodic line forms the opening theme of the first movement of a quintet for string instruments. The wide range—more than three octaves—is characteristic of instrumental writing; in this case the melody shifts from the upper middle range of the violin down to the lowest note but one of the viola.

The melody represents two different aspects of Mozart's writing: symmetry and freedom—or, to put it another way, eighteenth-century Classical style with a foreshadowing of Romanticism. The first twelve bars form three evenly balanced phrases of four bars each—a typical eighteenth-century structure. To complete the pattern, the composer might have written another four-bar phrase, and all would have been perfectly symmetrical in that most symmetrical of all possible worlds.

At this point the Romanticist in Mozart appears. In bar 14 the line surges chromatically upward, presenting at (*e*) a beautiful new motive that extends the final phrase out of all proportion to the others. The last segment occupies twelve bars—as long as the three preceding phrases put together.

Motive (*a*) provides the rhythm that repeats insistently throughout almost the entire melody, either in original form, [musical notation]

or in a slight variant. [musical notation]

It outlines the tonic chord in the first bar, is varied in bar 2 with a characteristically Mozartean chromaticism; and rests at the half cadence in the fourth bar. Phrase (*b*) starts with an inversion of (*a*), swoops up and down again to another half cadence in bar 8. Phrase (*c*) repeats phrase (*a*) exactly, an octave lower, for a change of color.

Then the last phrase (*d*) takes off on its venturesome course. At (*e*) the leap to the high point, the sudden change of rhythm from the original motive to a new pattern of dotted quarters and eighths, [musical notation]

and the intense chromatic movement combine in a telling climax. The bold harmonies are all the more effective at this point because the first twelve bars held to a conventional chordal framework.

The over-all melodic curve is a bowl, with widely contrasted peaks and valleys. This curve, together with the intensity of the climax, reveals the pre-Romantic "storm and stress" characteristic of many late Mozart compositions.

Schubert

Pre-eminently a lyricist, Schubert composed more than 500 songs, in a wide range of styles and moods. One of his many modes of expression reflected the popular music of his native Vienna.

Ex. 38   Schubert: *Heidenröslein*

Lieblich

(A) young man saw a rose-bud bloom grow-ing in the
Sah ein Knab'ein Rös-lein steh'n, Rös-lein auf der

mea-dow. Rose so new and sweet as dawn,
Hei - den, War so jung und mor— gen - schön,

He ran fast to see it there, Looked at it so
lief er schnell es nah'zu sehn, Sah's mit vie -len

joy-ful-ly. Rose-bud, rose-bud, rose so red,
Freu— den. Rös —lein, Rös-lein, Rös - lein roth,

Rose-bud on the mea - - dow.
Rös -lein auf der Hei - - den.

For sheer freshness and spontaneity, this song would be hard to equal. In three short phrases, all derived from the motive of the first two measures, Schubert's melody matches the folk imagery of Goethe's poem. The means are so simple that there is little need for commentary. Note, however, the charm of the C sharp in measure 6, leading the phrase away from the key of G major.* Observe, too, that the high note (G), touched lightly, provides an accent rather than a dramatic culmination of the phrase.

Tchaikovsky

In contrast to the fresh, almost naïve early Romanticism of *Heidenröslein*, we find in Tchaikovsky's melody late Romanticism at its peak. The difference lies not merely in the long, arching line, the curves within curves, or the sensitive chromatic touches; the *Romeo* theme offers another kind of beauty: a more complex, intense, bitter-sweet Romanticism.

* For this process, known as modulation, see Chapter II, Volume II.

Ex. 39   Tchaikovsky: Second theme, from *Romeo and Juliet* Overture-Fantasy

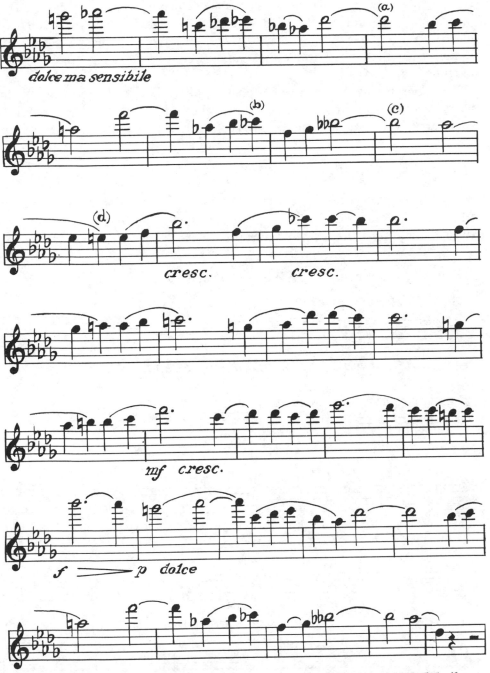

Starting *dolce ma sensibile* (sweetly but sensitively—how Tchaikov-skian an indication!) on a high G, the line drops in a long dying fall, with certain tones (*a*, *b*, and *c*) forming melancholy minor ninths with the bass line (not shown here). Although the melody remains complete in itself, it draws much of its meaning, in true Romantic fashion, from the rich harmonies underneath.

At (*d*) the falling wave gives way to a rising one. A two-bar motive reaches upward in chromatic waves typical of the nineteenth century. Mounting through six skillfully handled sequences, the phrase achieves a splendid climax on high B flat. A fine touch is the sudden reticence after the climax: the dynamic level and mood drop down immediately to *p dolce* for a return of the opening phrase.

Despite his Romantic emotionalism, Tchaikovsky leaned toward the Classical tradition; after thirty bars of melodic and harmonic motion, the final tonic arrives with as deliberate a perfect cadence as any Mozart ever wrote.

American Folk Song

As a lighthearted finale to this discussion of melodic styles, we consider a little-known American folk song. Or can this "Watermelon Cry," improvised casually on the streets of a Southern city, qualify as a song?

Ex. 40   American street cry: Fly Roun', L'il Ladies

Informal and evanescent, possibly never sung twice in the same way, the street cry reveals an image of music at the moment it springs to life—a distinctly American image. The Negro peddler who called his wares sang out spontaneously in syncopated rhythms, in changing meters, and in the blues mode (note the flatted sevenths at *a* and the variable thirds at *b*). The light, sarcastic tone of the words is matched by the odd rhythms, strange accents, and variable pitches of the music.

We have discussed seven melodies from different countries and historical periods.* In each, a combination of distinctive characteristics makes up the esthetic unity called style. Yet we must remember: when a melody has style, we do not think of its elements; we hear it as a whole. Style is more than an assemblage of techniques, it is their complete fusion.

Summary

1. The variety of melodic styles is practically infinite.

2. Style comprises a unity of various melodic and rhythmic traits plus indefinable historical and personal characteristics.

3. Various melodic styles found in plain chant, Josquin des Prés, Bach, Mozart, Schubert, Tchaikovsky, and American folk song form artistic unities, each blending various techniques in a unique manner.

* For discussion of more recent melodic styles, see Volume II, Chapter XIII.

Musical
Motion
Reviewed

At the beginning of this book melodic, rhythmic, and harmonic sources of musical motion were introduced. In subsequent chapters, these various kinds of motion were examined in some detail. Now we can draw up a broad summary of the forces that produce motion in music:

1. Rhythm creates motion by:
   a. Clearly articulated, or sharply accented patterns
   b. Insistent repetition
   c. Fast rhythmic values
   d. Fast tempo
   e. Acceleration of values or tempo
   f. Changing meter
   g. Syncopation
   h. Polyrhythm

2. Melody creates motion by:
   a. Frequent wide leaps
   b. Wide range
   c. Active intervals
   d. Strongly directed melodic curves
   e. Well-defined climaxes
   f. Motive repetitions varied by sequence, fragmentation, extension, and other techniques

3. Harmony creates motion by:
   a. Strong root movements
   b. Fast harmonic rhythm

    c. Active chords

    d. Dissonances

    e. Irregular or delayed resolution of dissonances

    f. A well-designed bass line

    g. A strongly directed line of broad harmonic movement

4. Rhythm, melody, and harmony can act separately or together in creating musical motion:

    a. One element can progress vigorously while the others remain relatively inactive.

    b. Two elements can progress vigorously, the third remaining quiescent.

    c. All three elements can combine in vigorous activity.

Appendix I
The Overtone
Series

For centuries, musicians have pondered over the relation between musical practice and the acoustical phenomenon known as the *overtone series*. This series is a group of harmonics or overtones that are sounded faintly along with every root or fundamental tone. While the fundamental tone always sounds the loudest, the faintly reverberating overtones add their color to the composite sound.

An overtone series may be built on any tone; generally C below the bass staff is used for purposes of illustration (Ex. 1). (The notes in boxes are out of tune, according to present tuning standards.)

Ex. 1   Overtone Series

Philosophers, physicists, and musical theorists ever since Pythagoras have been impressed by the apparent close relationship between the structure of the overtone series and familiar musical phenomena. Thus, the perfect intervals—octave, fifth, and fourth—are represented by the lowest numbers in the series, 1, 2, 3, 4. Many have speculated that these intervals won wide currency in music because they were the natural overtones formed by blowing a pipe or horn, or by dividing a string in the simplest mathematical proportions.

Rameau and many other theorists have carried speculation still further, finding in the overtone series a connection between traditional harmony and

456

natural law, especially the laws of acoustics. Even today, an excellent case can be made for a parallelism between the structure of the overtone series and the evolution of harmony. Thus, harmonics 1, 2, 3, and 4 formed the sole basis of medieval harmony, which consisted, as we have seen, of chords in octaves, fifths, and fourths. After 1200, harmonic 5 (the major third) was added, producing the triad. Around 1600, harmonic 7 contributed the dominant seventh chord, and, in the eighteenth century, harmonic 9 provided the ninth chord. Late in the nineteenth century, harmonic 11 was incorporated into the eleventh chord.

The view of harmony as derived from natural law, popular in the eighteenth and nineteenth centuries, seems to have passed its prime today. Although a relation between musical and acoustical phenomena no doubt exists, this relation is neither absolute nor thorough-going. Several thorny problems have vexed theorists for years. If, for example, nature is the basic source of harmony, why are certain tones of the harmonic series out of tune? If, as Rameau and later theorists have claimed, the overtone series furnishes the basis for the major scale, why is it that two notes of the scale—the fourth and sixth—are missing from the series, while other tones—the flat seventh and sharp fourth—are present in the series but not in the scale? If acoustics has been the root of music, why did the modal scales precede major in Western music by many centuries? Why is it so difficult to relate the minor mode to the series? How is it that the fourth—a basic interval of the overtone series and considered a fundamental consonance in medieval times—was for many centuries treated as a dissonance?

A knowledge of acoustics, as indeed of many other sciences, is obviously of value to the musician. Yet these questions suggest the pitfalls latent in any derivation of musical principles from scientific or other non-artistic disciplines. The evolution of melody and harmony, colored by many historical, social, and technological influences, should be understood primarily in musical and artistic terms.

Appendix II
Motive and
Germ

Many writers have described the motive as "the smallest unit of musical thought." Although perfectly adequate as a description of a great many motives, this definition seems inappropriate and misleading in others, where a motive may itself embody a repetition. In such cases, it would seem useful to draw a distinction between a motive—the *basic* unit of thought used in building a phrase or a composition—and a germ—the *smallest* unit of thought, often repeated within the motive itself.

Thus, the Chopin Waltz in A minor (Ex. 19, page 381), according to the common definition, would have a one-bar motive,

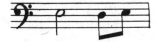

which recurs immediately in inverted form:

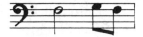

The original motive appears again, followed again by the inversion and then once more by the original.

Such a splitting up seems excessively microscopic. A more musical phrasing of the motive would describe it as a two-bar unit, with a slight dipping and rising inflection:*

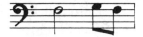

This conception of the motive not only coincides with the original phrasing of the composer, but simplifies analysis of the phrase. It makes possible a description of the theme as "a statement of the motive, followed by a repetition, and then an extension."

This broader type of motive identification leads to an analysis of the opening phrase of Mozart's Symphony No. 40 (Ex. 1) as a two-bar motive, ending in a leap of a sixth followed by a rest. The concept that views the first three notes of the phrase as the motive seems excessively fussy and, furthermore, obliges the analyst to identify the final leap of a sixth as a second motive.

* Note that Chopin writes a slur over the two bars, indicating that it be *played* as a unit.

It is preferable to consider the first three notes a germ, whose insistent repetition is an inherent characteristic of the motive. Since the two-bar pattern is constantly repeated as such, and followed each time by a rest, this concept leads to a more coherent analysis.

Ex. 1   Mozart: Symphony No. 40, K. 550

Several other motives, each enclosing a repetition of a germ, are given in Exs. 2–4 for the purpose of clarifying the distinction between motive and germ.

Ex. 2   Handel: Sarabande, from Suite No. 11

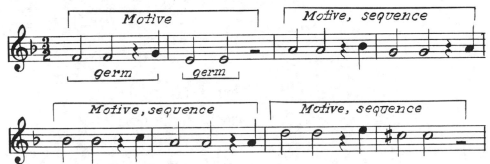

Ex. 3   Bach: Fugue in D major for Organ

Ex. 4   Bach: Toccata and Fugue No. 3 for Clavier

Indexes

Index of
Composers and
Compositions

Note: An (m) indicates a musical example in the text. Except for anonymous works, musical compositions are listed under their composers. **Boldface** type indicates pages on which the major discussion of a subject appears.

Index
of Subjects